A Guide to Common **Organic** GARDENING QUESTIONS

Step-by-Step Recommendations for Organic Vegetable and Fruit Gardening in Utah

Acknowledgment: Portions of this guide were originally published in *A Guide to Common Gardening Questions*. The guide has been revised and updated with an emphasis on research-based organic gardening practices.

I0809107

PUBLICATION TEAM

SENIOR WRITERS

Katie Wagner, *USU Extension Horticulture Faculty (Salt Lake County)*
Shawn Olsen, *USU Extension Agriculture Faculty (Davis County)*

CONTRIBUTING WRITERS

Dr. Dan Drost, *USU Extension Vegetable Specialist*
Dr. Diane Alston, *USU Extension Entomologist and IPM Coordinator*
Marion Murray, *USU Extension IPM Project Leader*
Britney Hunter, *USU Extension Horticulture Faculty (Davis County)*
Dr. Claudia Nischwitz, *USU Extension Plant Pathology Specialist*
Dr. Ricardo Ramirez, *USU Extension Entomology Specialist*
Dr. Mark Williams, *University of Kentucky Extension Landscape Horticulture and Weed Management Specialist*
Dr. Niel Allen, *USU Extension Irrigation Specialist*
James Barnhill, *USU Extension Agriculture Faculty (Weber and Morgan Counties)*
Dr. David Frame, *USU Extension Poultry Specialist*
Mike Pace, *USU Extension Agriculture Faculty (Box Elder County)*
Tamara Steinitz, *USU Clinical Associate Professor, Department of Nutrition, Dietetics and Food Sciences*
Dr. Carrie Durward, *USU Extension Nutrition Specialist*
Dr. Jennifer Reeve, *USU Associate Professor of Organic and Sustainable Agriculture*
Melanie Jewkes, *USU Extension Family and Consumer Sciences Faculty (Salt Lake County)*
Rick Heflebower, *USU Extension Horticulture Faculty (Washington County)*

GRAPHIC DESIGN & LAYOUT

Olivia Yeip, *Graphic Designer*

ISBN 978-0-9888891-2-5

Many thanks to the peer reviewers, staff assistants and volunteers who helped complete this guide. Special thanks to Tessa Groff, Stacie Stone and Shelley Ekman.

ORDERING INFORMATION

To order additional copies of **A Guide to Common Organic Gardening Questions,** contact Utah State University Extension Publications:

E-mail:
extension.publications@usu.edu

Website:
extension.cart.usu.edu

Phone:
(435) 797-2251
Monday - Friday 8 a.m. - 5 p.m. MST

CONTENTS

Top 10 Questions and Answers for Organic Fruit and Vegetable Gardening in Utah 1

Introduction 7

Introduction to USU Extension 9
Introduction to Organic Gardening 11
Nutritional Benefits of Fresh Produce 15
Kids and Gardening 19

Chapter 1: Garden Preparation 21

Getting Started and Site Selection 23
Variety Selection 27
Garden Layout and Planting 41
Starting Plants from Seed 53
Container and Raised Bed Gardening 57

Chapter 2: Organic Gardening Techniques 63

Organic Vegetable Gardening: An Overview 65
Tree Fruit and Small Fruit: An Overview 81
Pruning Fruit Trees and Small Fruit 99
Extending the Growing Season 107

Chapter 3: Garden Soil 113

Garden Soil and Soil Testing 115
Three Common Soil Problems 121
Organic Matter and Soil Amendment 125
Backyard Composting 131

Chapter 4: Organic Garden Care 137

Garden Soil Fertility 139
Garden Irrigation 167
Pesticide Application 179
Fall Garden Care 181

Chapter 5: Garden Pest Control 187

Integrated Pest Management 189
Beneficial Organisms 215
Organic Fruit Pest Control 233
Integrated Weed Management 249
Prevention and Management of Common Garden Diseases 257

Index 283

TOP 10 QUESTIONS AND ANSWERS FOR ORGANIC FRUIT AND VEGETABLE GARDENING IN UTAH

TOP 10 QUESTIONS & ANSWERS

1. Where can I find trustworthy organic gardening information?

It is easy to find organic gardening information on the Internet, in books, on television shows and so forth; however, the trick is finding information that is trustworthy and relevant to your local growing conditions. One benefit of land-grant universities' Cooperative Extension Services is that faculty advises residents on research-based, locally relevant gardening information. Other sources may or may not do the same. For example, gardening books and websites are great sources of information if the author is knowledgeable and the content is regionally relevant. If you can find a gardening book or website blog written by a local author who is also a knowledgeable gardener you are in luck! If the book or blog was written by a knowledgeable gardener located on the opposite side of the country, perhaps only a portion of the content is appropriate for your growing area. If the content was written by an unknowledgeable gardener or recommendations are based off of 'happen-chance' observations, well, I think you can guess where this is heading. Successful gardeners know that regional differences, like soil chemistries and climate, really make a difference when making good gardening decisions. Your local USU Extension office can help guide you through sound gardening choices and recommend research-based resources that will not leave you guessing.

2. How can I find out information about community gardening in my area?

One way to find out about community gardens in your area is to ask local gardeners or gardening groups. Wasatch Community Gardens (http://wasatchgardens.org) is a great resource for residents in and around Salt Lake County. The Salt

Lake County Urban Farming website offers a map of community gardens in Salt Lake County (www.slco.org/urbanfarming). Gardeners located in other areas of Utah or elsewhere in the U.S. might want to look up the American Community Garden Association (ACGA) online at www.communitygarden.org for a listing of registered ACGA community gardens. Your local USU Extension office is also always willing to help you locate the garden nearest you.

3. Does organic produce taste better than conventional produce?

Taste is tough to compare because it is subjective. Several research studies have shown that participants are not always able to determine organic from conventionally grown produce by taste alone. However, there is no doubt that gardeners may certainly be able to taste a difference between pre-ripe and fully ripe fruits and vegetables. For example, there is a world of difference between the taste of a pre-ripe and a tree-ripened peach. Taste is also variable among many varieties of garden plants. Which do you prefer, a Black Krim or an Early Girl tomato? Let your senses be the judge of what tastes best to you and never be afraid to explore delicious new options.

4. What is the best soil amendment for heavy clay?

Contrary to popular belief, clay is not necessarily "bad" for garden soil. True, too much clay (greater than 30%) is difficult to manage; however, some clay helps to ensure a reservoir of nutrients for garden plants and good plant support. The best amendment for clay is organic matter. Organic matter helps alleviate soil compaction and improve other soil qualities. Be careful if you plan to add sand to heavy clay soils. The

wrong proportion of sand and clay will produce a soil with a consistency similar to concrete. It is better to avoid adding sand to clay; choose to add organic matter instead. That said, adding too much organic matter at one time can be problematic as well. It is best to amend with 1 to 3 inches of organic matter annually.

5. How often should I water my garden?

This is probably the most commonly asked gardening question and unfortunately, one of the most difficult to answer. Water recommendations (how often and how much) are highly variable due to multiple impacting factors. Soil texture, slope, garden exposure, soil organic matter content, plant type, time of year and so forth all impact irrigation decisions. Although recommendations vary, one fact remains consistent (mostly); garden soil should dry out slightly between irrigation events. Most plants (excluding aquatic plants) do not grow well in constantly saturated soil. Under these conditions, the tips of root hairs may rot away causing plants to show surprisingly similar symptoms to under-watered plants. As a general rule, completely saturate garden soil in the root zone and then allow the top 2 to 3 inches of soil to dry out before saturating again. Ideal soil moisture resembles a wrung-out sponge. Be careful not to base your watering decisions off of sight alone; it is very difficult to "see" whether soil is dry or moist. Crusting or cracking at the soil surface is common with clay soils, wet or dry. Dig-in and feel down into the top inches of soil with your fingers. You will gain a knack

for "feeling" dry verses wet garden soil. Gardeners in Davis, Duchesne, Garfield, Iron, Juab, Morgan, Piute, Salt Lake, Summit, Uintah, Utah, Wasatch, Washington and Weber counties can sign up for a free water check at www.slowtheflow.org and receive a customized garden irrigation schedule.

6. What should I use to fill my raised bed garden boxes?

Many planting mediums can be used to fill raised bed garden boxes. Some gardeners choose to purchase a soilless growing medium (typically consisting of an organic matter source like peat moss, and a drainage material such as perlite or vermiculite) while others choose to amend existing topsoil with a composted organic matter source (like kitchen scraps or manure). Other gardeners might choose to purchase a topsoil blend from a reputable nursery. Research your choices before you fill your beds and select an option that fits both your preferences and your budget. Feel free to contact your local USU Extension office for pros and cons of various mediums or contact the company for details on product content and analysis. For more detail on container gardening, see the "Container and Raised Bed Gardening" section in Chapter 1 of this guide.

7. What is companion planting and how can it benefit my garden?

Companion planting refers to the idea that one plant benefits the growth of another. Many organic gardeners practice companion planting to improve pest control in the garden. Some companion planting recommendations are considered "garden myth" because they are not supported by research. See the "**Companion Planting: Myth or Reality**" section in Chapter 2 of this guide for more information on researched-based companion planting tips. It is always a good idea to create refugia, or habitat that supports natural enemies, by planting a diverse garden. Keeping these "good guys" around the garden will help to maintain pest populations at a tolerable level with no or minimal use of chemical control.

8. What are some examples of sources of organic matter?

Organic matter describes a soil amendment or mulch that came from a once-living source. A soil amendment is mixed in to improve soil qualities whereas a mulch rests on the soil surface. Organic matter sources include wood (shavings, soil pep or sawdust), kitchen scraps, grass clippings, manures, peat moss, leaves, straw and so forth. Non-living materials (plastics, perlite, vermiculite and other mined minerals) can also be used as soil amendments and mulches, but are not sources of organic matter.

9. What products can I use on my garden plants for insect control?

Organic gardeners can use any available organic product they want to use on garden plants. Some gardeners might choose to supplement non-chemical control practices with infrequent organic insecticide use. Others might choose to not use any insecticides at all. USDA certified organic growers can only use approved products listed on the Organic Materials Review Institute website (www.omri.org). Certified organic production restricts the use of certain active ingredients found in many pesticides; however, some insecticides, such as neem oil, insecticidal soaps and spinosad, are approved for use. Choose products that complement your gardening preferences. If you choose to use no chemical control, create refugia for natural enemies and monitor your garden frequently for insect pests; pick off and destroy insect pests as you discover them.

10. How do I know which nutrients I need to add to my garden plants?

It is important to have your soil tested before adding additional sources of nutrients, like fertilizers and manures. A routine soil test (soil texture, pH, salinity, available phosphorus and potassium and recommendations) will help you determine garden plant nutrient needs. If a soil test indicates your garden soil is adequate to high in phosphorus or potassium, it is best to not add amendments high in these nutrients if possible. Re-test your garden soil every 2 to 3 years unless you make major changes such as amending your soil with several inches of organic matter in a single season.

It is typically recommended that you add additional nitrogen to your garden plants one or more times during the growing season. Follow fertilization recommendations for each type of garden plant you decide to grow. See Table 18 in the "Chapter 4: Organic Garden Care" section of this guide for specific fertilizer recommendations for common fruits and vegetables.

GARDEN MYTH #1:

There is usually one correct answer to gardening questions.

Fact: There are no absolute gardening recommendations because there is an exception to almost every rule. I cannot count the amount of times I have given a research-based gardening recommendation to a client only to hear, "Actually, that has not been my experience in my garden." The high likelihood is that neither I, nor the gardener, were incorrect. We all know that nature is full of surprises and gardens are full of nature! Let this guide steer you in the right direction, but always feel free to contact your local USU Extension agent to help you troubleshoot any gardening surprises along the way.

INTRODUCTION

INTRODUCTION TO USU EXTENSION

INTRODUCTION

Utah State University (USU) Extension receives thousands of inquiries from Utah residents each year concerning common gardening questions. Callers express frustration over garden problems; there seems to be so much to learn! Insects, diseases, weeds, nutrient deficiencies, plant growth requirements, irrigation and other issues are all challenges to conquer in the garden. Extension faculty often hears "Why aren't my tomatoes producing fruit?" or "What is eating my bean sprouts?" USU Extension aids callers by answering gardening questions and providing diagnostic services for pest problems. In this way, USU Extension educates the citizens of Utah on research-based gardening practices. The goal of this guide is to help readers interested in organic gardening techniques troubleshoot common organic gardening problems. Although one can devote an entire career to better understanding the subtleties of organic gardening, this guide serves as a convenient and practical first step.

HOW TO USE THIS GUIDE

A Guide to Common Organic Gardening Questions is intended to walk readers through the basics of home and small-scale organic fruit and vegetable production in Utah. Sections throughout this guide were authored by contributors with expertise in their respective fields. Make sure to read the "Ask an Expert" sections authored by Extension specialists and researchers who have practical experience with organic production. At times, **hyperlinks indicated by bolded publication names** are provided to guide readers to additional fact sheets and reference materials available online. Note that even though not all referenced fact sheets have "organic" in their title, at least a portion of all materials contain information applicable to organic gardening. If you are referencing a paper copy of this guide, full web addresses for referenced online materials are listed at the end of this guide.

INTRODUCTION TO ORGANIC GARDENING

INTRODUCTION

Growing organically refers to the avoidance of synthetic products, such as pesticides and fertilizers. Upon searching for reasons why gardeners choose to grow organically, one is likely to encounter a variety of viewpoints; however, in reality, organic gardening is a personal preference. USU Extension does not advocate one gardening preference over another; it simply provides research-based, non-biased information on a wide range of gardening topics. A real attribute of organic food production is that it brings together gardeners with varying perspectives to support a common interest. For example, gardeners may choose to grow organically for health, environmental, ethical, economic, or traditional reasons. Whatever the motivation, organic gardeners share a love of harvesting the fruits of their labor and sharing their gardening experiences with others.

Goals of this Section:

- Learn basic principles of organic agriculture.
- Better understand the role of the U.S. Department of Agriculture (USDA) in regulating commercial organic operations.
- Learn the definition and purpose of the USDA Certified Organic label.

WHAT DOES IT MEAN TO GROW ORGANICALLY?

There are many definitions of organic gardening, and hence, any single definition may not be comprehensive or biased by an individual's perspective. Generally speaking, organic gardeners strive to sustain a

GARDEN MYTH #2:

Organic gardening is defined as gardening without the use of chemicals.

Fact: All organic gardeners use chemicals when growing garden plants. Nature is full of chemicals; in fact, water is a chemical compound and plants certainly need water to grow! Generally speaking, organic gardeners avoid the use of synthetically produced chemicals. Some organic gardeners choose to limit the use of all pest control and fertilizer products on and around edible plants while others feel comfortable regularly applying organic pesticides and fertilizers. A list of products approved for USDA certified organic agriculture can be found at the OMRI website (www.omri.org).

growing system through reliance on inputs from plant, animal and mineral products, and eliminate the use of synthetically produced chemicals. An example of a more broad definition of organic farming, provided by the National Sustainable Agriculture Information Service (ATTRA), characterizes organic farming through the following six principles:

- Build biodiversity within the ecosystem; for example, use plants from multiple families.
- Integrate the needs of farm enterprises; for example, use manure from livestock production to provide nutrients for plants.
- Embrace principles of sustainability; for example, limit non-renewable energy consumption when making farm management decisions.
- Apply natural sources of plant nutrients; for example, add mined nutrients and those harvested from plant and animal sources.
- Promote natural pest control; for example, attract natural enemies to control pest populations.
- Maintain integrity through a system that assures consumers they are purchasing products that are grown using organic methods.

For more information on these principles, visit **National Sustainable Agriculture Service**.

This sixth characterization differentiates most organic gardens from commercial organic farming operations since organic gardeners generally do not sell their plant and animal commodities to the public.

Organic gardening is not regulated unlike USDA certified organic agriculture. It is the role of the USDA to "develop and provide guidance, policies, and inspection methods and administer programs to protect consumers from misbranded and economically adulterated [products] ... to ensure all labels are truthful and not misleading" (**USDA Food Safety and Inspection Service**).

The USDA implemented the National Organic Program (NOP) in 2002 to "regulate the standards for any farm, wild crop harvesting, or handling operation that wants to sell an agriculture product as organically produced." The NOP defines the term "organic" as "a labeling term that indicates that the food or other agricultural product has been produced through approved methods that integrate cultural, biological, and mechanical practices that foster cycling of resources, promote ecological balance, and conserve biodiversity. Synthetic fertilizers, sewage sludge, irradiation and genetic engineering may not be used" (**USDA National Organic Program**).

Figure 1: *USDA certified organic label*

Therefore, the National Organic Program regulates inputs, like fertilizers and pesticides, for certified organic agriculture. A listing of farming inputs permitted by the NOP is available at the Organic Materials Review Institute website (www.omri.org). The NOP and USDA certified organic label (Figure 1) are important tools to protect the trust and promote understanding between producers and consumers. For more information on the NOP, visit National Organic Program. For an organic fundamentals fact sheet, see the Oregon State University Extension fact sheet Organic Gardening Fundamentals.

NUTRITIONAL BENEFITS OF FRESH PRODUCE

Tamara Steinitz, *USU Clinical Associate Professor, Department of Nutrition, Dietetics and Food Sciences*

INTRODUCTION

It is well known that fruits and vegetables are loaded with abundant nutrients and natural compounds. Those beautifully arranged piles of multi-colored fresh produce at the farmers markets or roadside stands look like they could be fountains of youth. That may be stretching things, but eating plenty of produce does reduce the incidence of many chronic diseases. Tips and tricks to eating more fruits and vegetables are widespread since most people do not eat as many servings of fruits and vegetables as they should. But making sure that the peach you eat contains as many healthful benefits as possible can be a bit fuzzy (pun intended). There are many factors from planting to plate that affect the nutritional profile of produce.

Goals of this Section:

- Learn about the effects of ripeness on the nutritional quality of fruits and vegetables.
- Learn how to minimize nutrient losses in freshly harvested produce.
- Discover the benefits of cooking with locally grown produce.

Plant varieties are often chosen for commercial production with an emphasis on yield and ability to survive transport rather than flavor and vitamin content. There is nothing tastier (and probably off the charts in Vitamin A) than a sun-warmed, juicy apricot from grandma's tree… but it is so fragile that it could not survive much more than a trip into your kitchen. The varieties in the grocery store are more resilient, but with a trade-off in flavor and tenderness.

Production methods are another variable. Methods that promote soil health such as cover crops, composted manures, crop rotation and integrated pest management can also enhance the nutrient content of the produce.

Ripening methods affect nutrient levels as well. Climacteric fruits (those that continue to ripen after harvesting such as melons and tomatoes) change in taste, aroma, color and

TABLE 1: LISTING OF CLIMACTERIC AND NON-CLIMACTERIC FRUITS AND VEGETABLES*

Climacteric (continue to ripen after harvest)	**Non-climacteric** (cease to ripen after harvest)
Apple	Blackberry
Apricot	Cherry
Banana	Cranberry
Blueberry	Cucumber
Muskmelon	Eggplant
Nectarine	Grape
Peach	Pea
Pea	Pepper
Plum	Raspberry
Tomato	Strawberry
	Summer Squash
	Watermelon

*Table referenced from Cornell University Cooperative Extension **2012 Production Guide for Storage of Organic Fruits and Vegetables**.

texture as they continue to ripen. If produce must travel many miles, it is often picked early in order to reach the final destination intact. Often the vitamin content does not reach the levels that would be attained while still attached to the plant.

The time period between harvest and consumption is also important when trying to protect nutrients. Maintaining proper temperature and humidity, avoiding bruising and purchasing minimally processed produce all minimize nutrient losses. Produce that has been cut, sliced, chopped or peeled is certainly convenient, but it costs more and likely contains fewer nutrients. Packaging methods, waxing, irradiation, chemical preservation, pH modification and addition of sugar or salt are some of the methods currently used to minimize losses.

So, back to that fresh, local produce. Yes, it is beautiful and appealing, and there are many benefits from eating produce that is not travel-worn. It is more likely to be a variety that has been selected with flavor as the top priority, grown in rich soil, picked at peak ripeness, handled gently and not pre-processed. Beware – it is tempting to buy more than you can carry (or fit into your fridge). But, bringing home that just-picked asparagus or parsnips... or beets... or leeks... and learning how to roast a big pan of vegetables just might get your family out of its dinnertime rut and turn the corner from "should-be" to "want-to-be" vegetable eaters.

Letting the season be your guide opens the door to trying new types of fruits and vegetables, which adds a little excitement to mealtime along with the nutritional benefits that come from a highly varied diet. And that is the best way to ensure that plenty of nutrients are being consumed in the produce section of your plate - know how to make them taste good and eat plenty!

ROASTED VEGETABLES

Serve these to vegetable "skeptics" and watch them become vegetable "lovers." The roasting process intensifies the natural sweetness in vegetables. They turn golden and crisp on the outside and tender in the middle... kids love them!

Try different combinations depending on what you have on hand or what is available seasonally. Asparagus is delicious in the springtime, and root vegetables are comforting during the "dark days of winter." Onions are fabulous year-round.

Scrub any combination of vegetables well – peeling is optional. Cut vegetables into fairly uniform chunks, slices or strips. The sizes are up to you, but remember that smaller pieces (~1 inch) will cook more quickly. Do not overcrowd the pan; vegetables should be in a single layer.

Vegetables that roast well:

- Parsnips
- Carrots
- Potatoes
- Radishes
- Turnips
- Rutabagas
- Beets
- Sweet potatoes
- Onions
- Peppers
- Eggplant
- Asparagus
- Green beans (whole)
- Winter squash (peeled)
- Cauliflower
- Broccoli

Preheat oven to 400 °F. Lightly coat a large roasting pan with olive oil. Add prepared vegetables. Drizzle with a small amount of olive oil and salt/pepper to taste. Toss with hands until uniformly coated. Roast in oven for 30 to 50 minutes (or until fork-tender and medium golden-brown), turning vegetables with spatula every 10 to 15 minutes. Sprinkle with fresh or dried herbs of choice. Add additional seasonings to taste and serve immediately.

PRESERVING YOUR HARVEST

Melanie Jewkes, *USU Extension Family and Consumer Sciences Faculty (Salt Lake County)*

Preserving fruits and vegetables is a great way to enjoy seasonal produce year-round; however, it is important to use safe and current preservation methods approved by the USDA to ensure food is not contaminated. Be aware that a simple Internet search for preservation tips is not the safest way to find a recipe to preserve your food. It could result in inaccurate preservation methods, putting you and those who consume the preserved foods at risk of foodborne illnesses. Be sure to use recipes and procedures that are scientifically studied and USDA approved. Keep in mind that canning is not cooking; it is a precise process that must be followed accurately to ensure food safety. For USDA approved preservation recipes, see the following resources:

- USU Extension: **canning.usu.edu**
- USDA Complete Guide to Home Canning: **USDA Complete Guide to Home Canning**
- The Ball Canning Company: Blue Book of Preserving: **freshpreserving.com**

KIDS AND GARDENING

Dr. Carrie Durward, *USU Extension Nutrition Specialist*

ASK AN EXPERT

INTRODUCTION

Do you struggle to get your children to eat their veggies? Starting a vegetable garden with your children may help. You probably already know that vegetables are an essential part of a healthy diet. Vegetables provide vitamins and minerals and are full of fiber so you feel full without eating too many calories. A good goal is to fill half of your plate with vegetables at every meal.

In homes with vegetable gardens, both the parents and children eat more vegetables. Growing a garden can increase the availability of vegetables at home and can help young children become more familiar with vegetables. It can also help parents' model healthy eating habits, since children learn what is good to eat by watching their parents eat. Getting your child involved in the garden may lead to even bigger rewards. Research shows us that children who garden are more willing to try new vegetables, increase their preference for vegetables and actually eat more vegetables!

Gardening with your child is a chance for hands-on learning and fun. In addition to eating more vegetables, children who garden improve social skills, self-esteem and interest in the environment. By starting a home garden, you can improve your family's diet while learning important life skills!

EATING LOCAL 1-2-3

Buying and eating locally grown foods is quite the craze these days! Fortunately, it is easy to access locally grown fruits and vegetables through one or more of the following three ways.

1. Grow your own at home. Even if you have limited space, you can still take advantage of shared spaces like community gardens. Gardeners can also successfully grow plants, like herbs, in containers positioned in a sunny spot on a porch or balcony.

2. Shop at your local farmers market. Farmers markets are popping up like weeds throughout Utah! Not only do farmers markets support local growers, they also provide shoppers with easy access to plant-ripened, seasonal fruits and vegetables. Not all vendors offer organically grown produce so be sure to ask if you prefer to solely purchase organic products.

3. Purchase a CSA share. CSA stands for Community Supported Agriculture. A CSA producer grows food locally and delivers shares (usually weekly) to customers at specified pick-up locations. Customers pay the producer at the beginning of the growing season which helps the producer cover farming risks associated with year-to-year growing variability. For example, if plants are set back by a hail storm or late freeze, customers receive less generous shares. On the other hand, if good weather provides a bumper crop, customers share in the season's bountiful harvest! For a listing of CSA growers in Utah, see www.csautah.org.

1 GARDEN PREPARATION

GETTING STARTED AND SITE SELECTION

INTRODUCTION

The key to a great garden starts with selecting a good growing location for plants. Garden plants grown under stressful conditions are at increased risk of garden problems. This may be especially challenging for urban gardeners who often face limited options for garden spaces. If possible, gardeners should position plants in a location with ideal growing conditions, even if it means limiting plant choices to those tolerant of your growing conditions. It is impossible to "force" healthy growth in garden plants, so it is best to carefully evaluate garden spot options and choose the best location available.

Goals of this Section:

- Identify the best site to grow your garden.
- Become familiar with growing criteria that impact the quality of fruit and vegetable plants.
- Become familiar with considerations that impact garden layout.

SITE SELECTION

Many types of garden sites may be considered for growing organic produce; however, the following criteria should be evaluated before final selection of a garden site: sunlight, soil, slope, water, annual and perennial weeds, air circulation and access.

Sun Exposure

Sunlight is an essential factor for quality growth of fruit and vegetable plants. Your garden plants have a lot of growing to do in a few short months and need the sun to produce the needed energy to do so! Most fruits and vegetables need a minimum of 6 to 8 hours of direct sunlight each day for optimal growth, including those that produce a fruit or a root, such as tomatoes, carrots and potatoes. Fruit trees, berries and grapes grow best in locations with more than 8 hours of sunlight. Vegetables that produce leafy foliage, such as lettuce or spinach, can

Figure 2: *Most garden plants require six to eight hours of direct sun daily*

Figure 3: *If positioned poorly, tall garden plants may shade lower growing plants*

tolerate less than 6 hours of sunlight but may grow slower and become more spindly than plants exposed to ideal amounts of sunlight. If your garden location receives less than 6 hours of direct sun a day, you may experience better success growing foliage plants, including many herbs, as opposed to fruit and root producing plants.

Another option is to rent a community garden space or share the care and harvest of an ideally positioned garden with a friend. It cannot be understated that ideal sun exposure is essential for healthy fruit and vegetable plant growth! Afternoon sun is preferable to morning sun for plant growth because afternoon sun is brighter and more intense. To reduce shading, consider the position of tall garden plants, vertical gardening structures, fencing and buildings (**Figure 3**).

Additional light sources, such as streetlights, may cause plants like spinach, lettuce, cabbage and radish to bolt (form seed heads) earlier in the growing season due to effects of a long-day photoperiod.

Garden Soil

Fertile, non-compacted and well-drained garden soil is as important a factor for growing healthy plants as ideal sun exposure. Although some organic gardeners may choose to leave the existing garden soil "as-is," most choose to improve the soil by adding organic matter such as composted kitchen scraps, wood chips or dried leaves. If you choose to use the existing soil on a site, have your soil tested before planting your garden (**www.usual.usu.edu**). The following are general guidelines on suitable concentrations of primary macro and micro nutrients in quality garden soils, $>$ 20 ppm (parts per million) nitrogen (N), $>$15 ppm phosphorus (P), $>$ 150 ppm potassium (K), and $>$ 10 ppm iron (Fe). It is important that garden soils have a low salt content and do not contain excessive amounts of clay or sand particles. See the USU fact sheet **Topsoil Quality Guidelines for Landscaping** for detailed information on evaluating topsoil quality. If soil contamination is of concern, contact your local USU Extension office for information on soil testing options for contaminates, such as heavy metals, or see the University of Minnesota Extension fact sheet **Urban Gardens and Soil Contaminants** for information on sources of soil contaminants and ways to reduce your exposure. See the "**Chapter 3: Garden Soil**" section of this guide for more additional information on soil.

Slope

Although a south facing slope can provide an ideal location for a garden, a garden bed should have a slope of less than 2%. A site that is too steep is difficult to irrigate, plant, harvest, weed and may be more susceptible to soil erosion problems. Furthermore, physically disabled gardeners or gardeners with limited mobility may find gardening too difficult or dangerous on a steep slope. Steep slopes can sometimes be terraced with walls or garden boxes. Avoid growing garden plants in windy areas at the top of a slope or low-lying areas near a stream or creek that periodically floods in wet weather. Soil located on the top and middle portions of the slope is typically drier, whereas soil located at the base of the slope is typically moister and plants located at the base may be more susceptible to frost injury. Some garden plants, such as fruit trees, may benefit from being planted on a slope. As cool air sinks, it drains down and away from frost sensitive fruit trees. Ideal placement of fruit trees may protect fruit buds from frost injury in some years. Frost sensitive fruit plants should be planted on east- or north-facing slopes that warm up more slowly in the spring. Fruit buds that break dormancy later in the spring may avoid early frost injury in some years on sensitive fruits such as apricots and cherries. For temperatures and pictures of evidence of frost damage on fruit trees see the USU Extension fact sheet **Critical Temperatures for Frost Damage on Fruit Trees**.

Water

Most fruits and vegetables require 1 to 1½ inches of water a week during the growing season. Fruit trees and established shrubs benefit from deep and less frequent irrigation. The term "established" refers to the plant's ability to explore surrounding soil for water and nutrients. Newly planted trees and shrubs must grow roots before they are able to "establish" themselves in the surrounding soil. In general, trees require one growing season per inch of trunk diameter to establish a sufficient root system to support canopy growth. For example, a 2-inch diameter trunk will take roughly two growing seasons to establish its root system after planting. A garden irrigation system should be designed and tested prior to planting garden plants. On smaller sites, culinary water can be used economically. On larger sites, it is more economical to use pressurized secondary water or ditch water from a canal if available. Irrigation water may be applied with sprinkler, drip, or flood irrigation or by hand watering. For more detailed information on watering your garden see the "**Garden Irrigation**" section in Chapter 4 of this guide.

Annual and Perennial Weeds

Weed control is a constant chore for any gardener; special consideration should be given to gardens located in areas surrounded by noxious weeds such as vacant lots or unmaintained fields. Weed seeds can move with water, wind, soil, compost, animals and birds. Introduction of weed seeds into your garden soil will result in years of weeding down the road. Secondary water sources and topsoil may introduce weed seeds into the garden. Initial weed control and garden maintenance practices can greatly impact weed seed germination. For more information on control of garden weeds see the "**Integrated Weed Management**" section in Chapter 5 of this guide.

Air Circulation

One of the challenges faced by organic gardeners is a restriction on use of synthetically produced chemicals for pest control. With limited pesticide options available, it is imperative organic gardeners use other means for controlling garden pests. One technique for controlling some garden diseases is to reduce the incidence of fungal disease by maintaining adequate air circulation. Good air circulation can reduce relative humidity and can be especially important for plants growing under enclosures and sites near large buildings. Good air circulation helps plant foliage dry quickly after a rainstorm or irrigation event, thus reducing the risk of some diseases. Avoid choosing a garden location surrounded by buildings or tall trees or shrubs with dense canopies. Canopies of large shade trees can be raised and thinned by a certified arborist to increase air flow to the area under the tree.

Access

Ideally locate the garden in an area easily accessed by the gardener. Consider locating your garden close to the house or near a patio, driveway or walkway for convenient movement to and from the garden area. Also, consider traffic through those areas to avoid damage to garden plants. Traffic considerations include movement of dogs and placement of garden hoses. Herb gardens are ideally positioned close to the kitchen for ease of harvest during food preparation. Vandalism and theft should be considered for at-risk gardens located near public areas. See Wasatch Community Garden's **From Neglected Parcels to Community Gardens** for innovative techniques to address vandalism at community garden spaces and gardens located near public areas.

Site Selection for Fruit Trees and Small Fruits

Sites for fruit trees, berries or grapes should be evaluated more critically because these garden plants are perennial and therefore require several years to reach full production. Fruit trees grow best on a site with good air circulation, soil drainage and protection from frost. Fruit trees require 4 to 5 feet of well-drained soil for adequate root growth. Berries and grapes need 3 to 4 feet of soil above a water table. See the "**Tree Fruit and Small Fruit**" section in Chapter 2 of this guide for more information on organic fruit production.

Figure 4: *Consider placement of garden pathways before planting garden beds*

VARIETY SELECTION

INTRODUCTION

There are numerous options when it comes to selecting seed and plant varieties for growing a garden or small farm. A plant variety describes a plant with characteristics such as fruit size, shape or color distinct from other varieties. Common desirable traits that lead us to choose one variety over another include taste, pest resistance, cold hardiness, days-to-maturity, color, size, scent or perhaps the origin or history of the plant. Many varieties of vegetables, tree fruit and small fruit grow well in Utah. This guide suggests a sampling of vegetable and fruit varieties that are well adapted to Utah. Do not fear if your favorite variety is not listed, as recommendations are not fully comprehensive. Vegetable varieties listed in Table 2: Suggested Vegetable Varieties for Utah were selected based on recommendations from local organic growers, retailers and experienced gardeners and are therefore subjective to individual preferences. There are many other varieties that also grow well in Utah including numerous hybrid fruit and vegetable varieties. This table lists several heirloom varieties and other open pollinated varieties due to strong interest among organic growers in these types of garden plants.

It should be noted that USDA certified organic producers are required to use certified organic seed, except when an "equivalent organically produced or untreated variety is not commercially available" (**Electronic Code of Federal Regulations**). Use of organically grown hybrid varieties is allowed; although, genetically modified (GMO) plants are not permitted in USDA certified organic agriculture. Non-commercial organic gardeners must decide whether or not they want to limit their seed and garden start selections to those that are certified organic. Gardeners who grow their own fruit and vegetable starts will enjoy the greatest selection of fruit and vegetable varieties. Gardeners who decide to purchase starts from a local retailer will be limited to the selection of varieties available. For more information on growing starts from seed, see the "Starting Garden Plants from Seed" section in Chapter 1 of this guide. It is important to consider local climatic factors and pest presence when selecting appropriate garden varieties. If you have questions regarding variety selection, consult your local USU Extension office.

Goals of this Section:

- Better understand why "days to harvest" requirements impact selection of non-perennial vegetable varieties.
- Better understand differences between the terms open pollinated, heirloom, hybrid and genetically modified organisms.
- Discover varieties of fruits and vegetables that are recommended for Utah gardens.

DAYS TO HARVEST

A gardener's selection of vegetable and fruit varieties is sometimes limited by local climatic conditions. Before selecting vegetable varieties, ensure your growing season is long enough to accommodate the days to harvest requirement. "Days to harvest" is the average number of days between a germinated seed or planted transplant and first harvest. This number will be most accurate when day time temperatures are conducive to growth. Days to harvest information can be found on the back of your seed pack, in a seed catalog, nursery plant tag or via the Internet. The growing season or frost-free period for many locations in Utah can be found in the Utah Climate Center publication Utah Freeze Dates.

SEED AND START TYPES

It is important to understand differences between types of seeds and starts (small plants, tubers and bulbs) when choosing fruit and vegetable varieties to plant in the garden. Examples of plant types available to gardeners include open pollinated, heirloom and hybrid varieties. By understanding benefits of various seed and start types, organic gardeners can choose garden plants that meet their expectations and are best suited to their site conditions.

OPEN POLLINATED AND HEIRLOOM VARIETIES

Like humans, when plants reproduce, each offspring has its own unique DNA and expression of traits. However, open pollinated seed varieties of fruits and vegetables usually express consistent traits from one generation to the next. Therefore, gardeners can expect similar taste, appearance and other traits from seeds collected from open pollinated varieties. Plants grown from seed of varieties not categorized as open pollinated, namely hybrids, seldom resemble the original parent plants and may also express traits unappealing to the gardener. One disadvantage of planting open pollinated varieties over hybrid options is that open pollinated varieties often have lower resistance to insects, nematodes and diseases as opposed to hybrid varieties selected for high pest resistance. Hence, if a gardener has known pest problems in the garden for which resistant plants are available, he or she may experience better success growing resistant hybrid varieties.

Sometimes gardeners interchange the terms "open pollinated" and "heirloom." It is true that all heirloom varieties are open pollinated, and hence seeds can be collected and replanted year after year. However, not all open pollinated varieties are heirlooms. Heirlooms refer to open pollinated fruit and vegetable varieties that were created prior to 1951 when hybrid varieties were first introduced. Seeds of some heirloom varieties have been exchanged for a hundred years or more whereas other heirloom varieties were created in the first half of the 20th century. Heirloom varieties are often selected for good flavor or unique appearance. For more information on heirlooms, see the Colorado State University Extension fact sheet **Creating an Heirloom Vegetable Garden**.

ASK AN EXPERT

CHALLENGES OF GROWING HEIRLOOM TOMATOES

Marion Murray, *USU Extension IPM Project Leader*

Don't let diseases like fusarium wilt hinder growing your favorite heirlooms.

In past seasons, the Utah Plant Pest Diagnostic Lab (UPPDL) has identified many tomato problems, including soil borne diseases and bacterial diseases. One reason for the increase in these diseases is the popularity of growing heirloom (open-pollinated) tomatoes, which lack genetic disease resistance, leaving them susceptible to epidemics.

Although hybrids are generally more productive and disease-resistant than open-pollinated tomato varieties, many varieties lack the rich fruit flavor that heirloom varieties deliver. There are several horticultural options that can help these plants prosper, resulting in reduced risk of disease, increased productivity and reduced fruit cracking.

When growing heirlooms, **pick cultivars** that have been shown to be successful in your area, which may take trial and error studies in your own garden. Some options include:

- **Green Zebra:** a prolific, medium-sized variety with good flavor
- **Cherokee Purple:** although a modest producer, this variety performs well in cooler climates, bearing purplish slicing fruit with a smoky flavor.
- **Caspian Pink:** beefsteak tomato similar to Brandywine but more prolific and suited to cool climates

Figure 5: Using good sanitation practices, like picking up and discarding fruit at the end of the growing season, is one technique to reduce the likelihood of pests popping-up in your garden

- **Wins All:** a disease-resistant heirloom with large, juicy fruit
- **Black Krim:** a productive variety less prone to cracking, with a deep purple skin and flesh producing a salty-sweet flavor

Since many open-pollinated tomato varieties tend to take their time ripening, they grow best where they get enough heat to allow them to fully mature. **Start plants early** in a cold frame, greenhouse or high tunnel to extend their season. Plants won't grow in the field until the soil has warmed, which can be helped by Wall-O-Water®, cages wrapped with plastic, thick row cover or mulches.

Heirloom tomatoes are vigorous growers and will need to be pruned regularly and spaced wider than hybrids. **Remove suckers and plant at a wide spacing** to provide better air flow, which helps prevent foliar diseases and encourages larger fruit production at the top of the plant.

When watering, **avoid overhead irrigation** because it increases humidity within the plants and splashes water, both of which improve conditions for spread of foliar diseases. Provide intermittent watering to reduce splitting skin, a common problem in heirlooms.

Monitor plants regularly for insect and disease problems (more than you would with hybrid varieties) and learn to identify tomato diseases.

Where soil borne diseases or poor production have put the kibosh on growing heirlooms, **consider grafting**. Grafted plants are made up of an heirloom scion (above ground part) and a hybrid rootstock, uniting disease resistance and enhanced vigor with fruit quality and taste. Grafted heirlooms can produce 30–50% greater yields than non-grafted heirlooms. In tube grafting, hybrid and heirloom seedlings are severed with a sterile knife at a slant just above the cotyledon. The heirloom scion is then secured to the root system of the hybrid with a tube or clip and allowed to heal before transplanting.

HYBRID VARIETIES

The term "hybrid" refers to seed and plant starts that were produced by crossing selected parents with desirable traits. Pollination occurs when pollen from male flower parts (stamen) fertilizes ovules of female flower parts (pistil). Hybrid parent plants can be pollinated manually or naturally. For example, a plant breeder (or a gardener) may take pollen from one parent and hand-pollinate female flower parts of the other parent plant. Hybrid parent plants can also be pollinated in the garden setting. For example, if a grower wants to create a hybrid corn plant, he or she may select two varieties of corn with desirable traits (parents) and remove the tassel (male flower parts) of one of the varieties. Corn is wind pollinated and the male (source of pollen) and female (produces seeds) flower parts are located on different parts of the plant; male flower parts are located on the top of the plant (tassel) and female flower parts are located on the ears (**Figure 6**). Pollen from the corn variety with remaining male flower parts will drift to female flower parts of the cultivar with the tassels removed. This ensures pollen from corn plants with the remaining tassels (male parent) is the only source of pollen that pollinates the corn ears (female parent) of the variety with tassels removed. In this way, a grower can select parents of hybrid offspring (seeds). For more information on hybrid production, see the Texas A & M Extension fact sheet **Hybrid Varieties and Saving Seed**.

USDA certified organic agriculture permits the use of organic hybrid seed and organically grown hybrid starts if the plants were grown from certified organic seed using approved growing methods. The desirable traits of the selected parent plants produce hybrid offspring with benefits to the gardener. The term "hybrid vigor" is often used to describe such benefits. Examples of hybrid vigor include increased production, increased disease resistance, optimal color and shape of fruit, fewer days to harvest requirement and so forth.

Figure 6: *Male and female flower parts on corn plants*

One common complaint made by organic gardeners of hybrid varieties is that hybrid fruits and vegetables do not taste as good as open pollinated varieties. Because taste is subjective, this may not be true based on individual preferences. However, taste is not always one of the qualities selected for by plant breeders. One major drawback of planting hybrids is that saved seed from hybrid plants is sterile or will not typically produce offspring that express the same traits as the plant from which it was collected. Planting seed collected from a hybrid plant is a gamble; gardeners may grow something great or something unappealing. Therefore, for hybrid plants, gardeners typically purchase new seed or plant starts each year to ensure consistency. For more information on hybrid verses open pollinated varieties, see the University of Illinois Extension fact sheet **Hybrid and Heirlooms**.

VFN VARIETIES

As mentioned previously, hybrid varieties offer many benefits to gardeners like increased pest resistance. Gardeners may notice some hybrid tomato varieties include the letters "VFN" after the name of the cultivar. VFN stands for "verticillium wilt," "fusarium wilt," and "nematode" resistance. VFN resistant varieties, such as "Celebrity" and "Better Boy," offer gardeners with the mentioned soil borne fungi or root knot nematode (microscopic roundworm) problems the ability to grow a more productive tomato crop. Your local USU Extension office can help you determine if you have these problems. For more information on common tomato questions and answers, including good plant selection tips, see the Texas A&M fact sheets **Tomato, Part 1** and **Tomato, Part 2**. For more information on fruit and vegetable pest management, see Chapter 5 "**Garden Pest Control**" section of this guide.

GENETICALLY MODIFIED ORGANISMS (GMOS)

Britney Hunter, *USU Extension Horticulture Faculty (Davis County)*

Genetically engineered plants, often referred to as genetically modified organisms (GMOs), are not permitted in certified organic agriculture. However, many gardeners, farmers and consumers are concerned with the use and safety of genetically engineered plants in agriculture. An introduction to understanding genetic engineering is provided below along with resources for further reading. The information on genetic engineering was compiled using peer-reviewed Extension publications from various universities and government agencies.

Definition

Genetically engineered or GE plants are products of biotechnology. Genetic engineering refers to the process of copying a gene from one living organism (bacteria, plant or animal) and adding it to another living organism using biotechnological methods. Genes are the instructions for all living things to build and maintain their cells. GE plants currently in commercial production include: soybeans, alfalfa, corn, canola, cotton, papaya, sugar beets and zucchini. GE seeds and plants of edible crops cannot be purchased at retail nurseries. GE seeds and plants are only available to commercial farmers.

How GE Plants are different

By inserting a new gene into a plant, a researcher can create a plant with additional nutrients, increased resistance to insects and disease, a higher tolerance of environmental stress or resistance to specific herbicides. Genetic engineering makes the process of moving desired genes into plants faster and allows for crosses that would not be possible under natural conditions. Methods of modern genetic engineering of plants vary. One example is exposing plants to bacteria that contain DNA with a desired trait. Bacteria can transfer DNA to other organisms. Once the bacteria deposit the DNA inside the plant, the DNA codes for a new protein that makes the plant express a desired trait, such as disease resistance. The novel protein within the plant differentiates the non-GE plant and a GE plant.

Safety and Regulation.
It has been estimated that 60 to 70% of food products in retail stores already contain genetically modified ingredients, largely due to the frequent addition of ingredients containing GE corn and soybeans. Three government agencies oversee the release of GM plants. The U.S. Food and Drug Administration (FDA) is the governing agency responsible for most aspects of food safety and health related issues. In some cases, such as when genetic engineering incorporates a protein with pesticide-like properties, the U.S. Environmental Protection Agency (EPA) has responsibility. The United States Department of Agriculture (USDA) oversees and regulates field testing, as well as the movement of GE crops and seeds.

The FDA assumes that DNA is safe for human consumption. If the novel piece of DNA in GE crops has the same chemical properties as DNA already present in food, it does not present any new health risk. Genetically engineered crops are not required to undergo formal long-term safety tests before marketing approval since they do not contain any new chemicals that have not already been widely consumed in other foods. An exception is "Bt" crops, which incorporate a protein toxic to insects, where the EPA oversees in long-term safety testing. U.S. regulators have concluded that GE foods are no more likely to have long-term health effects than conventional foods, and GE technology shows promise in solving many challenges in agriculture. However, environmental issues and consumer acceptance of GMOs in food will affect the continued use of genetic engineering in agriculture.

For more information on genetic engineering of plants, see the following online resources:

- University of California Agriculture and Natural Resources. **Safety of Genetically Engineered Food**
- Cornell Cooperative Extension. **Genetically Engineered Foods: Food Safety of Genetically Engineered Crops** and **Genetically Engineered Foods: In the Marketplace**
- USDA Agriculture Research Service. **What are GMO's?**
- University of Florida Institute of Food and Agricultural Science (IFAS). **Genetically Modified Foods**

TABLE 2: SUGGESTED VEGETABLE VARIETIES FOR UTAH*

Vegetable	Variety	Type
Asparagus	Jersey Giant	Hybrid
Asparagus	Purple Passion	Hybrid
Asparagus	Jersey Knight	Hybrid
Beans (Pole)	Blue Lake	Heirloom
Beans (Pole)	Cherokee Trail Black	Heirloom
Beans (Pole)	Kentucky Wonder	Heirloom
Beans (Pole)	Yardlong	Heirloom
Beans (Pole)	Scarlett Runner	Heirloom
Beans (Bush)	Dragon's Tongue	Heirloom
Beans (Bush)	Early Contender	Hybrid
Beans (Bush)	Jade	Hybrid
Beans (Bush)	Golden Wax-Yellow	Heirloom
Beans (Bush)	Maxibel	Heirloom
Beet	Burpee's Golden	Heirloom
Beet	Chioggia	Heirloom
Beet	Red Ace	Hybrid
Beet	Cylindra	Heirloom
Beet	Detroit Dark Red	Heirloom
Broccoli	Packman	Hybrid
Broccoli	Calabrese	Heirloom
Broccoli	Raab Rapini	Heirloom
Broccoli	Premium Crop	Hybrid
Broccoli	Waltham	Heirloom
Brussels Sprout	Long Island	Heirloom
Brussels Sprout	Jade Cross	Hybrid
Cabbage	Danish Ball Head	Heirloom
Cabbage	Golden Acre	Heirloom
Cabbage	Early Jersey Wakefield	Heirloom
Cabbage	Savoy Perfection	Heirloom
Carrot	Dragon	Heirloom
Carrot	Danvers Half-Long	Heirloom

Vegetable	Variety	Type
Carrot	Little Fingers	Heirloom
Carrot	Paris Market	Heirloom
Carrot	Scarlet Nantes	Heirloom
Cauliflower	Cheddar	Hybrid
Cauliflower	Self-Blanche	Hybrid
Cauliflower	Snow Crown	Hybrid
Celery	Conquistador	Hybrid
Celery	Tendercrisp	Hybrid
Celery	Utah 52-70	Hybrid
Cucumber (Slicing)	Sweet Success	Hybrid
Cucumber (Slicing)	Armenian	Heirloom
Cucumber (Slicing)	Straight 8	Heirloom
Cucumber (Slicing)	Sweeter Yet	Hybrid
Cucumber (Slicing)	Marketmore	Heirloom
Cucumber (Pickling)	Wisconsin	Heirloom
Cucumber (Pickling)	Cool Breeze	Hybrid
Cucumber (Pickling)	County Fair	Hybrid
Cucumber (Pickling)	Alibi	Hybrid
Eggplant	Rosa Bianca	Heirloom
Eggplant	Ping Tung Long	Heirloom
Eggplant	Florida High Bush	Heirloom
Eggplant	Black Beauty	Heirloom
Garlic	Siskyou Purple	Hybrid
Garlic	Spanish Roja	Heirloom
Garlic	German Hardy	Heirloom
Kohlrabi	Early White	Heirloom
Kohlrabi	Purple Vienna	Heirloom
Leek	American Flag	Heirloom
Lettuce (heading)	Tennis Balls	Heirloom
Lettuce (heading)	Oak Leaf	Heirloom
Lettuce (heading)	Iceburg	Heirloom
Lettuce (heading)	Red Sails	Heirloom
Lettuce (Romaine)	Winter Density	Heirloom
Lettuce (Romaine)	Paris White Cos	Heirloom
Lettuce (Romaine)	Paris Island Cos	Heirloom
Lettuce (Romaine)	Annapolis	Hybrid

Vegetable	Variety	Type
Lettuce (Romaine)	Crisp Mint	Heirloom
Lettuce (leaf type)	Cimarron	Heirloom
Lettuce (leaf type)	Mesclun Mix	Varies
Lettuce (leaf type)	Buttercrunch	Heirloom
Lettuce (leaf type)	Simpson	Heirloom
Lettuce (leaf type)	Green Salad Bowl	Heirloom
Muskmelon	Ambrosia	Hybrid
Muskmelon	Athena	Hybrid
Muskmelon	Minnesota Midget	Hybrid
Muskmelon	Hearts of Gold	Heirloom
Muskmelon	Hale's Best	Heirloom
Muskmelon	Crenshaw	Heirloom
Okra	Queen Silver	Heirloom
Okra	Clemson Spineless	Heirloom
Onion	Utah Sweet Spanish (yellow)	Heirloom
Onion	Copra (yellow)	Hybrid
Onion	Candy (yellow)	Hybrid
Onion	Walla Walla (yellow)	Heirloom
Onion	Borettana (yellow)	Heirloom
Onion	Candy Apple (red)	Hybrid
Onion	Super Star (white)	Hybrid
Onion	White Lisbon (bunching)	Heirloom
Parsnips	Horris Model	Heirloom
Parsnips	Hollow Crown	Heirloom
Parsnips	All American	Heirloom
Peas (snap)	Amish Snap	Heirloom
Peas (snap)	Sugar Snap	Heirloom
Peas (edible pod)	Oregon Sugar Pod	Heirloom
Peas (edible pod)	De Grace	Heirloom
Peas (shelling)	Tom Thumb (miniature)	Heirloom
Peas (shelling)	Green Arrow	Heirloom
Peas (shelling)	Little Marvel	Heirloom
Peas (shelling)	Lincoln	Heirloom
Pepper (mild)	Peruvian Aji Amarillo	Heirloom
Pepper (mild)	Sahuaro	Hybrid
Pepper (mild)	Anaheim	Heirloom

Vegetable	Variety	Type
Pepper (mild)	NuMex Joe E. Parker	Heirloom
Pepper (medium)	Serrano Del Sol	Hybrid
Pepper (medium)	Jalapeño	Heirloom
Pepper (medium)	Hungarian Yellow Wax	Heirloom
Pepper (very hot)	Thai Hot	Heirloom
Pepper (very hot)	Cayenne Long Slim	Heirloom
Pepper (very hot)	Red Mushroom Cap	Heirloom
Pepper (sweet long)	Aconcagua	Heirloom
Pepper (sweet long)	Corno di toro	Heirloom
Pepper (sweet long)	Carmen	Hybrid
Pepper (sweet long)	Pasilla Bajio	Heirloom
Pepper (sweet bell)	Purple Beauty	Heirloom
Pepper (sweet bell)	Merlot (purple)	Hybrid
Pepper (sweet bell)	Early Sunsation (yellow)	Hybrid
Pepper (sweet bell)	Gypsy	Hybrid
Pepper (sweet bell)	California Wonder	Heirloom
Pepper (sweet bell)	Yolo Wonder	Heirloom
Potato (white)	Yukon Gold	Heirloom
Potato (white)	Russets	Heirloom
Potato (white)	Cal White	Heirloom
Potato (white)	Kennebec	Heirloom
Potato (purple)	Viking	Heirloom
Potato (purple)	All Blue	Heirloom
Potato (red)	Red Norland	Heirloom
Potato (red)	Pontiac	Heirloom
Pumpkin	Musque de Provence	Heirloom
Pumpkin	Autumn Gold	Hybrid
Pumpkin	Howden	Heirloom
Pumpkin	Jack Be Little	Heirloom
Pumpkin	Cinderella	Heirloom
Radish	Champion	Heirloom
Radish	Cherry Bell	Heirloom
Radish	Cincinnati Market	Heirloom
Radish	French Breakfast	Heirloom
Radish	Rat Tail Radish	Heirloom
Specialty Melon	Tigger Melon	

Vegetable	Variety	Type
Specialty Melon	Canary Melon	
Spinach	Melody	Hybrid
Spinach	Red Cardinal	Hybrid
Spinach	Space	Hybrid
Spinach	Bloomsdale Long-standing	Heirloom
Sweet Potato	Georgia Jett	
Summer Squash	Juane et Verti	Heirloom
Summer Squash	Black Beauty Zucchini	Heirloom
Summer Squash	Gold Rush Zucchini	Hybrid
Summer Squash	Early Golden Crookneck	Heirloom
Summer Squash	Straight Neck	Heirloom
Summer Squash	Zucchini Elite	Hybrid
Winter Squash	Sweet Meat	Heirloom
Winter Squash	Delicata	Heirloom
Winter Squash	Argonaut (Butternut)	Hybrid
Winter Squash	Long Island Cheese	Heirloom
Winter Squash	Sunshine	Hybrid
Winter Squash	Spaghetti	Heirloom
Winter Squash	Pink Banana	Heirloom
Winter Squash	Waltham Butternut	Heirloom
Winter Squash	Buttercup	Heirloom
Winter Squash	Table Queen Acorn	Heirloom
Sweet Corn (se/sh2)	Serendipity	Hybrid
Sweet Corn (sh2)	Northern Extra Sweet	Hybrid
Sweet Corn (se)	Sugar Buns	Hybrid
Sweet Corn (se)	Ambrosia	Hybrid
Sweet Corn (se)	Double Delicious	Hybrid
Sweet Corn (se)	Peaches & Cream	Hybrid
Sweet Corn	Early Bantam	Heirloom
Swiss Chard	Bright Lights	Heirloom
Swiss Chard	Rhubarb	Heirloom
Swiss Chard	Lucullus	Heirloom
Swiss Chard	Fordhook Giant	Heirloom
Tomato (sauce)	Roma	Heirloom

Vegetable	Variety	Type
Tomato (sauce)	Amish	Heirloom
Tomato (sauce)	Polish Linguisa	Heirloom
Tomato (sauce)	Big Momma	Hybrid
Tomato	Jet Star	Hybrid
Tomato	Champion	Hybrid
Tomato	Big Beef	Hybrid
Tomato	Celebrity	Hybrid
Tomato	Better Boy	Hybrid
Tomato	Kellogg's Breakfast	Heirloom
Tomato	DX 52-12	Heirloom
Tomato	Black Krim	Heirloom
Tomato	Cherokee Purple	Heirloom
Tomato	Mortgage Lifter	Heirloom
Tomato	Rutgers	Heirloom
Tomato	Dixie Gold	Heirloom
Tomato	Green Zebra	Heirloom
Tomato	Brandywine	Heirloom
Tomato (cherry)	Mexico Midget	Heirloom
Tomato (small)	Patio	Hybrid
Tomato (cherry)	Chadwick Cherry	Heirloom
Tomato (cherry)	Yellow Pear	Heirloom
Tomato (cherry)	Sun Sugar	Hybrid
Tomato (cherry)	Juliet	Hybrid

*In spring 2013, Master Gardeners in Davis County and USU Extension Faculty were asked to list their top three vegetable varieties to grow. Recommendations were also provided by a Wasatch Community Gardens manager. This list was compiled by Britney Hunter, USU Extension Horticulture faculty in Davis county.

GARDEN LAYOUT AND PLANTING

INTRODUCTION

It is wise to carefully construct a garden plan prior to planting your garden. By mapping out the garden, a gardener will know how much room is necessary to grow desired plants. Different garden plants require different volumes of above- and below-ground space for adequate growth. For example, you would not want to grow pumpkin plants that sprawl several feet, 6 inches apart from one another. Furthermore, gardeners with limited garden space may want to try to grow as many garden plants as possible in a limited space. Others with unlimited space may choose to spread garden plants out to ensure easy access to each plant. Therefore new gardeners should consider both garden space constraints and which types of plants they want to grow before starting a garden. Territorial Seed Company offers a free online garden mapping program at http://gardenplanner.territorialseed.com/. See Figure 7 as an example of a garden plan.

Goals of this Section:

- Learn about spacing requirements for various vegetable plants.
- Become familiar with crop rotation practices.
- Learn when to plant cool and warm season plants outside.

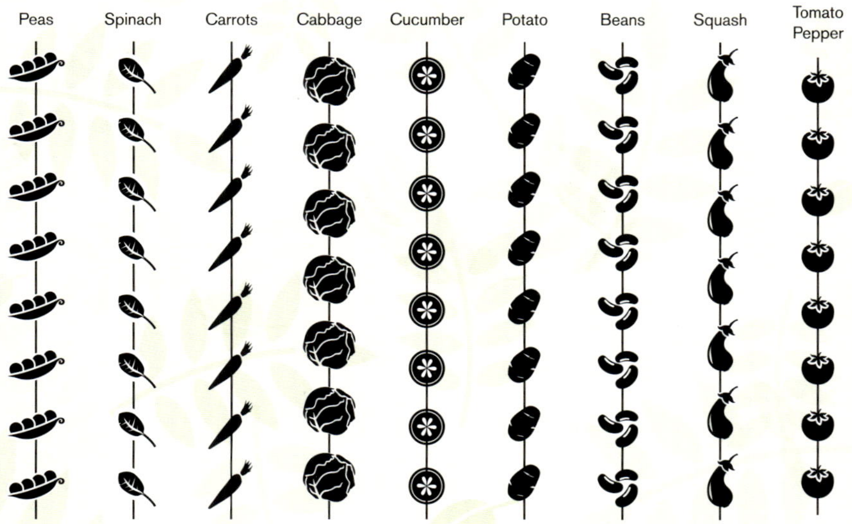

Figure 7: *Example Garden Plan*

VEGETABLE PLANTING DEPTH AND SPACING

Information on suggested plant spacing can be found on the back of seed packets, in various gardening books, online or from your local USU Extension office. Table 3 provides recommendations for traditional spacing of vegetable plants and Table 4 suggests closer vegetable spacing options for gardens with size constraints. A gardener may prefer to plant a garden using vegetable starts purchased from a local garden center. Select disease-free starts from a reputable garden center. If planting vegetable starts, plant in the garden at the same depth as the plant was grown in the container and follow recommendations for plant spacing in Tables 3 and 4.

TABLE 3: TRADITIONAL ROW SPACING

Use for large garden areas.

Vegetable	Planting Depth (in inches)	Planting Spacing (in inches)	
		In Row After Thinning	*Between Row*
Asparagus (crowns)	6-8	12-18	36-60
Beans			
Bush (green/wax)	1-2	3-4	18-24
Dry	1-2	3-4	18-24
Lima	1-2	3-4	18-24
Beet	1	2-3	12-18
Broccoli	½	18-24	24-30
Brussels Sprout	½	18-24	24-30
Cabbage	½	18-24	24-30
Carrot	¼	1-2	12-18
Cauliflower	½	18-24	24-30
Celery	¼	4-6	18-24
Cucumber	1	9-12	36-48
Eggplant	¼ - ½	18-24	24-30
Endive	¼ - ½	8-12	12-18
Garlic	1-2	3-4	12-18
Kale	¼ - ½	8-15	18-24
Kohlrabi	½	4-8	18-24
Leek	½	2-3	12-18
Lettuce			
Head	¼	8-15	18-24
Leaf	¼	6-8	18-24

Vegetable	Planting Depth (in inches)	Planting Spacing (in inches)	
		In Row After Thinning	*Between Row*
Muskmelon	1	24-36	36-48
Mustard	½	6-8	18-24
Okra	½ - 1	12-15	24-30
Onion			
Seeds	½	2-3	12-18
Sets	2	2-3	12-18
Transplants	1-2	2-3	12-18
Parsnip	½	3-4	18-24
Peas	1-2	2-3	12-18
Pepper	¼	15-18	24-30
Potatoe	4	9-12	24-36
Pumpkin	1	36-48	48-60
Radish	½	1-2	6-12
Rhubarb (crowns)	4-6	18-24	24-36
Spinach	½	3-6	18-24
Squash			
Summer	1	24-36	36-48
Winter	1	24-48	48-60
Sweet Corn	1-2	9-12	30-36
Swiss Chard	1	4-8	18-24
Tomato	¼	24-36	36-48
Turnip	½	4-6	18-24
Watermelon	1	24-48	36-48

TABLE 4: CLOSE-ROW PLANTING

Use for smaller gardens, raised beds, grow boxes and containers.

Vegetable	(in inches)	Planting Spacing (in inches)
Beans	½	6 or 4x12
Beet	1	3-6
Broccoli	½	18
Cabbage	½	18
Cantaloupe	1	24-36
Carrot	¼	2-3
Cauliflower	½	18
Chinese Cabbage	½	12
Corn	1-2	12x30 or 9x36
Cucumber	1	12-24
Eggplant	¼	18-24
Kohlrabi	½	7-9
Leaf Lettuce	¼	6-9
Leeks	½	2-6
New Zealand Spinach	1	12
Onion (dry sets)	2	4-6
Onion (green)	½	2-6
Parsnip	½	5-6
Peas	1-2	4-6 or 3x8
Pepper	¼	15
Potato	4	15 or 12x24
Pumpkin	1	36-48
Radish	½	2-3
Spinach	½	4-6
Summer Squash	1	30-36
Swiss Chard	1	6-9
Tomato	¼	24
Watermelon	1	24-36
Winter Squash	1	36-48

Figure 8: *Gardener planting onion sets*

CLOSE-ROW PLANTING TECHNIQUES

Square-foot gardening and other intensive planting methods, like spin-farming® (small plot intensive), practice close-row spacing methods. The objective of close-row planting is to gain maximum productivity in a limited garden space. Plants are spaced more closely than recommended spacing for a traditional garden area. One example of an intensive gardening technique is inter-planting cool season plants, like cabbage, chard, lettuce and spinach, with warm season plants, like beans, cantaloupe, peppers, sweet corn and tomatoes. As air and soil temperatures warm, cool season plant growth slows and warm season plant growth accelerates. Eventually warm season plants take over the space previously occupied by cool season plants. This technique allows the gardener to achieve more productivity out of less garden space by taking advantage of differences between ideal growing conditions for cool and warm season garden plants.

After harvesting from warm season plants, consider replanting the same area with a second crop of cool season plants in late summer to keep the soil covered and add an additional harvest to the growing season. For example, in one garden row, plant radishes in the spring, tomatoes in the summer and spinach in the fall. As a general rule, locate tall plants to the north or east (away from primary direction of the sun) of lower growing plants. Tall plants may shade lower

Figure 9: *Tomato plants trained-up a vertical structure with their lower branches pruned to provide ideal growing conditions for herbs planted underneath*

growing plants if poorly positioned. Shading restricts ideal sun exposure and may reduce air circulation to lower growing plants. Alternatively, in hot areas where shading will protect plants from heat stress, it may be useful to plant tall plants to the south of lower growing plants. Vertical growing structures, like trellises, stakes and cages, can be used to support plants and save space in the garden. If you are gardening in a raised bed, consider positioning trailing or vining plants, like squash and pole beans, toward the outside of the garden bed so plants can grow over the sides of the bed. For some plants, such as sweet corn and basil, it is helpful to replant every 1 to 2 weeks for a longer harvest period. This technique enables gardeners to enjoy smaller quantities of produce over several weeks as opposed to an excess of produce at one time. For more information on intensive gardening, see the University of Virginia Extension fact sheet **Intensive Gardening Methods**. For more information on growing needs of many fruit and vegetable plants see the **Fruit and Vegetable Production Fact Sheets**.

CROP ROTATION

Organic gardeners should exercise caution to avoid diseases and prevent insect pest infestations in the garden. One technique to reduce incidence of diseases and insects is proper crop rotation. When planning the garden space, it is important to consider the rotation of families to a different location in the garden every year. Plants in the same plant family often succumb to similar pests and should be rotated together as a group. Ideally, plants in the same family should not return to the same area where they were previously grown for at least three growing seasons. Proper crop rotation may be a difficult practice in a small garden; therefore gardeners who are unable to follow ideal crop rotation practices should be extra vigilant when scouting for garden pests. For more information on alternative management techniques, see Chapter 5 "**Garden Pest Control**" section of this guide. Below are common vegetable family groups:

- **Gourd** (cucumber, summer and winter squash, cantaloupe, watermelon, pumpkin)
- **Nightshade** (tomato, potato, pepper, eggplant)

CROP ROTATION DIAGRAM

Year 1	Year 1	Year 1	Year 1
Gourd, Nightshade	Mustard, Parsley	Legume, Goosefoot	Gourd, Nightshade
Legume, Goosefoot	Gourd, Nightshade	Mustard, Parsley	Legume, Goosefoot
Mustard, Parsley	Legume, Goosefoot	Gourd, Nightshade	Mustard, Parsley

*Perennial crops, such as strawberries, asparagus and raspberries, cannot be rotated every year but should be moved to another garden area if disease or insect pest levels exceed a reasonable threshold for control.

- **Grass** (sweet corn, popcorn)
- **Legume** (pea, bean)
- **Amaranth** (chard, spinach)
- **Chenopod** (beet)
- **Mustard** (cabbage, collards, Brussels sprouts, kale, cauliflower, broccoli, kohlrabi, rutabaga, turnip, cress, horseradish, radish)
- **Parsley** (carrot, parsley, celery, parsnip)
- **Composite** (chicory, endive, salsify, dandelion, lettuce, Jerusalem artichoke, globe artichoke)
- **Lily** (onion, garlic, leek, chives)
- **Mallow** (okra)

PLANTING OUTSIDE

Now that your garden is planned it is time to start planting! All gardeners must resist the urge to purchase the first tomato plant they see for sale. It is important to be patient and plant outdoors when conditions are appropriate for plant growth. Vegetables have varying degrees of tolerance to frost, cool temperatures and heat. Cool season plants 'grow best with temperatures of 60 to 65°F, tolerate light to moderate frosts, and are intolerant of high summer temperatures' (Iowa State University Extension). Conversely, most warm season plants survive 'under cool conditions but will not produce fruit until night temperatures reach 50°F, require warm temperatures to mature and grow, and require frost-free conditions for fruit formation' (Colorado State University Extension). Vegetables can be grouped into four groups, A-D, for spring planting (Table 5). Table 6 lists suggested vegetable planting dates for an average year in various Utah locations. Because each season has its own unique weather conditions, suggested planting dates may not be appropriate for all years. The 'Average Planting Date' describes timing of initial planting. For plants such as broccoli, radish, carrot, sweet corn and Swiss chard, several plantings can be made a few weeks apart and later than the average planting date for a longer harvest period. The average date of the last spring frost will vary with location and elevation.

TABLE 5: VEGETABLE PLANTING GROUPS AND SUGGESTED VEGETABLE PLANTING DATES FOR THE WASATCH FRONT (OUTDOORS)

Vegetable Plants Grouped by Tolerance to Cold (Cold Hardiness)

Group A: Hardy (Plant as soon as the soil dries out in the spring.)

Average Planting Date: March 15 – May 1
Artichoke, Kohlrabi
Asparagus, Onion, Rhubarb
Broccoli, Peas, Spinach
Cabbage, Radish, Turnip

Group B: Semi-Hardy (Plant a week or two after "A" group or about 2 weeks before average last spring frost.)

Average Planting Date: March 20 – May 1
Beet, Lettuce, Potato
Carrot, Parsley, Salsify
Cauliflower, Parsnip, Swiss Chard
Endive

Group C: Tender (Plant on the average date of the last spring frost–about when first apples reach full bloom.)

Average Planting Date: May 5 – June 1
Celery, Spinach
Cucumber, Summer Squash
Dry Bean, Sweet Corn
Snap Bean

Group D: Very Tender (Plant when the soil is warm, about 2 weeks after "C" group.

Average Planting Date: May 20 –June 10
Cantaloupe, Pumpkin
Eggplant, Tomato
Lima Bean, Watermelon
Pepper, Winter Squash

Group E: Planting for Fall Harvest

Average Planting Date
Beets July 1 – August 1
Cabbage May 1 – July 15
Kale July 1 – August 15
Lettuce June 1 – August 1
Onion August 1 – August 10
Rutabaga June 15 – July 1
Spinach July 1 – August 15
Turnip July 1 – August 1

TABLE 6: AVERAGE LAST SPRING FROST AND SUGGESTED VEGETABLE PLANTING DATES FOR VARIOUS LOCATIONS IN UTAH

City	Average Last Spring Frost	Vegetable Group and Average Date of Initial Planting			
		A	*B*	*C*	*D*
Beaver	June 6	April 15	April 25	May 20	June 1 (*P)
Castle Dale	May 25	April 15	April 25	May 25	May 15 (*P)
Cedar City	May 21	April 1	April 15	May 20	June 1
Coalville	June 18	May 1	May 10	June 10	May 15 (*P)
Duchesne	May 23	April 1	April 15	June 1	May 15 (*P)
Farmington	May 5	March 15	March 20	May 5	May 20
Fillmore	May 16	March 15	April 1	May 16	June 1
Heber	June 11	April 25	May 5	June 5	May 15 (*P)
Kanab	May 7	March 25	April 10	April 25	May 15
Laketown	June15	May 1	May 10	June 1	June 1 (*P)
Loa	June 15	May 10	May 20	June 1	June 1 (*P)
Logan – SW Farm	May 23	April 15	April 25	May 23	June 1
Logan - USU	May 7	April 1	April 10	May 7	May 20
Manila	June 2	March 15	April 1	May 20	June 1 (*P)
Manti	May 24	May 1	May 10	May 25	June 1 (*P)
Marysvale	June 3	May 1	May 10	May 20	June 1 (*P)
Midvale	May 13	March 15	April1	May 13	May 27
Moab	April 18	March 15	April 1	April 15	May 1
Monticello	May 28	April 1	April 15	June 1	May 15 (*P)
Morgan	June 6	March 15	April 1	May 20	June 1
Nephi	May 16	March 15	April 1	May 16	June 1
Ogden	May 3	March 15	March 20	May 3	May 20
Panguitch	June 21	May 10	May 20	June 7	June 1 (*P)
Price	May 12	March 15	April 1	May 12	May 27
Provo – BYU	May 1	March 15	March 20	May 1	May 20
Richfield	May 28	April 1	April 15	May 25	June 1 (*P)
Salt Lake Int'l Airport	April 26	March 15	March 20	April 26	May 15
Salt Lake County – Cottonwood Weir	April 30	March 15	March 20	April 30	May 15

City	Average Last Spring Frost	Vegetable Group and Average Date of Initial Planting			
		A	B	C	D
Santaquin	May 14	March 15	April 1	May 14	June 1
St. George	March 30	Feb. 15	March 1	March 15	April 1
Tooele	May 7	March 15	March 20	May 7	May 20
Tremonton	May 3	March 15	March 20	May 3	May 20
Vernal	May 27	April 1	April 15	June 1	May 15 (*P)
Woodruff	June 26	May 15	June 1	n/a	n/a

*P = Protected with cover

The occurrence of frost can vary over a short distance due to changes in elevation and topography. Keep records for your own garden area. For average freeze dates in other areas, see the USU Extension website: climate.usu.edu.

GARDENING IN WASHINGTON COUNTY

Rick Heflebower, *USU Extension Horticulture Faculty (Washington County)*

Vegetable planting dates for the Washington County area are different than most of the rest of the state. The last spring frost occurs much earlier in Washington County than in cooler locations in most other areas of Utah. The average last spring frost in St. George is March 30 and the average first frost in the fall is November 1. Cool-season plants such as lettuce, cabbage, broccoli and spinach may be planted as early as late February. Tender vegetables such as tomatoes can be planted as early as April 1. The desert heat in mid-summer causes severe plant stress affecting fruit set on many vegetables such as tomatoes, peppers, squash and sweet corn, so early planting is important. Higher elevation areas such as Enterprise and New Harmony have a shorter growing season than the St. George area. Visit the website: www.dixiegardner.org for suggested vegetable planting dates for different cities in Washington County and suggested fruit varieties for southern Utah.

PLANTING TIME BASED ON SOIL TEMPERATURE

One technique to ensure plants are planted in the garden during optimal growing conditions is to plant according to soil temperature. See Table 7 for optimal soil temperature ranges for seed germination and days to germination for common garden fruits and vegetables. Soil thermometers can be purchased from garden centers and hardware stores (Figure 10). Plants are often more sensitive to soil temperature than air temperature. Bare, dry soils will warm up more quickly than moist soils covered by plant foliage or mulch. Soil temperatures vary throughout the day with the highest temperature occurring at mid-afternoon and the lowest temperature after dawn. The standard soil temperature reading is taken around 8 a.m. by inserting a soil thermometer 4 inches deep into the soil. Record the soil temperature and wait until temperatures are consistent for 5 days before using soil temperature information to decide when to plant. Cool season plants will germinate when soil temperatures are 35-40° F. Warm season plants prefer a soil temperature of 55-60° F for germination or transplanting. If seeds are planted too far in advance of minimum germination temperatures, gardeners run the risk of poor germination success due to seeds rotting or desiccating in the soil.

Figure 10: *Soil Thermometer*

TABLE 7: OPTIMAL SOIL TEMPERATURE RANGES FOR SEED GERMINATION AND DAYS TO GERMINATION OF GARDEN PLANTS*

Fruit or Vegetable	Crop Type	Germination Minimum (°F)	Optimal Germination (°F)	Germination Maximum (°F)	Days to Germination
Asparagus	Perennial	50	75	95	---
Beans	Warm	60	80	95	7-10
Beet	Cool	40	85	85	7-10
Broccoli	Cool	40	80	90	3-10
Cabbage	Cool	40	85	100	3-10
Cantaloupe	Warm	60	90	100	3-10
Carrot	Cool	40	80	90	10-17
Cauliflower	Cool	40	80	100	3-10

Fruit or Vegetable	Crop Type	Germination Minimum (°F)	Optimal Germination (°F)	Germination Maximum (°F)	Days to Germination
Celery	Cool	40	70	85	10-14
Corn	Warm	50	95	105	5-10
Cucumber	Warm	60	95	100	6-10
Eggplant	Warm	60	85	95	7-14
Kohlrabi	Cool	40	80	90	3-10
Leek	Cool	40	80	90	7-12
Lettuce	Cool	35	70	85	4-10
Okra	Warm	60	95	105	7-14
Onion	Cool	35	75	95	7-12
Parsnip	Cool	35	65	85	15-25
Pea	Cool	40	75	85	6-15
Pepper	Warm	60	85	95	10-20
Pumpkin	Warm	60	90	100	7-10
Potato	Cool	45	---	---	---
Radish	Cool	40	85	95	3-10
Spinach	Cool	35	70	85	6-14
Squash Winter & Summer	Warm	60	95	100	3-12, 6-10
Swiss chard	Cool	40	85	95	7-10
Tomato	Warm	50	85	95	6-14
Turnip	Cool	40	85	105	3-10
Watermelon	Warm	60	95	105	3-12

* Table compiled from Texas A & M Extension fact sheet **Soil Temperature Conditions for Vegetable Seed Germination** and Colorado State University Extension fact sheet **Vegetable Planting Guide**.

STARTING PLANTS FROM SEED

INTRODUCTION

Growing your own garden starts can be both a rewarding and challenging experience. Gardeners experience many benefits from starting plants indoors; some enjoy increased access to a wide variety of vegetable varieties, while others enjoy growing plants prior to springtime weather. Indoor seed starting can also help gardeners get a jump-start on the growing season. Plants started indoors as opposed to direct seeding outdoors may allow an earlier harvest of 4 to 8 weeks and help gardeners save money by not buying transplants. Furthermore, indoor seed starting is fun and exciting!

Goals of this Section:

- Learn about soil, water, light and other growth requirements for indoor seed starting.
- Learn when to start different vegetables indoors and when to plant them outside.
- Learn how to harden-off transplants.

SOIL AND WATER REQUIREMENTS

It is important to select viable seeds and a commercial, high quality seed-starting mix. Seeds should be planted in a clean container with good drainage 2 to 8 weeks before outdoor transplanting is anticipated (Tables 5 and 6). Seed-starting mixes typically dry out rapidly so gardeners must check soil moisture levels daily to ensure seedlings do not fall victim to desiccation. Soil should be kept moist but not soggy, much like a wrung-out sponge. Consider your area's average last frost date and time seed planting dates accordingly. Frost-free dates for Utah can be found at the Utah Climate Center. Be careful to read the seed packet or contact your local USU Extension office for detailed information on starting seedlings indoors.

TABLE 8: SUGGESTED SCHEDULE FOR STARTING TRANSPLANTS INDOORS

Plant Indoors	Vegetable	Plant Outside
Mid-February	Broccoli	Early April (4-6 weeks old)
Mid-February	Cabbage	Early April (4-6 weeks old)
Early March	Lettuce	Early April (3-4 weeks old)
Early March	Caulifower	Late April (4-6 weeks old)
Mid/Late March	Eggplant	Late May (6-8 weeks old)
Mid/Late March	Pepper	Late May (6-8 weeks old)
Early April	Tomato	Mid/Late May (4-6 weeks old)
Early May	Watermelon	Late May (2-3 weeks old)
Early May	Cantaloupe	Late May (2-3 weeks old)

TABLE 9: SUGGESTED SCHEDULE FOR STARTING TRANSPLANTS INDOORS IN WASHINGTON COUNTY AREA

Plant Indoors	Vegetable	Plant Outside
Early January	Broccoli	Mid-February (4-6 weeks old)
Early January	Cabbage	Mid-February (4-6 weeks old)
February	Lettuce	Early March (3-4 weeks old)
February	Caulifower	Late March (3-4 weeks old)
Early February	Eggplant	Early April (6-8 weeks old)
Early February	Pepper	Early April (6-8 weeks old)
Early February	Tomato	Early April (6-8 weeks old)
Late March	Watermelon	Mid-April (2-3 weeks old)
Late March	Cantaloupe	Mid-April (2-3 weeks old)

For more information, see the USU Extension website: **http://www.dixiegardener.org/**.

LIGHT REQUIREMENTS

Many seedlings fail because of improper light levels during indoor growth. Special light arrangements are necessary to successfully start seedlings indoors. A sunny window by itself will not provide enough light for most seedlings. Seedlings need light as soon as they emerge from the soil; the optimal duration of light is 12 to 14 hours per day. Gardeners should supply light from fluorescent tubes or "grow lights" positioned 2 to 4 inches above seedlings. If the light source is farther away, the seedlings will reach for the light and become spindly. Florescent lights are ideally housed in a shop light on a frame and held by chains so the height of the lights can be adjusted as the seedlings grow. Do not allow plant leaves to touch the lights.

OTHER GROWING REQUIREMENTS

Seedlings and transplants prefer daytime air temperatures between 60-80° F and nighttime temperatures from 50 to 70° F. Some gardeners prefer to place a heat-warming pad under seed starting trays to warm the soil and promote rapid and uniform seed germination. Plant seeds at the depth suggested on the seed packet or according to Tables 3 and 4. Carefully moisten the soil and place a plastic dome or plastic bag over the newly planted seeds. Once the seedlings emerge from the soil surface, immediately remove the cover, but do not let the seedlings dry out. Keep the soil mix moist but not saturated. Newly emerged seedlings also need to be fertilized with a complete fertilizer [a fertilizer that contains Nitrogen (N)-Phosphorus (P)-Potassium (K)] in accordance

Figure 11: *Red spinach seedlings growing under florescent lights*

with the fertilizer label. Examples of organic fertilizers appropriate for indoor seedlings include fish emulsion (5-1-1) and seaweed extracts (9-2-7). These products are ideal because nutrients are more rapidly available for plant up-take than some other types of organic fertilizers. It should be noted many organic fertilizer products are available for purchase and will work well for seed starting. Check the product label for recommended uses.

Cool soil temperatures may delay plant up-take of available nutrients from organic fertilizers. Consider using a heat-warming pad or placing seedling trays on a warm surface, such as the top of an appliance, or keep them in a warm room while the plants are growing indoors.

Finally, young transplants should be hardened-off before planting them outside in the garden. Hardening helps young transplants adjust to outdoor conditions. Transplants should be placed outdoors for gradually increasing time periods over a week before permanently moving them outside. Be cautious of atypical minimum and maximum outdoor temperatures and other extreme weather (e.g., heavy rain or hail) during the hardening-off period. Be certain to water seedlings immediately after transplanting into the garden soil, and check soil moisture daily during the establishment period. For more information on starting indoor seedlings, see the USU Extension fact sheet **Growing Your Own Transplants At Home**.

CONTAINER AND RAISED BED GARDENING

INTRODUCTION

Container and raised bed gardening are popular growing methods. Container gardening is a great option for gardeners who do not have access to a garden site but do have a sunny patio or porch, or those who wish to restrict growth of aggressively plants like mint. Container gardens provide an attractive accent to your home and fresh produce. Raised bed gardens provide gardeners ease of weeding and reduced soil compaction, the ability to grow on sites with difficult or contaminated soils and can be constructed to be accessible based on American Disabilities Act (ADA) standards.

Goals of this Section:

- Become familiar with container garden growing requirements.
- Better understand advantages and disadvantages of raised bed gardens.
- Learn how to construct a raised bed garden.

CONTAINER GARDENING

Container gardens located close to the house provide the gardener convenient access to fruit, vegetable or herb plants. The following factors should be considered before planting your container garden: sunlight, container size and drainage, potting soil, fruit or vegetable type and access to water. Ideally your container garden should be located in a site that receives 6 to 8 hours of sunlight daily with convenient access to a water source. If you decide to hand water your containers, make sure to

Figure 12: *A container garden*

position the containers close enough to the house so you can easily monitor the soil moisture level. The container must have adequate drainage to allow excess water to escape out the bottom of the container. Consider placing stones or a mesh screen over the drain hole before adding potting mix so the drain hole does not become clogged with soil or soil does not wash out of the container over time. If you choose to use a pot without a drainage hole, call local pottery shops or hardware stores and ask if they have a drill bit designed to drill holes in pottery. Your container garden must have drainage holes before adding the potting mix!

CONTAINER AND SOIL SELECTION

Select weather-resistant containers that are large enough to house plants when they reach maturity. Consult the seed packet or plant tag for mature plant size. Fill your container with a high quality potting mix. Make sure to select a potting mix that is specifically sold for use in containers. Do not attempt to use garden soil in containers. Check to see if the potting mix you selected contains fertilizer. If you want to use an organic fertilizer, check the product label for the fertilizer source. You can always opt to buy a potting mix that does not contain fertilizer and mix your fertilizer of choice into the growing medium. For a listing of organic fertilizers, see the USU fact sheet **Selecting and Using Organic Fertilizers**. For more information on growing container plants, see the USU Extension fact sheet **Herb Container Gardens**.

RAISED BED GARDENING

A raised bed garden is built on top of the surrounding soil and may be filled with an enriched mixture of compost and soil. Raised bed gardens offer both advantages and disadvantages. Advantages of raised bed gardening include:

- Control of soil quality,
- Good soil drainage,
- High productivity in a small area,
- Warmed soil early in the spring allowing for early planting dates,
- Minimal soil compaction,
- Accessible gardening for physically disabled or individuals with limited mobility,
- Reduced weed growth,
- Ability to extend the growing season with attached season extension structures.

With all these advantages, raised bed gardening may seem like a no-brainer! However, disadvantages should be considered before building a raised bed garden. Disadvantages of raised bed gardening includes:

- Expense of construction materials,
- Mandatory pathways between beds,
- Gardening area restricted to the size of the bed,
- Labor involved in the assembly of the raised bed,
- Increased water use due to rapid drainage of water through soil.

HOW TO BUILD A RAISED BED GARDEN

Perhaps you have considered your options and committed yourself to building a raised bed garden. First, you need to select an appropriate site. Consider the growth requirements of the plants. See previous section on "**Garden Site Selection**." Next, you need to select a construction method. The simplest and least expensive method is an unframed raised bed (**Figure 13**). Unframed raised beds are constructed by tilling the existing soil 6 to 12 inches deep, incorporating 1 to 2 inches of organic matter and mounding the soil into beds 6 to 12 inches above the un-raised soil level. Be cautious of applying too much compost in one application. Improvement of soil quality through the addition of organic matter takes time! It is better to apply 1 to 2 inches of organic matter once a year over many years than to dump huge quantities of organic matter in one application. Excessive compost can cause a nitrogen deficiency in garden plants or may increase the salt levels in the soil. Leachate from some organic matter sources can also contribute to pollution of nearby water sources.

Figure 13: *Unframed raised bed*

Figure 14: *Raised bed made of lumber*

Raised bed gardens can also be constructed as more permanent structures from non-toxic, durable materials such as rot-resistant lumber (cedar or redwood), concrete blocks, brick, stone or synthetic lumber (**Figure 14**). Be cautious if using old lumber; USU Extension does not recommend using chromated copper arsenate (CCA) treated lumber. Pressure treated lumber and non-oozing railroad ties are acceptable construction materials if the beds are lined with heavy gauge plastic to avoid potentially hazardous compounds in the lumber from leaching into the garden soil. When lining the beds with plastic, make sure the beds have adequate drainage before filling with garden soil. Construct the raised bed box to measure at least 6 to 12 inches high to accommodate the rooting depth of most vegetables. Raised beds should be 3 to 4 feet wide and any length for easy garden access from all sides. Make sure to reinforce the corners of the bed so the structure can withstand the weight of wet soil. A rectangular-shaped block of wood can be placed in the corner and secured to both sides for adequate support. When setting the boxes in place, make the walkways wide enough for a wheelbarrow, tiller and gardener to work around and between the raised beds. Spread a layer of mulch, such as weed-free straw, wood chips, leaves or landscape fabric over the walkways to reduce weed growth and mud problems. Raised beds are generally planted in a block pattern (see Table 4) as shown in **Figure 15**.

Figure 15: *Raised bed planted in block pattern*

RAISED BED SOIL MIX OPTIONS

The boxes are now ready to be filled with garden soil! Either compost-enriched topsoil or a soil-less potting mix can be used in raised bed gardens. Native soil or topsoil that has been amended with organic matter contains valuable minerals, encourages beneficial microorganism activity, improves soil aeration and drainage, provides excellent plant support and improves the nutrient and water-holding capacity of the soil. Consider a ratio of 50 to 70% native soil or topsoil to 30 to 50% compost. Avoid planting in 100% compost because compost is lightweight and may not provide adequate plant root support to top-heavy plants or under windy conditions. Incorporate an annual addition of compost (1 to 2 inches per year as needed) to the raised bed as the soil level settles in the bed. If you are concerned about salts in the compost, have the **USU Analytical Laboratory** perform a soil test before planting your garden. A soilless potting mix is typically more expensive and may become nutrient deficient over time; however, soilless mixes are loose or friable in texture and retain good soil moisture. Soilless mixes are typically composed of peat, perlite or vermiculite and compost. If you have questions concerning the contents of a purchased soil mix, contact the company selling the product for a list of ingredients. For more discussion on raised bed garden mixes, see the USU Extension fact sheet **Raised Bed Gardening**.

RAISED BED IRRIGATION & FERTILIZATION

Most watering systems can be used for raised bed gardens; however, a soaker hose or drip irrigation system is an ideal and inexpensive choice. Drip systems use less water than overhead sprinklers since water is

Figure 16: Soaker hose placed around tomato plant

applied directly to the plant root zone. Drip systems also suppress weed growth because water is not delivered to bare soil between plants. For more information on construction of a basic drip system, see the "**Garden Irrigation**" section in Chapter 4 of this guide or see the USU fact sheet **Designing a Basic PVC Home Garden Drip Irrigation System**. Overhead sprinklers can be used, but they wet plant foliage which may encourage some fungal diseases on fruit and vegetable plants. If using overhead sprinklers, water in the morning hours to allow foliage to dry throughout the day. Fertilization should be based on soil test results and applied according to each plant's specific nutrient needs. For more information on fertilization see Chapter 4 "**Organic Garden Care**" section of this guide.

ORGANIC GARDENING TECHNIQUES

2

ORGANIC VEGETABLE GARDENING: AN OVERVIEW

Dr. Dan Drost, *USU Extension Vegetable Specialist*

ASK AN EXPERT

INTRODUCTION

Growing vegetables organically is not exceedingly difficult if you pay attention to details. While very few gardeners go through the trouble of certifying their garden as USDA certified organic, it is important to pay attention to the fundamentals of what it means to grow "organically." Growing organically means that you are committed to promote diversity, enhance biological cycles and improve soil health in the garden.

Goals of this Section:

- Learn tips for growing organic transplants
- Learn how to maintain adequate soil fertility
- Learn basic pest management techniques

DEVELOPING AN ORGANIC GARDEN

To legally sell organic produce, vegetables must be grown in accordance with federal and state regulations that govern the use of the term "organic." If you intend to label and sell your produce as organic, you must follow guidelines and be certified by an official certification agency. Small growers who profit less than $5,000 gross annual income are exempt, but even these growers should closely follow organic production practices. See the "**What Does It Mean to Grow Organically**" section in Chapter 1 of this guide for more information on the USDA National Organic Program and the USDA certified organic label.

An organic garden takes time to develop, focuses on the whole system and uses natural approaches to manage the system. Gardens do not become organic by just changing one or two practices. Often gardeners change garden management practices in stages. They may convert from using commercial fertilizer to integrating composts and cover crops for improved soil fertility. Pesticides may be eliminated and exchanged with multiple biological approaches for management of diseases, insects and weeds. Over several years, the system will gradually convert from a more conventional to an organic system. In order for the garden to remain organic, all of the practices, inputs and approaches need to adhere to accepted organic production practices. The remainder of this section outlines a sampling of things one needs to consider when planning and maintaining an organic garden.

SEEDS AND TRANSPLANTS

The seeds you directly plant in your garden or use to grow transplants need to come from certified organic sources. Most seed companies stock a selection of many different vegetable seeds that have been grown organically. Table 10 provides a short list of seed companies that have organic seeds for sale; many companies sell organic seeds so this list is not comprehensive. It is useful to search for organic seeds via the Internet because the selection at local nurseries, greenhouses and retail outlets may be limited.

Most nurseries or greenhouses do not grow or sell organically raised transplants. Therefore, if you choose to plant transplants strictly from organic seeds, you may have to grow your own plants. This is particularly true if you want to maintain your organic certification or intend to sell your produce as organic. Most commercial outlets that grow transplants apply non-organic inputs when raising plants, for example, treated seeds, synthetic fertilizers, wetting agents in the soil media and insecticides and fungicides to control pests.

To grow organic transplants you need to start with good growing media, use organic fertilizers and provide a suitable environment to grow the plants. Greenhouse-grown transplants are commonly grown in peat- or compost-based growing media. Do not introduce garden soil into the growing media as you may introduce diseases or weeds that affect plant growth. There are many recipes for mixing your own growing media. Growing media can be purchased, but most purchased mixes are not certified organic because they contain fertilizers or wetting agents not permitted by organic regulations. If you are using compost as the primary ingredient in the "soil mix," it is wise to have it tested by the **USU Analytical Laboratory** for pH, soluble salts and major nutrients.

TABLE 10: ONLINE RETAILERS THAT SELL USDA CERTIFIED ORGANIC SEED

Retailer
Johnny's Selected Seeds **www.johnnyseeds.com**
Park Seed Company **www.parkseed.com**
High Mowing Organic Seeds **www.highmowingseeds.com**
Seed Savers Exchange **www.seedsavers.org**
Territorial Seed Company **www.teritorialseed.com**
Sustainable Seed Company **www.sustainableseedco.com**
Peaceful Valley Farm Supply **www.groworganic.com**
Baker Creek Heirloom Seed Co. **www.rareseeds.com**
Burpee Seed Company **www.burpee.com**
Seeds of Change **www.seedsofchange.com**
Snow Seed Company **www.snowseed.com**
Mountain Valley Seed **www.mvseeds.com**

Figure 17: *Seedling emerging from potting mix*

USU Extension faculty has had good success growing organic transplants using a soilless mix plus additional fertilization with fish emulsion (see recipe in Table 11). If using composts, the compost should be well-aged (composted for more than 6 months), screened to remove coarse materials and mixed with knowledge of all composted materials. Aging ensures that the materials are completely broken down. Screening ensures that larger particles are excluded and that the flats or pots fill properly. Using known materials ensures consistent quality and production from plant to plant and year to year. It cannot be stressed enough how important compost consistency is when trying to grow high quality transplants. For more information on making your own growing media, see the ATTRA publication **Potting Mixes for Certified Organic Production**.

TABLE 11: SOILLESS POTTING MIX RECIPE

Transplant Soilless Mix Recipe

- 1 bale of peat (3.8-4.0 cu. ft bale)
- ½ bag coarse vermiculite (4.0 cu. ft bag)
- ½ bag coarse perlite (4.0 cu. ft bag)
- 3 quarts of fertilizer mix

To make the fertilizer mix, blend together:

- 15 cups steamed bone meal
- 10 cups kelp meal
- 10 cups blood meal
- 7 cups dolomitic limestone (80 mesh)

Transplants require additional fertilizer to ensure plant growth remains vigorous. Start applying supplemental nutrients 2 to 3 weeks after the seedlings emerge. Most vegetables require additional nitrogen (N) to ensure strong growth. Weekly additions of fish emulsion (2-3-2 (N-P-K) analysis) at 250-500 ppm N (2-4 Tablespoons/gallon) will maintain healthy plant growth.

Finally, transplants need an environment that is appropriate for the type of vegetable being grown. Pay attention to growing temperatures, light levels, air quality, humidity and soil moisture levels. Ideally the growing environment for cool season vegetables (i.e., cabbage and other brassica vegetables, leafy greens like lettuce or spinach, onions, etc.) is cooler than what is needed for the warm season vegetables (i.e., tomato, pepper, melon, squash, etc.). Plant production times also vary so timing plant growth in the greenhouse relative to transplanting outside in the vegetable garden is critical. See Tables 5 and 6 for suggested plant dates of different fruits and vegetables for multiple locations throughout Utah. For additional information on indoor seed starting, see the "**Starting Garden Plants from Seed**" section in Chapter 1 of this guide.

SOIL FERTILITY

Organic vegetable production improves when plants are grown in a fertile, biologically active and diverse soil environment. Fertile soil should have high levels of organic matter, an acceptable pH and a balance of nutrients suitable for healthy plant growth. Soils throughout Utah generally test very low or low in organic matter. Over time, regular additions of organic materials will help to build soil organic matter.

Good organic materials to add to soil include suitable, well-aged compost, animal-based manures and cover crops. Be careful when adding composts (plant or animal-based) or manures. Regular additions over time can result in the accumulation of excessive quantities of certain nutrients. This can create nutrient imbalances that affect plant growth or may lead to excessive leaf growth or nutrient accumulation within the plants grown. Soil and compost testing will help determine if the soil is balanced and will ensure that the proportion of nutrients is appropriate for proper plant growth. Growing summer or winter cover crops helps trap excessive soil nutrients and adds organic matter back into the soil. Good winter cover crop choices include wheat, hairy vetch or winter brassica's (mustards or rapes). Summer cover crops that grow well include millet and buckwheat. Summer cover crops are particularly good at helping control weeds. Be careful not to let the cover crops go to seed and incorporate them back into the soil 4 to 6 weeks before you plan to plant the vegetable garden. See the "**Integrated Weed Management**" section in Chapter 5 of this guide for more information on using cover crops for weed control.

Figure 18: *Earthworms are an indication of soils with adequate organic matter content*

Utah's soils tend to have a high pH value. Soil pH is a measure of the acidity or alkalinity of the soil and pH is indicated by a range of numbers from 1 to 14. A soil pH of 7 is considered neutral and many soils in Utah range from 7.5 to 8.5. While changing the soil pH is possible, it is often not necessary or recommended unless the pH value is excessively low or high. Most vegetables grow well in pH values between 6.5 and 7.8. If your soil pH tests above 8.5, follow the recommendations provided in your soil test results or consult your local USU Extension office on methods to lower the value. See the "**Three Common Soil Problems**" section in Chapter 3 of this guide for additional information on soil pH.

Finally, vegetable garden soil needs to have a balance of nutrients. Regular soil testing is critical to ensure that the ratio of different nutrients in the soil stays in balance. Over application of composts, manures or concentrated organic fertilizers may result in the buildup of excess levels of one or more nutrients. Excessive nutrient build up can lead to pollution of ground or surface waters. Excessive build up may also cause nutrient deficiencies of other elements needed by plants or interfere with plant establishment and growth. Determining how much nutrient to apply depends on your experience, the stage of plant growth, knowledge of soil qualities and its supply capabilities, plant nutrient needs and the nutrient supply capabilities of the fertilizer source. See the "**Soil Fertility**" section in Chapter 4 of this guide for more information on fruit and vegetable nutrient needs.

PESTS (DISEASES, INSECTS AND WEEDS)

Disease Management can be challenging in organic production systems. Once a plant is diseased there are few options for controlling the problem. Therefore, it is best to know which vegetable diseases are common in your production area and what management options are available for their control. Ideally, disease management starts with good planning and record keeping, use of resistant vegetable varieties, proper water use and good sanitation practices before resorting to some type of chemical treatment. If your plants and soil are healthy, you may not observe problems with diseases.

Many disease causing organisms survive in plant debris so planning and record keeping is needed to ensure you do not continually grow the same plants in the same areas of the garden year after year. Plant resistant (tolerant or partially resistant) varieties since disease organisms do not grow well on these plants. Unfortunately, not all varieties have disease resistance. Those with some resistance may not be the most desirable or they may not have resistances to all the different pathogenic strains of a disease. However, disease resistances are a good place to start controlling plant pathogens.

Many disease problems arise due to improper irrigation practices. Over irrigation and excessive leaf wetness are the primary causes of many disease outbreaks. Wet soils cause seed and root rots that affect plant performance. Most diseases require free moisture to grow, so water early in the day rather than in the late afternoon or evening. Morning watering allows the leaves to dry and minimizes the potential for a pathogen to grow.

Finally, good garden sanitation practices are critical if diseases are to be managed. Remove obvious

Figure 19: *Lady bird beetle adult gorging on aphids*

diseased plants to keep the problem from spreading. Bury diseased plant material with tillage so that soil organisms can decompose the tissue containing the pathogen problem. If all else fails, rouge out diseased plants and dispose of them rather than incorporating them into the soil or compost pile. For examples of common garden diseases, see the "**Prevention and Management of Common Garden Diseases**" section in Chapter 5 of this guide.

Insect Management is best in organic systems through prevention of the problem rather than gardeners being reactive to the pest problem. The garden should be designed so the insect pests cannot find the plants of interest, by creating environments that favor beneficial insects and allowing some damage to occur before taking a reactive approach using chemical control.

Designing the garden so pests cannot find host plants is accomplished first by creating a diverse environment, then by companion planting (intercropping) and correctly timing plantings. By creating a diverse environment, natural control options are greatly increased. Diversity increases the likelihood that natural predators will take up residence in the landscape. Create habitat for birds, bugs, beetles, flies, spiders and wasps that feed on common garden pests. These biological control options thrive in diverse plantings. See the pull-out section "**Gardening for the Good Guys**" in Chapter 5 for additional information on creating attractive habitat for beneficial insects.

One problem with the vegetable garden is that it often lacks diversity. Many vegetable plants are closely related and thus prone to the same pest problems. Companion planting or intercropping involves diversifying garden plants so that pests have trouble finding the plants they like to feed on. Consequently pests may spend time moving around looking for something favorable to eat. If insect pests have trouble finding host plants, they do not grow and reproduce as quickly. Wandering pests are also more likely to encounter natural predators living in your garden. Think about ideal combinations of vegetables to grow near one another when planting intercropped plants. Vegetables should be from different families or groups and should not interfere with each other's growth requirements. For example, since pepper, tomato, potato and eggplant are all from the same family, plant these plants in separate areas of the garden if tomato hornworm is a persistent problem in the garden each year. See the "**Garden Layout and Planting**" section in Chapter 1 of this guide for a listing of vegetable family groups.

Finally, if possible, time your planting dates to avoid exposing the plants to specific insect pests. While corn earworm infestations occur every year, there are windows of time when the pest populations are very low. With good record keeping, you can plant corn to mature when this lull in the pest population occurs. By learning more about a pest and its life cycle, you can plant slightly earlier or later in the growing season, thus avoiding the problem.

While a diverse garden can minimize pest problems, gardeners will inevitably regularly encounter insects that feed on plants in the garden. Try using trap crops, barriers and other physical and cultural control approaches before resorting to the use of organic pesticides. Trap crops are designed to lure the pest to their favorite host plant and away from a plant desired by the gardener. The trap crop is deemed expendable and is usually destroyed along with the pest infestation. For example, squash bugs prefer to lay eggs on crookneck squash over other squashes like zucchini, acorn and butternut squash.

ASK AN EXPERT

COMPANION PLANTING: MYTH OR REALITY?

Marion Murray, *USU Extension IPM Project Leader*

Companion vegetable planting for home and local markets is a historical concept, passed between generations and from neighbor to neighbor. The idea is that the presence of one plant species improves the growth of another. Many recommendations are based on folklore and tradition rather than scientific research. There are, however, valid mechanisms of certain plant associations that can lead to minor pest suppression and greater crop yields.

Documented benefits from plant associations include physical, chemical and biological alterations that can improve the establishment and survival of desired plant species. The mechanisms of plant interactions are not completely understood, but there are several scientific conclusions that explain the process:

Trap cropping occurs when one plant species or variety is attractive to a pest and is not affected by yield loss, or is used as a "sacrificial" crop. The trap crop is either treated or removed after infestation, and pest pressure on the desired crop is reduced. An example is using Petunia 'Carpet Blue' to attract thrips away from tomatoes or peas.

Nitrogen fixation by roots of legumes (peas, clover) adds nitrogen to the soil, reducing the need for nitrogen fertilizer, which is helpful for vegetables like corn, tomato or cabbage.

Nurse cropping by using tall or dense plants can protect tender plants through shading and wind breaking. Oats, for example, are used to help establish alfalfa by preventing weeds from establishing.

Pest suppression can occur through a variety of mechanisms:

a) **Chemical exudates** from parts of certain plants may have pesticidal properties. In two studies examining the chemical compounds of marigold (Tagetes spp.), one found that naturally occurring compounds in flowers and foliage were lethal to Mexican bean weevil, and another found that root compounds were lethal to cabbage maggot larvae. Another example is the use of mow-killed rye grain as a mulch. The chemicals from the rye residue prevent weed germination and do not harm transplanted vegetables.

b) **Mixing plant species** may cause an interference with visual or olfactory orientation of pests to their host plants.

c) **Mixing plant varieties** of the same species circumvents insects' ability to adapt to natural plant defenses. For example, mixing field-planted barley cultivars resulted in reduced aphid feeding as compared to a planting of a single cultivar.

d) **Refugia** (beneficial habitats) provide desirable environments of plant material and shelter for predator and parasitic insect species such as syrphid flies, parasitic wasps, lacewings and robber flies. One research project showed that the addition of chicken wire plus bedding straw in tilled soybean fields reduced pest injury by 33% by providing habitat for spiders and predatory beetles.

Table 12 provides examples of plant associations that have traditionally been followed. Some home gardeners have reported benefits by mixing certain plant species while others see no difference. Understanding how plant associations work can improve their use and consistency of effects.

References:

Halaj, J. 2000. Modular habitat refugia enhance generalist predators and lowers plant damage in soybeans. Environmental Entomology. 29:2, pp 383-393.

Leger. 2009. Evaluation of marigolds and entomopathogenic nematodes for control of the cabbage maggot (Delia radicum). Journal of Sustainable Agriculture. 33: 2, pp 128-141.

Ninkovic. et al. 2002. Mixing barley cultivars affects aphid host plant acceptance in field experiments. Entomologia Experimentalis et Applicata. 102: 2, pp 177-182.

Weaver, D.K., et al. 1994. Insecticidal activity of floral, foliar, and root extracts of Tagetes minuta against adult Mexico bean weevils. Journal of Economic Entomology. 87: 6, pp 1718-1725.

TABLE 12: TRADITIONAL RECOMMENDATIONS OF COMPATIBLE PLANT ASSOCIATIONS

Note that these relationships are based on the mechanisms mentioned above, such as trap cropping, disruption in host-finding, shading, chemical exudates and habitats for beneficial insects; not on whether plants "love" or "hate" one another.

Crop	Compatible
Asparagus	Tomato, parsley, basil
Beans	Most vegetables & herbs
Beans (bush)	Potato, cucumber, corn, strawberry, celery, summer savory
Beans (pole)	Corn, summer savory, radish
Cabbage Family	Aromatic herbs, celery, beet, onion family, chamomile, spinach, chard
Carrot	English pea, lettuce, rosemary, onion family, sage, tomato
Celery	Onion & cabbage families, tomato, bush beans, nasturtium
Corn	Potato, beans, English pea, pumpkin, cucumber, squash
Cucumber	Beans, corn, English pea, sunflower, radish
Eggplant	Beans, marigold
Lettuce	Carrot, radish, strawberry, cucumber
Onion Family	Beets, carrot, lettuce, cabbage Family, summer savory
Parsley	Tomato, asparagus
Pea (English)	Carrot, radish, turnip, cucumber, corn, beans

Crop	Compatible
Potato	Beans, corn, cabbage family, marigold, horseradish
Pumpkin	Born, marigold
Radish	English pea, nasturtium, lettuce, cucumber
Spinach	Strawberry, fava bean
Squash	Nasturtium, corn, marigold
Tomato	Onion family, nasturtium, marigold, asparagus, carrot, parsley, cucumber
Turnip	English pea

Source: George Kuepper & Mardi Dodson. 2001. Companion Planting: Basic Concepts & Resources. Appropriate Technology Transfer for Rural Areas. Horticultural Technical Note.

Barriers and other physical controls may prevent some insect pests from accessing the host plant. Floating row covers are a common example of a physical barrier (**Figure 20**). Since the weave of the fabric is very tight, small insects like flea beetles, leaf hoppers and moths cannot see the plants they want to feed on or cannot gain access to the plant when they do find it. Other examples include cardboard collars placed around tomato, broccoli or pepper transplants. These collars keep cutworms from feeding on the stems during plant establishment. Milk jugs, tin cans, copper strips and sticky traps all can be used to repel, trap or exclude unwanted garden pests. See the "**Integrated Pest Management**" section in Chapter 5 of this guide for more information on physical techniques for garden pest control.

Figure 20: *Floating row cover*

Do not forget to use crop rotation, good sanitation and mulching as preventative techniques to keep pesky "pests" in check. Growing the same vegetable in the same garden spot year after year will only create problems. If possible, vegetables in the same family should be rotated every year and not return to the same garden spot for 3 years to help break disease and insect cycles. Clean up the area after the plants are finished producing edible portions. Good sanitation is a very effective method of pest control. Till under or compost old plants after they have been harvested. Do not let those old broccoli plants become a cabbage worm hotel and bean plants a bean beetle haven! Good sanitation will go a long way to keep pest problems in check. Although organic mulches, like straw and grass clippings, (**Figure 21**) are great weed barriers, they can also become a safe haven for insect predators like beetles, spiders and centipedes.

Figure 21: *Straw mulch*

Organic pesticides should only be used as a last resort. If your garden is healthy and well-maintained, you should experience less pest problems and the controls outlined should be sufficient to control the problem. Organic-based chemicals are derived from plants (pyrethrums, rotenone, azadirachtin), organisms (diatomaceous earth), bacteria or fungi (Bacillus thuringiensis, Beauveria bassiana), nematodes, or from soaps and oils (insecticidal soap or horticultural oils). They act as contact poisons, as repellents, as suffocates or by other modes of action. Make sure you select the correct organic pesticide for the pest of interest. Always read the product label first before applying any pesticide and carefully follow the directions for use.

Weed Management in organic systems relies on a combination of methods to keep weeds in check. Weed control requires an understanding of weed species and weed types (annuals, biennials, perennials, broadleaf, grasses). Furthermore, over time, the mix of weed species and types is likely to change. Some weeds are more difficult to manage while others are seasonal; however, all weeds interfere with the growth of desired vegetable plants. Therefore, the more diverse the management program, the better your chances of keeping weeds in check.

Timing is important for successful weed control. Small weeds are easier to manage and cultivation is quite effective when weed plants are small. If you can keep weeds under control during the first 4 to 6 weeks after planting your vegetable garden, most vegetables can tolerate some weed pressure later in their growth. The following are strategies and techniques that can help gardeners successfully control most weeds. Recommendations include preventative approaches, land preparation tactics and mechanical controls.

Figure 22: Asparagus, a long-lived garden perennial

PREVENTATIVE APPROACHES

Preventing weeds from getting established or entering the garden is one of the first steps toward creating a less weedy garden. Weeds enter the garden by wind, water and mechanical means. Many weed seeds blow into the yard (dandelion or elm seed pods) which make it difficult to control their germination in the garden. Other weeds travel in with the irrigation water. If you have a secondary water source, you may consider screening it to try to trap weed seeds before they enter your garden. Other seeds move in on clothes (burrs and sticktights), wrap around the tiller tines (bindweed or purslane) or hitch a ride on soil encrusted tools. Regardless of the mode of entry, by practicing good garden hygiene, fewer outside weeds will germinate in your garden.

LAND PREPARATION TACTICS

There are a number of different soil preparation techniques that help reduce weed pressures. They include crop rotation, cover crop use, stale seedbeds and mulching. If you regularly grow the same vegetables in the same area of the garden, weeds adapted to those crops and crop production practices gain a foothold. For example, since asparagus is a perennial vegetable, perennial weeds like bindweed, thistle and quackgrass often become established in the patch. While you cannot rotate where asparagus is grown, you need to be careful not to let these types of weeds get established. Fall or summer planted cover crops can also help control weeds. Cover crops should be planted so they establish and grow quickly. When cover crops are planted densely, they effectively crowd-out weeds.

A stale seedbed is prepared weeks prior to the time you want to plant your garden. Weeds are allowed to emerge, then are controlled with shallow cultivation or flaming. Once the weeds are killed the site is planted without tilling or excessive digging to prevent exposure of dormant weed seeds buried deep in the underlying soil. This will reduce the number of weeds that germinate after the vegetable plants are planted. Finally, use various mulches to control weed establishment. Mulches block sunlight from reaching the soil surface as many weeds need the sun to germinate. Black plastic, cardboard and newspaper layers, straw, grass clippings and killed cover crops (vetch, wheat or buckwheat) all make very effective mulches. However, if you use grass clippings or straw, make sure you are not introducing new weed seeds into your garden!

If you have a really bad weed problem, you may want to solarize the soil. Work up the problem area, smooth the soil surface, water it, and then cover the area with a sheet of clear plastic mulch making sure to seal the edges. The plastic should remain in place for six to eight weeks. Solariziation is generally done during the months of July and August. Soil solarization super-heats the soil and effectively kills problem weeds, certain soil diseases and some insect pests. Since the area will be reasonably free of weeds and pests, make sure you do not re-introduce new weed seeds to the same area after you worked so hard to control them!

MECHANICAL CONTROLS

Finally, there are numerous mechanical approaches for keeping weeds at bay. Besides hand weeding, you can till, hoe or cultivate with a variety of tools to kill small weeds. Flame weeding can also be used with caution. Quickly direct the hot flame over weeds when they are small seedlings. Flaming can be used in conjunction with the stale seedbed approach or immediately after planting. Choose alternative weed control techniques after desired vegetable plants emerge. Be careful when using flames! Flaming will kill desired plants just as easily as weeds, and may cause dried residues (mulches, etc.) to burn and create a fire hazard. Always check if local ordinances restrict the use of open flames. You may want to mow large weeds and use debris as mulch. Be sure to mow weeds before they set seeds to reduce the addition of new weed seeds back into the garden.

If a weed-free garden is your goal, it is important to use a variety of approaches for weed management. All of the practices described help to create biological diversity and consequently reduce weed seed survival. Regardless of the weed control approach, vigilance is the key to keeping all garden problems in check. For more information on weed control, see the "**Integrated Weed Management**" section in Chapter 5 of this guide.

Record Keeping is one of the central tenets of organic gardening. Good records are invaluable to the gardener and help build on successes and avoid repeating mistakes. There are so many things that occur during the growing season that without written record, you are sure to forget something! Keep a log of what you purchased, what you did and when it occurred. Start with a garden map and note what you planted (location, dates, varieties, etc.) and how you prepared for planting. Record what you added (composts, fertilizers, etc.), what problems showed-up (diseases, insects, etc.), and when things happened (emergence dates, flowering and harvest dates, levels of productivity, etc.). A few minutes spent recording your activities will provide a wealth of useful information for the next growing season. Knowing what to expect will help you grow a more productive garden in the future. Keep your camera handy to photo-record your observations. A photographic record is a great way to visually track gardening memos. Photos also help you remember what things look like and can be emailed to your local USU Extension office for help in diagnosing garden problems.

ASK AN EXPERT

TRANSITIONING TO ORGANIC AGRICULTURE

Dr. Jennifer Reeve, *USU Associate Professor of Organic and Sustainable Agriculture*

Organic agriculture is a frequent topic of conversation today among consumers and producers. With rising costs of inputs and a steady demand for organically grown products, growers are increasingly wondering if "going organic" might be worth it. The process can no doubt seem daunting and there can be a steep learning curve. In the past there has been a scarcity of reliable information on the farming practices involved in organic agriculture, but that is changing.

The first thing to consider is the size of your current operation and potential market you wish to access. We recommend to initially transition a small portion of the farm to organic. During the 3-year transition period, no inputs of conventional fertilizer or pesticides are allowed and no price premiums are available until the field or operation is fully certified. Problems such as reduced yields and increased pest pressures are often enhanced during the transition period as the farm adapts to the new management practices.

Organic production relies on the inherent fertility of the soil to a much greater degree than conventional agriculture. This fertility is based on the organic matter content of the soil, which provides a warehouse of slow-release nutrients. As such, choose your best land to transition to organic agriculture to minimize the expected yield losses that may occur before organic matter in the soil is replenished. While fast-release sources of fertilizer, such as fish meal, are available for organic production, they are expensive, so it is unwise to rely too heavily on these products and instead focus on long-term building of soil fertility. The same is true for weed control. Organic management relies on minimizing the weed seed bank, so starting out with minimum weeds can help enormously in the long run.

One of the best ways to build long-term soil fertility is through addition of perennial crops in the rotation. Perennials have much deeper root systems than annuals, and deposit organic matter deep within the soil profile. Choosing a field that has been in long-term alfalfa production or grass clover hay would be an ideal place to start.

Otherwise, if you have the land available, focus on including as many soil-building cover crops in the rotation as possible. The exact approach to take depends on the crop and cropping system you have in mind.

The Website of the **National Sustainable Agriculture Information Service** (ATTRA) is probably the best source of detailed information on organic practices for a large selection of crops and organic production systems.

Utah State University also has an emerging research program in organic production practices tailored specifically to local conditions. Experiments with season-extension for organic vegetable production have proven to be very successful. New research plots are currently being established to study organic transition strategies for organic field crops and vegetables, selecting cover crops for weed control, and input reduction and orchard floor management strategies for organic stone fruit production. All these systems need to be optimized to the challenges of Utah's climate where alkaline soils are low in organic matter, and the short growing season and limited water supply can make the use of cover crops challenging. Conversely, the climate provides important benefits to the organic grower in that the dry, sunny growing season usually limits disease pressure.

While no one would claim that organic production is an easy approach, it certainly can be very rewarding. In order to be an effective organic farmer, an understanding of the seasonal cycles involved in pest dynamics, crop rotations and nutrient management is necessary. The learning and understanding involved in developing such a relationship with the land can be a source of increasing satisfaction. In addition, many growers have found that the organic label has enabled them to expand into niche markets and increase the profitability of their farms. Ultimately, a successful organic grower requires a combination of biological-based farming knowledge, and marketing and business expertise.

Figure 23: *USU Student Organic Farm*

TREE FRUIT AND SMALL FRUIT: AN OVERVIEW

Mike Pace, *USU Extension Agriculture Faculty (Box Elder County)*

INTRODUCTION

Growing fruit at home is a rewarding experience for many gardeners. Organic fruit production requires knowledge of:

- Good varieties for your area
- Organic pest control techniques
- Proper pruning
- Good plant maintenance practices

Gardeners are often surprised by the extent of care necessary to maintain a healthy and productive home orchard. If you plan to grow fruit at home, it is strongly recommended that you research the fruit production considerations or contact your local USU Extension office for recommendations on tree and small fruit care. See the USU Extension publication, **Utah Home Orchard Pest Management Guide** for detailed information on pest control and the USU Extension publication, **Pruning the Orchard** for recommended tree pruning techniques.

Goals of this Section:

- Become familiar with important questions to consider prior to planting a home orchard.
- Better understand tree fruit pollination and chilling requirements.
- Learn how to maintain tree and small fruit plants.

Before selecting and planting fruit trees or small fruit, homeowners need to answer the following important questions:

- What type of fruit would you like to grow?
- How are you going to use your fruit (canning, drying, fresh eating, etc.)?
- What size of plants do you have room to grow?

- How will you harvest the fruit?
- Who will prune and maintain the trees? How will you control insect and disease problems?
- How will you irrigate the plants?
- How cold hardy are the fruit varieties you would like to grow?

See "Variety Recommendations" below for suggestions on tree and small fruit varieties that grow well in Utah. Average ripening dates and descriptive information is available for apples, apricots, cherries, nectarines, peaches, pears and plums at the USU Extension online resource **Tree Fruit Recommendations**. Detailed information on apple production and variety recommendations is available from the USU Extension fact sheet **Apple Production and Variety Recommendations for the Utah Home Garden**. You may also want to visit the **USU Botanical Center** (USUBC) in Kaysville to view the demonstration orchard. The orchard is open to the public and demonstrates several varieties of heirloom and modern apples, peaches, apricots, Asian and European pears, plums, grapes and novelty fruits like plum-apricot hybrids. For information on strawberry and red raspberry production, see the USU Extension fact sheets **Strawberries in the Garden** and **Red Raspberry Production in Utah**.

SITE AND VARIETY SELECTION

Fruit trees prefer deep, well-drained soils and full sunlight exposure. Common site factors that impact fruit production include date of last spring frost, frost pocket locations, growing season length and low winter temperatures. It is essential to select tree varieties that grow well in your area. Gardeners must know their USDA cold hardiness zone to select plants that will survive low winter temperatures in their area. You can find your USDA cold hardiness zone number by visiting **http://planthardiness.ars.usda.gov**

GARDEN MYTH #3:

It is just as easy to grow organic fruit as it is inorganic fruit.

Fact: For some types of fruit, this assumption is true, but for other types, it is unfortunately not the case. For example, some crops, such as apples, do not lend themselves to organic management as well as others like raspberries. Even the most experienced organic apple growers still suffer significant losses due to codling moth and fire blight, whereas raspberries are relatively pest-free. If you plan to grow fruit, it is important that you take action to prevent against pests. Untreated plants can harbor garden pests which become problematic for neighbors and nearby commercial orchards. For more information on common pests of fruit trees and small fruit, see Chapter 5 "**Garden Pest Control**" section of this guide.

Figure 24: *Demonstration orchard at the USU Botanical Center*

and entering your zip code. A cold hardiness zone is a number which corresponds with the range of low temperatures a plant can withstand without severe or lethal damage. For example, a zone 5a tree can withstand a winter low temperature range of -20 to -15°F. It is okay to select a variety with a cold hardiness zone number lower than the zone number listed for your area, but risky to select one with a higher number. For example, if your garden is located in an area with a cold hardiness zone of 5a, a zone 4a or 4b tree will be tolerant of your winter temperatures in most years. However, it might be risky to plant a tree with a cold hardiness zone number of 6a or 6b. Keep in mind that the USDA cold hardiness zone for your area is based on averaged temperature data from the past 10 years.

Hardiness zones periodically change as maps are updated and, since they are an average, marginally hardy trees may not survive in extreme years. Most reputable nurseries will carry trees adapted to your area; however, if you are ordering trees online, make sure you purchase varieties appropriate for your hardiness zone. The date of last spring frost can often be more important than hardiness zone in determining what to plant, as some fruit trees such as apricots will survive very low cold winter temperatures, but will not set fruit in some years due to spring freeze damage to developing flower buds. Some summers in Utah are hot and dry which can be stressful for fruit trees. Varieties also differ in their heat tolerances. Gardeners need to select appropriately adapted varieties to keep trees well irrigated during hot summer months to tolerate this stress.

FRUIT TREE POLLINATION REQUIREMENTS

Before planting your trees, it is important to consider the pollination requirements of various types of fruits. Some fruit trees, such as peach and certain apricot varieties, set fruit with their own pollen (self-fruitful) meaning you only have to plant one fruit tree to produce fruit. Other fruit trees, such as apples, most pears, some plums, and some cherries, require cross-pollination (self-incompatible or self-unfruitful) for the transfer of pollen between varieties of the same fruit type (two apple or two pear tree varieties) for fruit development. See the Colorado State University Extension fact sheet **Pollination of Fruit Trees** and the Washington State University Extension fact sheet **Pollination of Fruit Trees** for pollination charts of apple, cherry, pear and plum trees. If these two publications do not list your preferred variety, search online using the name of the variety you are looking for along with the term "pollination chart." Sometimes a neighbor's tree located on the same block will serve as a compatible pollinizer tree as long as both trees are the same type of fruit and bloom at the same time (apples pollinize apples, pears pollinize pears, etc.)

Bees are the main pollinating insects of fruit trees and can fly 2 to 4 miles in search of pollen and nectar under sunny and warm conditions. Compatible pollinizer trees need to have overlapping bloom times for

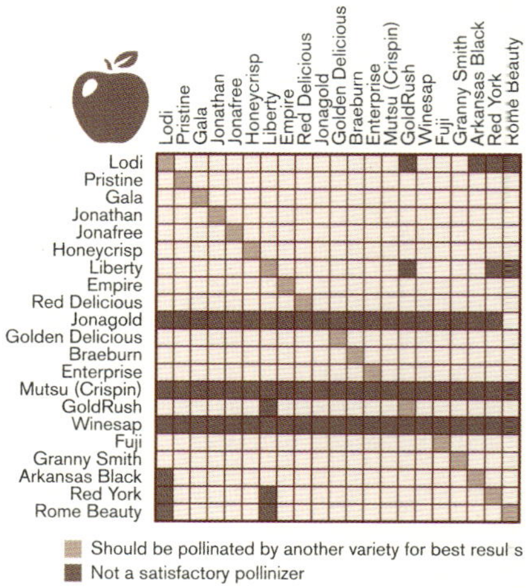

Figure 25: *Pollination chart of apple varieties*

cross-pollination. Cross-pollination will not occur between two trees of the same variety (a red delicious apple tree will not pollinize another red delicious apple tree). Furthermore, varieties of fruit that require cross-pollination may or may not be compatible if the selection is made without the aid of a pollination chart (**Figure 25**). For example, a Jonagold apple will not pollinize a red delicious apple tree even though they are different varieties and may bloom at the same time, because the pollen of a Jonagold tree is sterile. Many ornamental crabapple and flowering pear trees provide a good source of apple and pear pollen for edible tree varieties if both trees are in bloom at the same time. Commercial apple orchards sometimes interplant crabapples with their apple trees. See Table 13 for a summary of pollination requirements of several fruit tree types.

TABLE 13: TREE FRUIT POLLINATION GUIDE

Crop	Cross-Pollination
Apple	Requires cross-pollination.
Apricot	Most are self-fruitful. Perfection, Riland and Rival require cross-pollination.
Cherry, Sweet	Stella and Lapins are self-fruitful. Most require cross-pollination.
Cherry, Tart	Common varieties, such as Montmorency, are self-fruitful.
Peach, Nectarine	Most are self-fruitful. J.H. Hale is not.
Plum	Some prune types such as Stanley and Damson are self-fruitful. Most either require or do better with cross-pollination. European varieties require other European varieties as cross-pollinizers. Likewise, Japanese plums need pollen from a different Japanese variety.

FRUIT TREE CHILLING REQUIREMENTS

Deciduous fruit trees need a period of exposure to cool air temperatures, termed chilling requirement, to break dormancy and begin spring growth. The chilling requirement allows growth inhibiting hormones to break down within the tree. For example, apples require exposure to a temperature range of 35 to 54 ° F for a set number of hours. Chilling requirements vary between fruit tree types and varieties and can range from 200 to more than 1,000 hours. Lower chilling requirements result in earlier spring bloom. Typically trees with low chilling requirements are grown in areas with warmer climates. Longer chilling requirements result in later spring bloom. Trees with longer chilling requirements produce best in areas with colder climates. Most reputable nurseries, staffed by nurserymen with good knowledge of local growing conditions, will carry varieties with chilling requirements that are appropriate for your area. If you plan to order trees over the Internet, make sure you choose varieties with suitable chilling requirements for your area. One way to quickly check this is to find out what varieties are sold at reputable local nurseries and compare their chilling requirements with the variety you plan to purchase. A variety with a low chilling requirement planted in a cold area might be continually damaged by spring frosts. A variety with a high chill requirement planted in a warm area may have no blooms or uneven blooms and delayed foliation. Do not worry if you select a variety with a high chilling requirement as many areas in Utah accumulate an excess of chill hour units each year. For detailed information on chilling requirements, see the Arizona Cooperative Extension fact sheet **General Chilling Requirements of Various Fruits and Nuts**.

FRUIT TREE ROOTSTOCK

Fruit production has advanced considerably from Johnny Appleseed's days of spreading seeds along his path, because today most fruit trees purchased at the local nursery are grafted onto a rootstock. Rootstocks are dissimilar to the fruiting cultivar. In other words, the roots of a grafted tree are a different variety than the portion of the tree that bears fruit. Rootstock selection impacts the mature size of the tree and other qualities such as disease resistance, cold tolerance and adaptability to various soil conditions. When shopping at the nursery, you may have the option to choose from various mature sizes of trees; dwarf, semi-dwarf and standard sized. Do not be fooled by terminology, as dwarf trees still grow 6 to 12 feet tall; semi-dwarf trees grow 12 to 21 feet; and standard trees may grow higher than 21 feet depending on variety and rootstock. A 15-foot, semi-dwarf tree is a large plant! Rootstock selection particularly impacts the mature size of apple and cherry trees. If you are looking for certain characteristic like fire blight resistance or tolerance of poorly draining soils, it would be wise to research available rootstocks online or contact your local USU Extension office. Dwarf fruit trees are typically not free standing and generally require a trellis, stake or some other type of support for the entire life of the tree. See the University of Maine Cooperative Extension publication **Rootstocks and Dwarf Fruit Trees** for more information on various rootstock characteristics.

Figure 26: *Effect of different dwarfing rootstock on the same apple variety*

PURCHASING TREES

It is important to purchase your fruit trees from a reputable nursery or trusted online retailer. There is nothing more frustrating than putting forth 5 to 6 years training and developing a fruit tree only to find out it is not the variety or size of tree you wanted or the tree variety is not well-suited to your local growing conditions. Life is too short for such nonsense! Make sure you purchase trees within a few days of when you plan to plant them. Compare the branching patterns of trees while at the nursery and select the ones with the branching you like best. Spring and fall are both good times to plant fruit trees as cool and wet conditions allow for root development before the hot and dry summer months. Most nurseries will have a better selection of trees to choose from in the spring, but gardeners might have the best shot at purchasing deeply discounted nursery stock in the fall. Shoppers might also have a choice between bare-root or containerized fruit trees in the spring; bare-root plants are not available for purchase at nurseries in the fall.

PROPER PLANTING

An important factor for woody plant health (plants that produce woody roots, trucks, branches or vines) is digging a great hole! If planted incorrectly, woody plants become stressed and more vulnerable to pest problems. Gardeners sometimes forget that the portion of the plant growing underground is just as important as the visible portion growing above ground. In order for plants to grow healthy root systems, they must be planted correctly in a soil environment suitable for healthy root growth. Follow these planting tips:

- Dig a hole wider than deep (2 to 3 times wider than the root ball width) with sloping sides.
- Dig the hole so that the base of the root ball sits on undisturbed soil and the root flare* is exposed (do not bury the root flare).
- If you are planting a grafted tree (most fruit trees are grafted), make sure the graft union is located above the soil surface.
- Remove packaging material (burlap, wire caging, string or twine) prior to planting.
- As a general rule, use no more than one-third organic matter when backfilling the hole (two-thirds of the backfill material should be soil you removed when digging the hole).
- Thoroughly mix all backfill material to avoid layering in the hole.
- Deeply water the plant immediately!
- Read the USU Extension fact sheet **Planting Landscape Trees** for detailed information on planting newly purchased trees, woody shrubs and vines.

*The root flare describes the section on the plant where trunk or stem tissue transitions into root tissue.

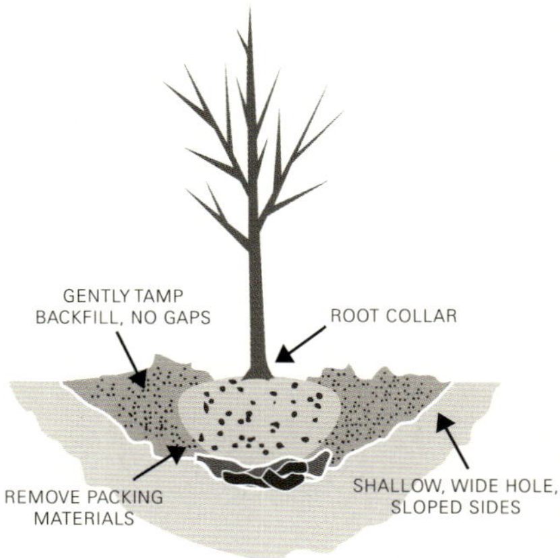

Figure 27: *Illustration of a tree planting*

VARIETY RECOMMENDATIONS

Some of the trees listed below are available for viewing (and the fruit available for sampling) at the USUBC demonstration orchard in Kaysville. The following is a list of some fruit tree varieties that grow well in Utah. Not all varieties below grow well in all parts of Utah, check with your local USU Extension office for varieties that grow best in your area. For information on cider apple varieties, see the Washington State University Extension fact sheet **Apple Varieties for Cooking, Baking, and Cider**.

	Description
Apples	
Akane	Best used for baking or desserts due to its slightly tart flavor and texture that holds up well when baked. It has a sweet, spicy flavor and distinct aroma, but does not store well. Apples are firm with smooth, clean skin and have good bright red color.

Variety	Description
Arkansas Black	When first picked, fruit is very crisp (almost hard) and somewhat tart. Its flavor improves after a few months of storage. A seedling of Winesap.
Blondee	Completely yellow apple with cream-colored flesh and texture similar to a Gala. It has sweet, rich flavor similar to Golden Delicious. Flesh has good resistance to browning. Stores well.
Braeburn	Fruit is predominantly orange-red blush over a yellow background color. Due to its sweet, yet complex flavor, this apple is popular worldwide. It can be frozen, cooked, used in sauce and eaten fresh. The fruit may drop prematurely in hot climates, but can be prevented by thinning. It can be stored for several months.
Cameo	Discovered by chance in a Washington orchard in 1987. It may be a cross between a Red Delicious and a Golden Delicious, since it was found near orchards of those fruits; it also appears similar to the original Delicious cultivar. It is bright red striped over creamy orange, firm and crisp with an aromatic flavor. It is rapidly becoming a favorite, and is now among the top ten most grown apples in Washington.
Cortland	After the many attributes of McIntosh were discovered, plant breeders began crossing it with other varieties to enhance its traits. One of the earliest was the Cortland, combined with the Ben Davis variety. Its flavor is sweet compared to McIntosh, and it has a flush of crimson against a pale yellow background sprinkled with short, dark red stripes and gray-green dots. Cortland has very white flesh and is an excellent dessert apple.
Fuji	One of the more attractive modern apple varieties. Lovely pink speckled flush over a yellow-green background. Crisp and juicy, with dull white flesh which snaps cleanly. The flavor is predominantly sweet, very refreshing, but not particularly outstanding.
Gala	Native to New Zealand, this apple is now grown extensively in the United States since its introduction in the 1970s. Excellent for both eating and baking. Most Gala apples are yellow-gold with pink to red stripes, while some Gala strains may be nearly solid red. Good-quality Gala apples will be firm with smooth and clean skin.
Gibson Golden Delicious	A very sweet apple with smooth, thin skin. Less prone to russeting than Golden Delicious.
Ginger Gold	Discovered as a chance seedling in Virginia, this Golden Delicious-type apple ripens 6 weeks ahead of Golden Delicious. Ginger Gold exhibits all the qualities of a fall variety with sweet, crisp, slightly acidic fruit. It is the highest quality early season yellow dessert apple available. The apple, once cut, has very little tendency to turn brown. Limbs of the tree are well-spaced, resulting in less work for the orchardist. Great for eating or in salads.
Golden Delicious	When picked fresh from the tree the flavor is exceptionally sweet and rich, almost like eating raw sugar cane. Golden Delicious is also a versatile apple and can be used both for dessert and cooking purposes. It has an attractive appearance which can indeed be golden if left to mature on the tree.

Variety	
Granny Smith	Has a tart flavor and is an excellent cooking apple. Unfortunately, it ripens late, even in warmer areas of the Wasatch Front.
Honeycrisp	Fruit is has an exceptionally crisp, juicy texture and mildly aromatic flavor. Flesh is cream colored and coarse. A nearly solid red coloration develops only if the fruit is well exposed to the sun. The outstanding flavor and texture can be maintained for at least 6 months in refrigerated storage without atmosphere modification. Exhibits strong cold hardiness.
Jonathan	A classic American variety, widely regarded as one of the best flavored with a good sweet/sharp balance. Can be used fresh, in baking and frozen.
Jonagold	A cross between Golden Delicious and Jonathan developed in 1953 in New York. Fruit is large and sweet with a thin skin. Apples have a green-yellow basic color with crimson brindle cover. It is crisp with juicy, aromatic, sweet-sour taste. Jonagold is triploid, and requires a second type of apple for pollen and is incapable of providing pollen for other trees. Is excellent for salads, pies and baking purposes.
Jonamac	Jonamac is similar in flavor to McIntosh, but has a more tart flavor. Excellent for cooking, in desserts and salads.
JonaPrince	Fruit is firm, complex in flavor with sour-sweet high taste qualities and a deep red skin. JonaPrince are early ripening and store very well.
Macoun	A cross between McIntosh and Jersey Black, developed at the New York State Agricultural Experiment Station, first introduced in 1923, and has been regarded as one of the finest eating apples in the Northeast. Macoun tends not to produce reliable crops each year, with a good harvest followed by a sparser one. The skin is a dark red with a purplish flush. Its very firm flesh is juicy and snow white, tasting sweet with a hint of berry.
McIntosh	Fruit has a red and green skin, a tart flavor and tender white flesh. Well known for being juicy and aromatic, it is a superior eating apple and well suited for applesauce. Comes from a hardy tree.
Mutsu	Fruit has a sweet flavor with firm, juicy and creamy white flesh. It is similar to Golden Delicious but more complex in flavor. Its skin color is a yellowish green with an orange blush. The Mutsu apple is also known as Crispin. This apple is vigorous, fairly early, and the fruit is large and oblong shaped. It is excellent for fresh eating, sauces, baking and freezing. This apple stores and keeps well.
Northern Spy	Skin color is a green ground, flushed with red stripes where not shaded. The white flesh is juicy, crisp and mildly sweet with a rich, aromatic flavor, noted for high vitamin C content. Its characteristic flavor is more tart than most popular varieties, and its flesh is harder/crunchier than most, with a thin skin. It is commonly used for desserts and pies, but is also used for juices and cider. Further, the Northern Spy is an excellent apple for storage, as it tends to last longer due to late maturation.

Variety	Description
Red Delicious	Excellent for eating fresh and in salads; poor for baking. Good-quality Red Delicious apples will be firm with smooth, clean skin and have a rich red color that is sometimes streaked lightly with yellow or with a yellow cheek. Popularity has declined with new introductions.
Rome Beauty	A popular apple for baking due to its slightly tart flavor, but is also tasty eaten fresh. Consider using this apple where Granny Smith will not ripen.
Sansa	A sweet-tart apple with flavor resembling a Gala. Medium in size. Red in color with a firm and juicy yellow flesh. Stores for 6 to 8 weeks.
SnowSweet	SnowSweet is bred for colder climates. Fruit can be used fresh, for cooking and for processing. The fruit can also be stored for 4 to 8 weeks.
Sweet Sixteen	Popular apple for very cold northern regions. A good all-purpose apple. It ripens in early fall, just ahead of Honeycrisp. It is crisp and juicy with an exotic yellow flesh and rosy red, smooth textured finish. A very sweet, unusual sugar cane or spicy cherry candy flavor. Fruit is medium to large sized. Trees are moderately resistant to fireblight. The fruit stores for 5 to 8 weeks.
Winesap	Fruit has red flesh and a tart flavor with undertones of wine. It is a popular choice for making cider and can be used in salads. Winesap will not pollinate other apple varieties.
Zestar	Ripens early and is crisper than other summer apples. It can be eaten fresh or used for cooking. Can be stored for up to 2 months. This apple is better suited to colder climates.
Apricots	
Chinese	Early bearing, heavy producing, good quality with medium to large fruit. Skin and flesh color are yellow to medium-orange. Good flavor and texture. Pollinates other apricot varieties. Blooms late avoiding damage from late frost. Pit can be dried and cracked open, yielding a sweet, edible nut.
Harcot	Medium to large fruit often blushed with red. Firm flesh with sweet, juicy, rich flavor. Good fresh quality.
Harglow	Medium to large sized, full flavored, juicy fruit. Texture makes them great for fresh eating, cooking and preserving. Requires no other variety for pollination.
Goldcot	An open-pollinated seedling of Perfection. Fruit is medium-sized, nearly round. Skin color is golden and moderately tough. Flesh is firm and medium-orange in color. Somewhat self-fruitful.
Goldrich	Large, oval fruit develops a waxy bright orange ground color. Flesh is deep orange, firm with a fine texture. Resistant to winter injury. Requires pollinator, not Perfection.
Moorpark	A large yellow, juicy, sweet tasting fruit. Good fresh or dried. Poor canner. Very productive. Self-pollinating, good pollinator for late varieties.

	Description
Perfection	Large, oval to oblong fruit. Flesh and skin color clear, yellow-orange to deep orange at full maturity. Good quality, texture and flavor. Very hardy.
Rival	Large, oval fruit. Skin is light orange and develops a blush on exposed cheeks. Mildly flavored deep orange flesh. Low acid. Vigorous, productive tree which requires cross-pollination. Flowers early and may not pollinate well with later flowering varieties.
Royal	Sweet, aromatic and flavorful.
Tilton	Leading commercial variety for drying and canning. Medium to small fruit with fine flavor. Golden yellow with a dark red blush.
Tomcot	Light orange color with trace of blush. Fruit medium to large, orange, firm flesh. Dessert quality. Tree is vigorous, early bloomer.
European Plum	
Damson	Oval, blue plums used mainly for preserves.
Green Gage	Greenish yellow fruit with amber flesh. Fruit is good fresh, cooked or preserved. Self-pollinating.
Italian	Dark blue in color. Very sweet and good for dessert, canning or drying. Self-pollinating.
Stanley	Most widely planted European plum has large, dark blue fruit with richly flavored yellow flesh. Oval in shape. Good fresh, preserved or dried. Self-pollinating.
Japanese Plum	
Duarte	Large, heart-shaped, deep red fruit. Sweet red flesh that is excellent fresh or for canning.
Elephant Heart	Mottled dark crimson colored skin, rich firm, red, juicy flesh. One of the best tasting plums with extremely sweet flavor. Japanese variety has clingstone fruit.
Santa Rosa	Large plum with deep crimson skin. Flesh is purple to yellow. Good for dessert or canning.
Satsuma	Fruit is small to medium with dull, dark red skin. It has mild red flesh, small pit and produces red juice. Use for dessert or preserves.
Shiro	Medium to large round plum. Yellow in color with good flavor. Use fresh or for cooking. Heavy producing tree.
Peaches	
Angelus	A yellow peach with a slight red blush. Fruit flesh is yellow in color and has a low acid flavor.
Blushingstar	A medium to medium large white-fleshed peach. Firm with very good flavor.

	Description
Canadian Harmony	Late-blooming, vigorous tree. Cold hardiness comparable to Redhaven. Medium to large, firm, yellow freestone with red near the pit. Skin almost entirely blushed red. Ripens just before Halehaven. Use fresh and for freezing. Self-fertile.
Cresthaven	Medium to large freestone fruit is bright red over a gold background. Flesh is yellow and non-browning. Good for canning and freezing.
Contender	Very cold hardy, tolerant of late spring frosts. Skin is red-orange color with sweet, yellow flesh. Self-pollinating.
Early Elberta	Large golden yellow peach with very little or no blush. Golden yellow flesh with rich, sweet flavor. Excellent for fresh eating and canning. Most popular variety in the area.
Elberta	Large, golden yellow fruit blushed with red. Firm, rich, sweet, yellow flesh. Excellent for fresh eating and canning. Hardy and productive. Self-fertile.
Flamin Fury PF 24C®	A medium large to large fruit. Yellow-green skin with crimson red overtones. Firm, melting, yellow flesh with sweet/acidic flavor.
Hale Haven	Medium to large fruit with red over yellow skin. Very sweet skin. Yellow, freestone flesh is juicy and flavorful. Tree is vigorous and productive
Interpid	An excellent yellow peach variety producing large, firm, freestone fruit.
J.H. Hale	Extra large, round fruit with golden skin, mostly covered with red blush. Sweet, firm, yellow flesh. Requires pollination from another variety. Very popular late peach.
Loring	Medium-sized freestone has a red blush over yellow background. Yellow flesh is firm, medium textured.
O'Henry	Large, freestone fruit with yellow flesh.
Red Globe	Very large, round peach. Skin is highly blushed red over golden color. Firm, yellow flesh with excellent sweet flavor. Excellent for fresh eating, canning or freezing. Self-fertile.
Redhaven	Medium sized, freestone, round fruit. Golden-yellow skin with attractive red blush. Non-browning, sweet yellow flesh is firm and smooth textured. Good for canning, freezing and fresh eating. The tree is vigorous and early bearing. Self-fertile.
Redstar®	A medium fruit with scarlet orange-red over a greenish-yellow skin. Firm, yellow flesh with good flavor. Productive, but must be thinned hard and early to get larger fruit.
Reliance	Late blooming. Very cold hardy/frost hardy. Sweet, flavorful yellow freestone. Best choice for climates having severe cold in winter and spring. Harvest 2 to 3 weeks before Elberta. Self-fruitful.
Risingstar™	Medium orange-red fruit with good blush.

Roza	Large, round peach with medium blush. The flesh is deep yellow, very firm and slightly coarse in texture. Fruit flavor is excellent and can be used fresh or for canning.
Saturn	Large, white-fleshed fruit. Very sweet in flavor with high sugar content.
Suncrest	Large, freestone fruit with yellow flesh.
Pear	
Barlett	Medium to large, thin skinned familiar pear. Sweet, tender flesh is fine for eating and canning. Trees bear when young and are very productive. Partially self-fertile, but produces more with cross pollination.
Bosc	Long, narrow fruit with russet color. Flesh is firm, crisp with heavy perfume. Good fresh, canned and especially fine for cooking.
Comice	Rotund body with a short defined neck. Green with red blush or red in color.
Concorde	Round bottom with exceptionally long neck that tapers to point. Yellow-green skin with dense flesh that is sweet and juicy. Excellent all-purpose pear. Slow to brown once cut.
D'Anjou	Large, green fruit. Firm flesh has a mild flavor and is not especially juicy. Stores well, good for fresh eating or canning.
Seckel	Small in size with rotund body, small neck and short stem. Olive green in color with a maroon blush.
Sensation	Red in color. Good when fresh or canned. Sweet with higher sugar content than a Bartlett.
Sweet Cherries	
Bing	Exceptionally large fruit with dark burgundy skin – almost black when fully ripe. Firm, sweet, juicy, purplish flesh. Excellent for eating, canning and preserving. Will not pollinate Lambert or Royal Ann.
Lambert	Very large, firm, heart-shaped cherry with black skin and very dark, sweet flesh. Lambert is hardy and vigorous. Will not cross-pollinate with Bing or Royal Ann.
Lapins	Very large, dark purple to black cherry with firm, sweet, delicious purplish flesh. Bears heavy crops. Self-fertile. Excellent pollinator for other sweet cherries.
Rainier	A large crack-resistant cherry. Skin color is golden yellow with a considerable red blush. Firm fruit with distinctive sweet flavor. Higher sugar and lower acid than Bing. Vigorous, hardy, productive variety. Excellent pollinator for most varieties.

Variety	Description
Stella	Large, heart-shaped cherry with dark red, nearly black skin. Firm, sweet, dark red flesh with good flavor and texture. Fruit is of excellent quality and very similar to Lambert. Resistant to cracking. Tree bears at a young age. Self-fruitful. Good pollinator for all sweet cherries.
Utah Giant	More flavorful, sweeter and larger than Bing or Lambert. Dark red flesh holds color when processed. Disease-resistant tree needs a pollinator such as Van or Stella.
Van	Medium to large size cherry with dark, almost black skin. Firm, dark, semi-sweet flesh. Excellent pollinator for other sweet cherries. Tree is hardy, vigorous and a very prolific bearer.

Figure 28: *Apple cluster that should have been thinned to one fruit earlier in the season*

GARDEN MYTH #4:

If a newly planted fruit tree does not grow new branches or bear lots of fruit the first few seasons, it means there is something wrong with the tree.

Fact: Remember that woody plants, like fruit trees, must balance root growth with shoot growth. If a tree fails to grow lots of new branches and leaves the first few seasons after planting, it is likely putting the majority of its resources into root development. This is a good thing! It is best to not fertilize newly planted trees for the first few seasons. It is also recommended to remove young fruit for the first few seasons so the plant can channel its resources into root development, not fruit production. Sometimes this is a very hard thing for gardeners to do; we want that fruit so badly! Also keep in mind that some types of fully ripe fruit (like apples and pears) are very heavy. If branches are too weak to the support the fruit, they might break under the weight, ultimately damaging the plant.

FRUIT THINNING

Gardeners may not realize they need to thin fruit on apple, peach, pear, nectarine and sometimes apricot trees. Fruit thinning is important to produce large fruit and for consistent production every year. Without thinning, apple and pear trees may enter an alternate-year bearing cycle where the tree fruits heavily one year and very little the following year. This pattern will continue until the gardener correctly thins fruit from the tree. Time thinning when the fruit is dime to quarter sized in diameter. If fruit has formed in a cluster, you will want to remove the smaller fruit in the cluster and leave a single fruit spaced at every 5 to 6 inches along the branch. If fruit is spaced too closely, the tree will not have the resources to properly ripen the fruit.

SMALL FRUIT PRODUCTION

Small fruits (raspberries, blackberries, strawberries and grapes) are a great option for gardeners with limited space. Grapes can be trained to trellises, strawberries can be grown in parking strips, and a small raspberry patch can produce enough berries for

Red Raspberries Fall Bearing	
	Description
Anne	Large fruit size with good flavor, firmness and appearance. Anne berries are a pale yellow variety moderately susceptible to sunburn.
Autumn Bliss	Early season, fall-bearing variety. Fruit is produced 2 to 3 weeks before Heritage. Fruit can get dark if not picked regularly. Large and flavorful fruit.
Caroline	Large, attractive, glossy, firm berries with excellent flavor that tend to be more tart.
Fall Gold	Gold-colored berries.
Goldie	Apricot in color when fully ripe. Other than color, Goldie has similar characteristics to Heritage.
Heritage	Very productive and durable. Fruit is small to medium and mildly flavored. One of the oldest fall raspberry varieties.
Polana	High yielding, fall bearing berries. Low percentage for sunburn injury.
Redwing	Small fruit that is less firm than Heritage and has flavor that is not rated as highly as Heritage.
Ruby	Firm, large berries. High risk for sunburn injury and late fruiting.
Summit	Soft textured, small to medium sized berries. Good flavor.

*See the USU Extension fact sheet "**A Comparison of 10 Fall Bearing Raspberry Cultivars for Northern Utah**" for descriptions of fall bearing raspberry varieties.

both fresh eating and making jams and jellies. Small fruits grow best in well-drained loam or sandy loam soils with full sunlight exposure. It is important to control weeds prior to planting small fruits because weeds are difficult to control once plants are established.

Red Raspberries June Bearing	
Variety	**Description**
Canby	Fruit is large and flavorful. Susceptible to powdery mildew.
Cascade Bounty	High yield producing. Fruit is not recommended for fresh use due to softness and acidity.
Cascade Delight	Berries are large and firm. It is productive with long fruiting laterals.
Chilliwack	Medium-large size fruit that is excellent fresh or processed. Good, very sweet flavor.
Lantham	Full flavor.
Reveille	Large bright red berries with elongated cup shape.
Royalty	Very large, conic, purple berries that produce excellent processed products.
Titan	Berries are large, dull red and have acceptable flavor at best flavor.
Tulameen	Produces large, firm fruit with excellent, non-traditional raspberry flavor.

FALL BEARING RASPBERRIES

Fall bearing raspberries produce fruit on current year's growth (primocanes). Early producing varieties start to fruit in early September. Later producing varieties fruit in late September or early October and continue to produce fruit until the first hard frost. If primocanes are not removed in the fall, they will produce a small crop the following summer, lower on the cane. After this second harvest, the canes should be pruned to the ground because they will not produce fruit again. If old canes are left on the plant, they will become vulnerable to pests.

SUMMER AND JUNE BEARING RASPBERRIES

Unlike fall bearing raspberries, summer or June bearing raspberries bear fruit once during the summer months on second-year canes (canes grow the first season, over-winter, and produce fruit the following year). After the canes produce fruit, they must be pruned to the ground because they will not continue to bear fruit.

STRAWBERRIES

Strawberries are an excellent fruit choice for almost any garden space because:

1. Strawberries require minimal space to grow.
2. Once established, strawberries require minimal maintenance.
3. Strawberries are an early bearing fruit.
4. Strawberries can be grown in a container.

If gardeners decide to plant a strawberry patch, they should locate it in an area that receives at least 8 hours of direct sun a day. Strawberries grow best in loamy or sandy soils that have been amended with organic matter. Strawberry plants require minimal additional fertilizer but may need to be relocated every 5 years to avoid soil borne diseases and plant crowding. Gardeners have a choice on the types of strawberries they want to grow: June-bearing, ever-bearing and day neutral varieties. June-bearing strawberries bear fruit late May to June, ever-bearing strawberries bear fruit in the

Strawberries	
Variety	**Description**
Earliglow June Bearing	Among the earliest fruiting and is considered by many to be the gold standard of flavor.
Chandler June Bearing	Yields well and has large fruit. The plant is vigorous and adapts well to a range of conditions, but may not be hardy enough for the coldest regions of Utah.
Honeoye June Bearing	The most popular home variety in the U.S due to high yields of large fruit that ripen in early mid-season. This variety is not well suited to many parts of Utah as it does not do well on heavy soil and the fruit develops off flavor when it ripens in hot weather.
Allstar June Bearing	A good choice for midseason fruit as the plants are more tolerant of hot weather. Fruit is large and sweet.
Jewel June Bearing	A cold hardy variety that produces late season large fruit of excellent quality.
Sparkle June Bearing	Produces a medium-sized fruit that is very flavorful and prized for jams and freezing. The plants are cold hardy, vigorous and show resistance to at least one type of root rot.
Ogallala Ever Bearing	An ever bearer that produces medium-sized, flavorful, dark red fruit. The plants are vigorous, productive and somewhat drought tolerant.
Seascape Day Neutral	Proven to be productive in a wide range of climates. Fruit are large, flavorful and good for fresh consumption. Plants are resistant to Verticillium wilt.
Tribute Day Neutral	Vigorous, productive plant resistant to gray mold fruit rot, Verticillium wilt and red stele root rot. The fruit is medium sized with good flavor.
Evie 2 Day Neutral	Recently imported from England, this variety produces medium to large fruit.

spring and the fall, and day neutral strawberries bear similarly to ever-bearing strawberries in some areas of Utah. Day neutral strawberries do not fruit when daytime temperatures consistently exceed 85°F. For many areas in Utah, including the Wasatch Front, gardeners can expect poor fruit production with this type. It is this author's personal suggestion to experiment with a few plant types for great season-long picking!

SMALL FRUIT MAINTENANCE

Small fruits vary in their care from irrigation to fertilization and pruning needs. In general, irrigate small fruits when the top 2 to 3 inches of soil has dried out. Do not irrigate wet soil because plants will grow poorly and become vulnerable to pests if they are overwatered. As with tree fruit, it is essential to familiarize yourself with common pests of small fruits and respective organic controls. This information is available in the fact sheets referenced below and Chapter 5 "**Garden Pest Control**" section of this guide. In general, fertilize small fruits as recommended by a soil test; most small fruits grow well with little additional fertilizer. See the "**Soil Fertility**" section in Chapter 4 of this guide for more information on garden nutrient needs. Most small fruits benefit from a layer of mulch from an organic source (wood chips, straw, etc.). Grapes are an exception; grapes require less annual irrigation (20 to 25 inches) than fruit trees (30 to 40 inches) and should only be fertilized in the case of a nutrient deficiency. Grapes are highly susceptible to iron chlorosis. The following fact sheets give suggestions on soil, planting, fertilization, pruning and variety selection for grapes, raspberries and strawberries: **Colorado Grape Grower's Guide**, **Red Raspberry Production in Utah**, **Strawberries in the Garden**, and **Pruning the Home Orchard**.

ADDITIONAL CONSIDERATIONS

Before you plant an orchard it is essential to ask yourself; do I have time to care for the plants? It is likely that unmanaged fruit will harbor pest problems that may invade neighbor's plants or a commercial orchards. If you are unable to grow plants yourself, you can still take advantage of local fresh fruit. Purchase seasonal fruit from a commercial grower or visit a U-pick farm. See the "**Buying and Eating Local is as Easy as 1-2-3**" section in Chapter 1 of this guide for additional ways you can enjoy fresh local fruit.

GROWING FRUIT IN WASHINGTON COUNTY

Rick Heflebower, *USU Extension Horticulture Faculty (Washington County)*

A wide variety of tree fruits and small fruits can be grown in Washington County. Be sure that you have a good irrigation system to keep plants adequately irrigated during the heat of the summer. For a list of suggested fruit varieties and helpful growing tips, go to: **dixiedgardener.org/htm/fruits**.

PRUNING FRUIT TREES AND SMALL FRUIT

INTRODUCTION

Pruning fruit is both an art and a science. Pruning is art because each plant has unique branching characteristics and therefore your plant will not look exactly like the examples illustrated in this guide. Furthermore, a fruit tree located in a gardener's front yard or manicured landscape must maintain aesthetic appeal; who wants to show off an ugly plant? Pruning is a science because plants respond to pruning with new growth; it is a gardener's goal to control the direction of new growth. The general purpose of pruning is to remove unwanted branches and improve fruit production, while the term training refers more specially to directing plant growth of a young tree into a well-developed structure. Pruning can be intimidating at first, but once it is mastered, it is a skill that becomes second nature. Start by studying pruning basics and then dig in and try! Observe where you made previous cuts and how your trees or small fruits responded to your pruning cuts. Do not be afraid to try your hand at pruning; plants are usually very forgiving and will recover and fill in from most mistakes.

Goals of this Section:

- Learn the basic tools needed for pruning
- Learn the basic training systems for tree fruit
- Learn how to prune small fruit such as berries and grapes

PRUNING TOOLS

Basic pruning tools include by-pass hand pruners, loppers, hand saws and curved saws. By-pass pruners should be used for branches with a small diameter, loppers for slightly wider branches, hand saws for large

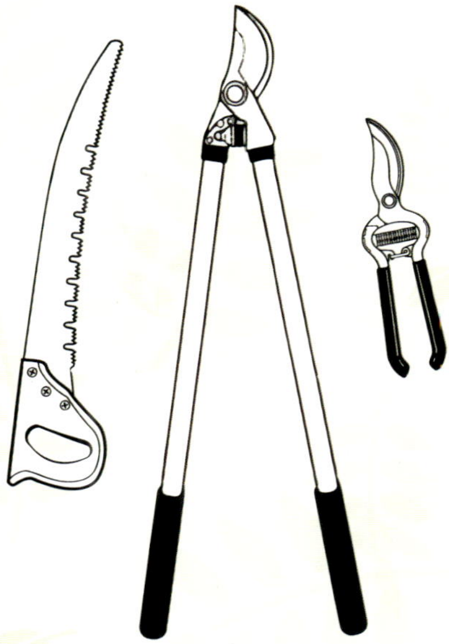

Figure 29: *Basic pruning tools*

branches or small trunks and curved saws for large diameter trunks. Chain saws are useful tools for large jobs; however, make sure you are comfortable handling a chain saw as it can be dangerous if used improperly. If a job is large enough to warrant use of a chain saw, consider calling a certified arborist. Never work around power lines. Hiring an arborist will always be less expensive than a trip to the emergency room! Local certified arborists can be found by visiting the International Society of Arboriculture (ISA) and searching within your local chapter (**www.isa-arbor.com**). Always wear protective equipment appropriate for the job (close-toed shoes, gloves, eye protection, ear protection, long pants) and remember, if you have to fight back nasty words, you probably need to select a better tool for the job!

BASIC PRUNING GUIDELINES

Contrary to popular belief, plants do not enjoy being pruned. However, gardeners may decide to prune plants for the following reasons:

- To increase fruit production and fruit size,
- To remove dead, diseased and broken branches,
- To control height and width of plants,
- To train plants to grow with an ideal branching pattern,
- To increase light penetration to all plant parts.

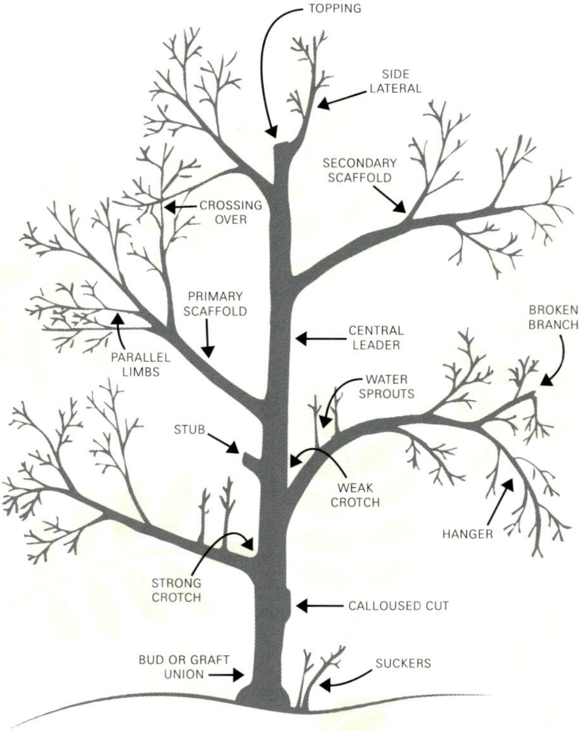

Figure 30: *Basic plant framework*

Some general pruning guidelines include:

- Cut branches on a 45-degree angle just outside of the branch bark ridge and branch collar
- Cut close to a bud or branch and avoid leaving long stubs
- Keep tools sharp to make clean cuts

Figure 31: *Basic pruning cuts Left: Thinning, Right: Heading*

HEADING BACK VS. THINNING OUT CUTS

There are two basic types of pruning cuts. The first is called heading back; with this type of cut, a branch or shoot is shortened. A heading back cut is made to encourage lateral growth (side growth) and additional branching. A heading cut can also be made to balance main branch growth or to remove a major branch that is competing with the main trunk. The second type of pruning cut is called thinning out; with this type of cut, an entire shoot or branch is removed. A thinning cut is used to remove undesirable growth such as water sprouts (suckers located in the canopy of the tree) and root suckers (suckers located around the base of the tree) as well as competing parallel branches. Thinning cuts are also helpful to remove branches with narrow crotch angles that compete with the leader.

GETTING STARTED PRUNING

Spring is just around the corner and it is time to prune your trees. You may be asking yourself, how do I get started? If you feel confident you know what to do, get pruning! If you have questions, ask if your local county Extension service office plans to offer public pruning demonstrations. Another way to get some hands-on training is to ask a certified arborist to come and prune your trees with you. Perhaps after some one-on-one training, you will be ready to prune your trees yourself the following year. Trees are best pruned when dormant (before they grow

Figure 32: *Prune fruit trees when buds are dormant*

leaves or flowers) and with care. As a general rule, never remove more than one-third of a plant in a single season. If more pruning is required, space-out necessary pruning over several seasons. Some exceptions exist, for example grapes and stone fruits may need more aggressive pruning, but be careful not to prune too much in a single season. If you over-prune, you could harm your plant, or even worse, prune off all your fruit buds! Your local Extension agent or certified arborist can help you master pruning decisions. Here are some general guidelines to the pruning process:

- Start with the easy decisions–remove dead, broken, crossing and diseased branches.
- Remove branches or twigs growing too close together.
- Remove branches with weak crotch angles.
- Remove root suckers and water sprouts.
- Cut back main branches so they are about the same length and the tree is balanced.
- Thin and shape according to plant type and location.

TRAINING FRUIT TREES

Fruit trees are generally trained to one of four main structure types based on their growth and branching habits: central leader, modified leader, open center and quad V. These systems are suggestions; fruit trees will still produce fruit if alternate training systems are used. It is important to maintain well-spaced and balanced branching patterns for good light penetration and access to fruit for thinning and harvesting. Choose a

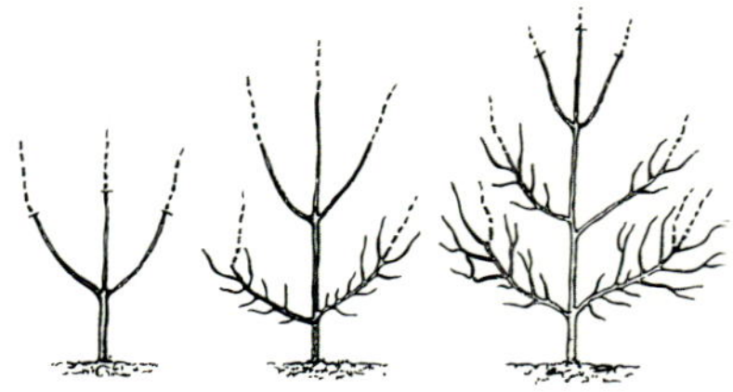

Figure 33: *Central Leader*

training system and proceed to train your tree immediately after you plant it.

1. In the central leader system, the main trunk is surrounded by layers of lateral (side) branches that whorl around the trunk. The first layer of whorls should start 30 to 36 inches above the ground. The next layer should be spaced 20 to 24 inches above the previous layer and so forth. When the tree reaches the desired height, the central leader (tallest vertical branch) is cut back to a short lateral branch, or in other words, the top growth is reduced. Cutting back the central leader will stimulate the tree to produce vertical growth in order to maintain the desired height upright growth should be removed as necessary. The shape of the tree is maintained in a pyramidal Christmas tree shape. This system is used for semi-dwarf apples.

Figure 34: *Modified Leader*

2. The modified leader system involves selecting four to five of the best lateral branches and removing the rest. Ideally, all of the lateral branches should be spaced every 8 to 10 inches vertically along the main trunk. The top lateral branch, or leader, is left about twice as long as the next longest lateral branch. Each lateral should occupy a specific sector, or compass direction, of the tree so that it is balanced. This system is typically used for standard-size apples, pears, sweet cherry, tart cherry, apricot, walnut, pecan and European plums such as Italian prune and Stanley. This system works well for European plums because these trees grow more upright than Japanese plums.

Figure 35: *Open Center*

3. In an open center system, three to four main lateral branches, growing at equal spacing around the trunk, are selected and pruned equal in size. Selected branches should be located 18 to 24 inches above the ground. The preferred crotch angle of the branches is 60 to 90 degrees. This system is typically used for peach, nectarine, apricot, sometimes tart cherry and Japanese plum such as Santa Rosa, which grows in a more spreading form.

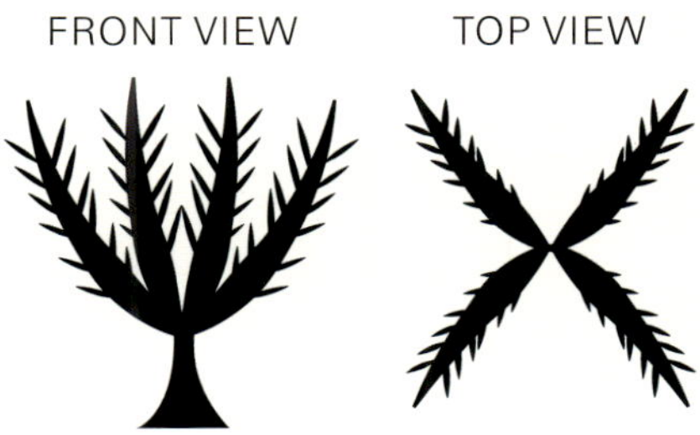

Figure 36: *Quad V*

4. The Quad-V system allows for higher density branching. Four main lateral branches with equal spacing around the trunk are selected. The branches are trained to grow more upright than in an open center system. Fruiting wood (branches that bear fruit) is renewed from the main branches each year. It is important to note that stone fruits, such as peaches, apricots and cherries, bear fruit on fruiting wood. Pome fruits, such as apples and pears, bear fruit on spurs. Make sure you know the difference before pruning your fruit trees. Research at the USU Extension Kaysville Research Farm has found the Quad-V system works well for training peaches. For more information on fruit tree pruning, see the USU Extension publication **Pruning the Orchard**.

PRUNING SMALL FRUIT

Grapes

Grapes require support from a trellis or fence. The four-cane Kniffin system is a simple training system that has worked well in Utah. Set 5 to 6 foot tall support posts and attach heavy gauge wire at 2 ½ and 5 foot height increments above the ground. Fruit

Figure 37: *Four-cane Kniffin system for grapes*

clusters grow on current-season leafy shoots that arise from buds which are borne on woody canes produced the previous season. The goal of pruning is to balance foliage and wood growth. Start the first year by training the main trunk. In subsequent years, attach developing side canes with plastic ties to support structure. Prune to 4 lateral arms or fruiting canes. Select fruiting canes that are pencil sized. A vigorous vine can support 30 to 40 buds or 12 to 15 buds per lateral. Leave fewer buds on less vigorous vines. Also leave 2 renewal spurs of 1 to 2 buds for each lateral arm. Select renewal buds that are close to the main trunk; fruiting canes for next season grow from these renewal buds. Proper pruning necessitates removal of 80 to 90 percent of the wood.

June-bearing Raspberries

Summer bearing (June bearing) raspberries, such as Canby and Newburgh, produce fruit on 1-year old wood. Canes grow the first year

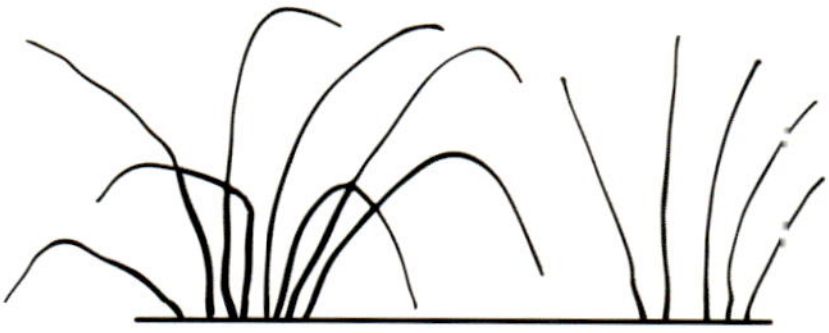

Figure 38: *Pruning raspberries*

without producing fruit and should be trimmed back in the fall to 4 to 5 feet high to avoid winter damage. These same canes will bear fruit the next year around June. In early spring, develop a hedgerow system by removing all canes that are growing outside of an 18 to 24-inch wide row. Then, within the row, thin out canes so there is no more than 3 to 4 canes per row. Select the larger canes and remove the smaller canes. In late summer, after the canes are done fruiting, cut them to the ground to make room for new cane growth.

Ever-bearing raspberries

Ever bearing or fall bearing raspberries, such as Heritage, Caroline and Joan J, will produce fruit in June and September. For two harvests, prune canes the same way as summer bearing varieties described above. For a fall harvest only, cut all canes to the ground in late winter. This practice reduces winter injury and may be less time consuming for the gardener.

Figure 39: *Pruning black and purple raspberries*

Black and Purple Raspberries

Black and purple raspberries generally do not spread much beyond the place they are planted. If needed, they can be supported by a stake or a two-wire trellis with wires at 15 inches and 30 inches above the ground. Tie new shoots to the support structure when they are 24 to 30 inches tall. Next, cut off the growing tip to stimulate side branch growth. The following spring, cut the side branches back to about 12 inches. Keeping the side branches shorter helps balance the number of buds on the plant so berries develop well. Leave 4 to 6 main canes per foot of row.

Blackberries

Upright thorn-less blackberries, such as Navajo, Arapaho and Apache, are pruned similarly to black and purple raspberries except plants grow vigorously and can be topped at 30 to 36 inches above the ground. Thin out suckers during the summer to leave 3 to 6 plants per foot of row.

Semi-erect thorn-less blackberries, such as Chester, Triple Crown, Black Satin, Dirksen and Thornfree, grow best when trained on a trellis. Allow

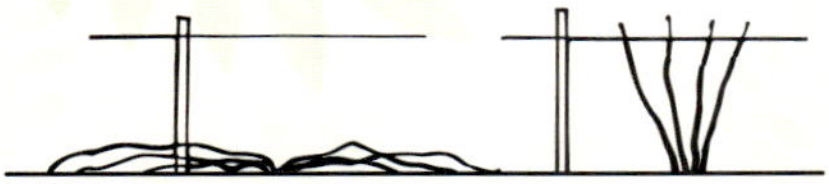

Figure 40: *Pruning trailing blackberries*

Figure 41: *Blackberries growing on a trellis*

5 to 8 canes per foot of row to grow on a trellis that is approximately 6 feet high; thin-out all other canes. Tip the primocanes when their growth extends above the trellis.

Trailing blackberries, such as Boysen, Marion, Logan and Black Diamond, are tender and require protection most winters. An easy way to protect plants is to allow 1-year old wood to grow on the ground and then cover it in the fall with straw mulch for winter protection. In the spring, lift the canes up and tie them to a trellis or stake. Remove dead and diseased wood and weak canes. Wrap canes around the trellis wires of the support structure.

EXTENDING THE GROWING SEASON

Britney Hunter, *USU Extension Horticulture Faculty (Davis County)*

INTRODUCTION

Once gardeners begin to master basic gardening techniques, many build a desire to learn more about season extension. Some beginning gardeners assume they need a heated greenhouse to grow vegetables year-round; however, the truth is they can get away with much less expensive and less permanent structures. Gardeners may ask themselves if they could get their lettuce to grow earlier next year or harvest broccoli in the winter months. With the right knowledge, gardeners can extend their growing season and reap the rewards of "bonus" harvests.

Goals of this Section:

- Learn about using plastic mulches.
- Learn about using floating row covers.
- Learn about using season extension structures.

UTAH'S GROWING SEASON

The growing season for a given location is defined as the period of time between the last spring freeze (32°F or below) and the first fall freeze. This is also known as the freeze-free period. Specific weather information for your area is available through the USU Utah Climate Center (climate.usu.edu). All plants have their own unique temperature requirements for growth but are generally divided into two categories; warm season and cool season plants. Warm season plants only survive during the freeze-free period and prefer temperatures between 55°F and 85°F for optimum growth. Cool season plants prefer temperatures between 40°F and 70°F, and certain cool season plants, like spinach, can survive freezing temperatures. See the "**Garden Preparation**" section in Chapter 1 of this guide for more information on planting dates and cold hardiness of vegetable plants.

USE OF PLASTICS IN ORGANIC GARDENING

Using synthetic plastics for organic farming and gardening is generally considered acceptable and creates opportunities for increased production. Using plastics to cover soil as mulch can greatly decrease weed growth without the use of chemical herbicides. However, plastics can persist in the environment for a long time, and not all plastics are easily recyclable. For example, polyethylene is a common plastic used for greenhouse coverings and mulches and can be recycled by repurposing into other plastic products, but is not accepted in curbside recycle bins. Greenhouse plastic covering can be recycled locally by Rocky Mountain Recycling if delivered separately; however, plastic mulches are not recyclable at this time.

SEASON EXTENSION TECHNIQUES AND DEFINITIONS

A variety of materials and structures can be used to give gardeners the benefit of earlier planting in the spring and later harvest in the fall. Such materials include plant covers, row covers, plastic mulches, cold frames, hotbeds, high tunnels and greenhouses. Also, raising your garden bed above ground level creates a smaller volume that allows soil to warm for earlier planting and keeps the root zone warmer to promote faster growth. However, earlier in the season, plants in raised beds are more susceptible to damage from spring freezes.

Plastic Mulches

Black or clear plastic can be spread over the garden area as mulch in the spring to warm the soil and enable earlier production (Figure 42). Plastic is used most often with warm season transplants such as eggplant, tomatoes, peppers and melons. Typically, plastic comes in 3 or 4-foot wide rolls that can be cut to the length of the garden row. Secure the plastic using heavy objects or by shoveling soil onto the edges of the plastic to hold it in place and prevent it from blowing away. Make a small x-shaped slit in the plastic, then seed or transplant fruits and vegetables through the opening. When using solid plastic between plants, it is best to use drip irrigation underneath the plastic to ensure adequate watering. Some plastics have small holes that allow water to penetrate through so overhead irrigation is possible. It is also a good idea to make sure that the mulch is in good contact with the soil. Where plastic mulch tents-up and leaves air pockets, the temperature of the trapped air can get extremely hot and damage seedlings.

Figure 42: *Lettuce planted in black plastic mulch*

Black plastic warms the soil 6 to 8°F and eliminates weeds, while clear plastic can warm the soil 8 to 10°F. Unfortunately, weeds will grow under clear plastic. When clear plastic is spread over the garden in the spring, the fruit and vegetable plants grow quickly and shade the plastic so over-heating is not a problem. Clear plastic can be used in summer to over-heat the soil on purpose for soil solarization to help destroy weed seeds and soil borne diseases.

Individual Plant Covers

Individual plant covers are one of the simplest materials to use for season extension. Commonly used plant covers include plastic coated hot caps, empty milk bottles and Wall O'

Water®. Hot caps and bottles placed over young plants help conserve soil moisture, increase temperatures inside during the day and provide a few degrees of frost protection at night. Non-vented plant covers such as glass jars should be used with caution since heat builds up very quickly during the day and can easily become too hot for plants inside. The Wall O' Water® product is a self-standing, 18-inch high cylinder made of small tubes that are filled with water, and is open at the top for ventilation. The water absorbs heat during the day to help maintain warmer nighttime temperatures and protect plants from frost down to about 16°F.

Cloth "Floating" Row Covers

Cloth floating row covers include plastic and spun polyester materials that are placed on top of plants to promote warmer temperatures. Floating row cover is made of lightweight polyester fabric that does not require supportive hoops and can rest directly on plants. Floating row cover transmits 80 to 95% of sunlight and is also very porous to allow water to penetrate through the fabric and reach the garden soil. Floating row covers are self-ventilating and provide 4 to 7°F of frost protection which allows earlier planting in the spring (1 to 3 weeks) and later harvest in the fall. Although floating row covers are not needed in the summer for temperature protection, they can be left on plants to exclude certain pests. See Chapter 5 "Garden Pest Control" section of this guide for more detail.

Plastic Row Covers or "Low Tunnels"

Low tunnels are made of UV stabilized greenhouse plastic that requires

Figure 43: *Looking inside a plastic low tunnel*

some support to keep the plastic from damaging plants. The support is generally shaped like a half circle or tunnel that is low to the ground. Support for plastic row covers can be made of plastic, wire or steel and ranges from 15 to 36 inches high in the center (Figures 43 and 44). Plastic row covers are ventilated with small slits in the plastic or by rolling up the sides of the covers. Plastic row covers provide a similar frost protection to floating row cover. However, plastic covers are preferable over cloth because plastic traps solar heat during the day to create a much warmer environment for plant growth. Plastic also provides a better wind break from cold winds in spring and fall.

Figure 44: *Plastic low tunnel over raised bed*

Figure 45: *Cold frames in front with greenhouse in back*

Cold Frames

Cold frames are rectangular boxes made of wood or brick that are used to protect plants from cold and frost injury (Figure 45). The box is constructed to be higher in the back than in the front, and the box is covered with glass, plastic, double-wall polycarbonate or fiberglass sash. A cold frame should be oriented to face south for best sun exposure. Plants can be planted in a cold frame up to 6 weeks earlier than outdoors. Cold frames are typically used to grow short vegetables to maturity and to start transplants of warm season vegetable plants. On warm, sunny days, cold fames need to be ventilated by manually opening the top sash or with an automatic vent opener. A hotbed is simply a cold frame that is heated by placing fresh manure in the bottom of the box, or by using electric heat cables to warm the soil inside. If using manure, place 12 to 16 inches of the manure 8 to 10 inches below the soil surface.

High Tunnels and Greenhouses

High tunnels, or hoop houses, are walk-in structures covered with UV protected greenhouse plastic, without any electrical heating or cooling components (Figure 47). High tunnels are passively heated by the sun and passively cooled by manual ventilation. At night when the passive heat source (sun) is gone, air

Figure 46: *Looking inside a plastic high tunnel*

temperatures within the tunnel will be close to the outside air temperature. A greenhouse is a walk-in structure passively heated by the sun that includes additional heating, cooling and lighting controls to create an optimal growing environment for plants. Greenhouses are commonly covered with greenhouse plastics, glass or other synthetic materials such as polycarbonate. Greenhouses are most commonly used to grow potted annual flowers and vegetable transplants for gardening and landscaping. Galvanized steel is the most common material used to create the structure of a greenhouse or high tunnel. Some low-cost high tunnel designs use PVC pipe instead of steel, but can be less rigid against high winds and heavy snow loads. The plastic is secured to the structure with twine or clips.

Many season extension structures can be used in combination. For example, low tunnels can be used within high tunnels to further protect plants from cold night time temperatures (**Figure 46**).

For more information on high tunnels and greenhouses, see the following online and printed resources:

- Utah State University Publications: **tunnel.usu.edu**
- Cornell University Publication: **Greenhouses for Homeowners and Gardeners**
- Mississippi University Extension Greenhouse Design Publications: **msucares.com/pubs/plans/books/greenhouses**

Figure 47: *High tunnel made of PVC pipe hoops and covered with plastic*

GARDEN SOIL 3

GARDEN SOIL AND SOIL TESTING

INTRODUCTION

Soil science is a complex field of study that encompasses the sciences of chemistry, hydrology, physics, biology and ecology. Sometimes soil scientists grimace when people call soil "dirt" because the noun implies a lifeless, stagnant physical medium. The truth is actually quite the opposite; soil is a dynamic, living and constantly changing ecosystem. Furthermore, the key to a great garden is the quality of the soil. Avid gardeners know that by continuously improving their garden soil, they are ensuring a productive garden for years to come.

Goals of this Section:

- Discover the beneficial roles of soil.
- Become familiar with the three soil components that define soil texture.
- Discover the benefits of soil testing.

BENEFICIAL ROLES OF SOIL

Soil serves many roles: it is a medium for plant growth, it is a recycler of raw materials, it functions as an environmental filter, it regulates underground water supplies, it provides habitat for soil organisms and it performs as an engineering medium. Without soil, our planet could not support life! Even humans depend on soil for our existence. Plants use nutrients from the soil to produce the food we consume in our diets. Therefore, understanding the needs of a healthy soil is an important first step toward growing a successful garden. For those with limited knowledge of soil, here is a basic overview of soil science concepts important for gardening.

SOIL TEXTURE

Soil texture is described as the proportion or percent of three particles: sand, silt and clay.

GARDEN MYTH #5:

The amount of soil organic matter is defined by the soil texture.

Fact: Soil texture is independent of the percent of organic matter in the soil. Soil texture defines the relative proportions of sand, silt and clay. Even though the percent of soil organic matter does not affect the soil texture, organic matter is a very important component of a healthy garden soil.

Figure 48, known as a soil texture triangle, illustrates the relationship between particle size distribution and soil texture classes. A common misconception is that the percent of organic matter is described in soil textures. Although organic matter is an important component of soils, it does not contribute to soil texture. Differences between sand, silt and clay particles are most simply described by their relative sizes. Most soils contain a mixture of sand, silt and clay particles but may be dominated by one or more particle types. A dominating particle type can determine properties of the soil such as water infiltration and nutrient retention. See the USU Extension fact sheet **Topsoil Quality Guidelines for Landscaping** for a summary of topsoil quality guidelines including desirable soil textures.

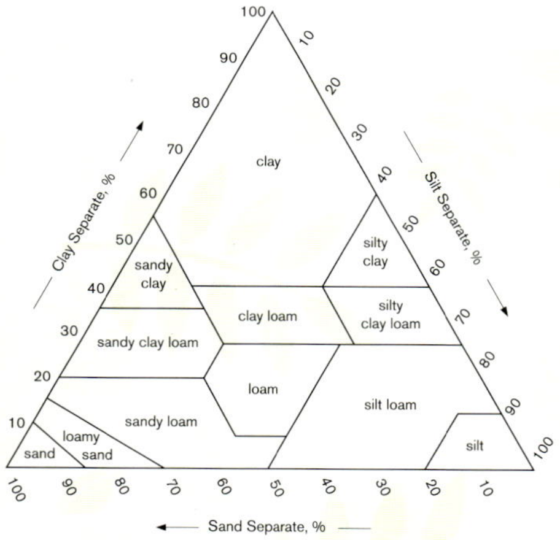

Figure 48: Soil texture triangle

Sand

Sand, the largest particle size (2 to 0.05 millimeters in diameter), can be seen by the naked eye and has a gritty texture when rubbed between fingers. Without a binding agent, sand particles do not stick together or form the many small capillary pores that bind water, like finer textured soils. Sand also has a low nutrient holding capacity. Therefore, sand particles generally do not provide plants with adequate nutrients for optimal growth. Think of a sand dune; does vegetation grow densely on sand dunes? Although some exceptions exist, most plants will not thrive in sand-dominated growing mediums unless the medium is amended with organic matter and/or regularly supplied with nutrients. Sand does provide excellent drainage for plants. Most plants are not adapted to conditions where roots are growing in stagnant water. Again, some exceptions exist like plants adapted to wetland conditions, but typically poorly draining soils or constantly saturated conditions are stressful on plant growth. Sand-dominated soils prevent this stress by rapidly draining water away from the plant's root-zone; consequently sand-dominated soils require more frequent irrigation and fertilization for adequate plant growth. Sand-dominated soil textures include sand and loamy sand.

Silt

Silt, the middle particle size (0.05 to 0.002 millimeters in diameter), is so small that individual particles are not visible to the naked eye. Silt particles feel smooth but not sticky when wet and rubbed between your fingers. Silt particles have a higher water holding capacity than sand; however, silt-dominated soil textures are also improved with the addition of organic matter. Because silt particles alone are only moderately attracted to one

Figure 49: *Loam textured garden soil*

another, the addition of organic matter assists in building soil structure in silt-dominated soils. Dry silt appears powdery with some clods. Silt is commonly transported via water in streams and rivers or windblown as loess. Perhaps you have noticed that more turbulent sections of streams often appear cloudy. Silt particles suspended in turbulent water quickly settle as the stream flow slows leaving a soft and silky layer on the river bottom. Silt-dominated soil textures include silt and silt loam.

Clay

Clay (less than 0.002 millimeters in diameter) is the smallest of the three soil particle sizes and feels sticky when wet. Soil samples high in clay can be formed into a ball, like Play-Doh®, when they are moist. Clay has high water retention and nutrient adsorptive properties. This means clay-dominated soils have a tendency to hold onto water and nutrients. While these are the positive characteristics, clay-dominated soils also have some drawbacks. Clay soils form clods easily and can be difficult to work down to a fine seed bed, especially if they are tilled while wet. In the spring, when gardeners are anxious to get their gardens planted, clay-dominated soils are slow to dry out. Oftentimes there are only a few days when clay soils are at an appropriate moisture level for tilling. Once they dry out, they become hard and difficult to work. Gardeners often misconceive clay soils as "bad" or "unfertile" and are tempted to start-fresh by bringing in outside topsoil or building raised beds to avoid planting in clay-dominated soils. While these options are certainly a possibility, the shortcoming of poor workability can usually be corrected with annual amendments of organic matter. Clay soils are not unfertile. Remember, clay has a high ability to hold onto nutrients; therefore, amended clay soils are a rich source of plant nutrients and can provide an excellent garden soil.

When adding amendments (like hauled-in topsoil) to existing soil, thoroughly mix them with existing soil to avoid layering of different soil components (**Figure 50**). Gardeners should be cautious when adding sand to clay-dominated soils. Although sand does improve drainage, only medium-grained sand should be added and the sand should always be pre-mixed with organic matter before incorporating it into clay-dominated soils. Failure to do so can yield a medium with a soil structure similar to concrete! Organic matter alone will improve soil structure in clay-dominated soils without the risk associated with adding sand. If sand is selected as the preferred amendment, it should be added in amounts large enough to make a difference, usually 2 to 3 inches of sand per 6 inches of soil. Adding a small amount of sand is like putting a handful of marbles into a bucket of flour; it does not improve the structure or drainage. Clay-dominated soils include clay, clay loam, sandy clay and silty clay.

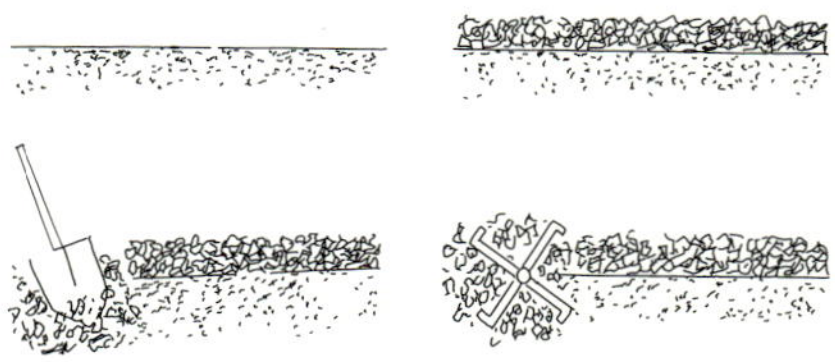

Figure 50: *Till or mix amendments into existing soil*

Loam

Loam soils are a composition of sand, silt and clay percentages that form an ideal, "best-case scenario" plant-growing medium. Loam soils provide adequate drainage, water retention, and nutrient adsorptive properties for

GARDEN MYTH #6:

A soil test will tell a gardener exactly what is wrong with his or her garden plants.

Fact: Soil test results are one piece of information a gardener can use to determine the source of garden problems. Soil test results are important to help gardeners know how to best fertilize garden plants. However, sometimes gardeners will have their soil tested with the expectation that recommendations will tell them what they are doing wrong; imagine their disappointment when test reports make no mention what happened to create the problem. This is where your local USU Extension office can help; sometimes soil test results indicate a clear stress, such as high salinity, while other times results rule out evidence of common problems. USU Extension is not in the business to sell residents services they do not need; talk with your local USU Extension agent or Master Gardeners prior to testing your soil to see if a soil test will aid you in solving your garden problem. See the USU Extension fact sheet **Understanding Your Soil Test Results** for more information on soil testing and result interpretations.

ideal plant growth. Nationally, most soils are loams although loam soils may be dominated by a particular soil particle size such as sandy loam, silt loam or clay loam. Even though loam soils are considered ideal garden soils, loam soils still benefit from the addition of organic matter. Loam soils include fine sandy loam, very fine sandy loam, silt loam, sandy clay loam and silty clay loam.

Soil texture can be determined by feel; however, the more accurate method to determine soil texture is to have your soil tested by the nearest land-grant university soil testing laboratory. Soil texture can also be determined by viewing the Web Soil Survey online (**USDA-NRCS Web Soil Survey**), although actual soil texture may not be reflected in the Web Soil Survey if the soil on the property was recently modified; for example, outside soil was brought in to build up an area. However you determine your soil texture, remember to keep your fingers crossed that the results reveal you live in loamville!

SOIL TESTING

Although differences in soil textures might seem obvious from the descriptions above, correctly identifying a soil texture by feel takes the expertise of a trained professional. Fortunately, having your soil tested by a professional is both inexpensive and convenient! USU Extension often recommends having your soil tested if you are planning a garden or experiencing problems growing fruits and vegetables. It is ideal to have your soil tested by the local land-grant university because the tests

Figure 51: *Soil test in progress*

performed and recommendations provided are adapted to your local growing area. Tests range from a basic analysis (phosphorus and potassium only) to a complete analysis (pH, salinity, texture, phosphorus, potassium, nitrate-nitrogen, micronutrients, sulfate and organic matter). For organic gardeners on a budget, USU Extension usually recommends a routine soil analysis (pH, salinity, texture, phosphorus, potassium and recommendations from the soil testing technician on advised nutrient additions). Garden soil should be tested every two to three growing seasons. Mail soil samples to the USUAL Soil Testing Laboratory (**www.usual.usu.edu**) in Logan, Utah. The site will provide instructions on how to prepare and mail soil samples. You can also contact your local USU Extension office for more information on how to prepare soil samples and interpret soil test results. For a more detailed discussion on interpreting soil test results and an example soil test report, see the USU Extension fact sheet **Understanding Your Soil Test Report**.

THREE COMMON SOIL PROBLEMS

INTRODUCTION

Sometimes gardeners bring samples of their problematic garden soil into the Extension Service office and want it tested to figure out why their plants are growing poorly. Unfortunately there is not one diagnostic test that can determine all potential problems. Plants may be stressed by drought, disease, insect pests, improper care or all of the above! Before you throw your hands up in the air in defeat, rest assured that some soil problems are more common than others. This section will explore three common soil problems and how they can be managed.

Goals of this Section:

- Better understand the impact of pH on soil.
- Better understand the impact of salinity on soil.
- Better understand the impact of compaction on soil.

1) SOIL PH

Soil pH impacts garden plans because variations in pH affect plant nutrient availability and soil microorganism activity. The pH scale ranges from 0 to 14 with 7 being neutral. Values above 7.0 are considered alkaline and pH values below 7.0 are considered acidic. A one point increase in pH represents a ten-fold increase in alkalinity. Utah soils tend to be slightly alkaline with pH values of 7.5 to 8.5. Fortunately pH values in this range are suitable for production of most fruit and

GARDEN MYTH #7:

Additions of acidic materials, like pine needles or peat moss, is a great way to lower soil pH.

Fact: It is very difficult to permanently lower the pH of Utah soils. Soil has a high "buffering capacity" meaning it resists change in pH. Acidic additions, like pine needles and peat moss, may only slightly and temporarily lower soil pH (if they have any affect at all) but the pH level will revert back to the original level over time. Irrigation water comes in contact with the parent materials (weathered rock) that built Utah soils. Therefore, unless irrigation water is acidified, you can count on a soil pH level around that which is average for Utah soils. USU Extension encourages gardeners to embrace local conditions and plant garden plants that thrive in our soil chemistries.

Figure 52: *Plant wilting can be a symptom of multiple garden stresses*

vegetable plants; however, some pH sensitive plants, such as berries and grapes, may show signs of nutrient deficiencies. Phosphorus, iron, manganese, molybdenum, copper, boron and zinc deficiencies are possible with soil pH values above 7.5. Soil pH values above 8.2 make it difficult to grow some plants. Check with your local county Extension service office if your soil test results measure above this pH value.

Adjusting Soil pH

It is possible to slightly lower pH values (0.2 to 0.5 units) over a period of time through the addition of organic matter or elemental sulfur; however, making a significant reduction of soil pH is generally not practical. Soils resist change in pH due to their high buffering capacity. Lime should never be added to Utah soils because lime tends to raise the soil pH. One method for controlling soil pH is to use a more acidic soil medium, like peat moss, in a raised bed garden. However, the pH of Utah irrigation water tends to be slightly alkaline, so if irrigation water is not acidified before watering acidic soils, the soil pH values will eventually increase to the pH range typical of Utah soils. It is recommended to plant garden plants that are tolerant of slightly alkaline soils instead of trying to decrease the soil pH for acid-loving plants like cranberries and blueberries. Soils with a pH over 8.5 may be sodic. Sodic soils contain high levels of sodium (Na), which interfere with plant growth and reduce soil aggregate stability. Plants grow poorly or not at all in sodic soils. Gypsum has no effect on soil pH but is used, along with leaching, to reclaim sodic soils. For detailed information on growing acid-loving blueberries in Utah, see the USU Extension fact sheet **Blueberries in Utah? Difficult, But Maybe Not Impossible**. For more information on managing soil pH, see the USU Extension fact sheet **Solutions to Soil Problems II. High pH (Alkaline Soil)**. See the USU Extension fact sheet **Understanding**

Your Watershed: pH for additional information on the effect of pH on the environment.

2) SOIL SALINITY

Salinity is a measure of the soluble salts in the soil. Saline soils are not the same as sodic soils. Sodic soil properties are dominated by an excess of exchangeable sodium (Na) while saline soils contain high levels of salts of other cations as well, like chlorine, potassium, magnesium and calcium. High salinity concentrations inhibit seed germination of sensitive plants and can suppress growth due to increased water stress. Such stress is sometimes referred to as "chemical drought" because affected plants look as if they are suffering from a lack of water. Fortunately, it is possible to move salt away from the root zone of garden plants. Soluble salts can be leached or washed from the soil during an extended irrigation event. Water should be added to the soil surface in one continuous irrigation event over an extended period of time. The idea is that water will super-saturate the soil, dissolve soluble salts and carry the salts down through the soil and away from the rooting-zone of plants. As a general reference, to leach 1 foot of soil with good internal drainage, apply:

- 6 inches of water to cut salts by 50%
- 12 inches of water to cut salts by 80%
- 24 inches of water to cut salts by 90%

If deeper leaching is necessary, a proportional increase in water will be needed. It is vital to irrigate with a water source that is low in salts, and with the soil freely draining to allow movement of soluble salts away from the leached area. Irrigation water coming from a secondary source such as a well or canal should be tested for salinity levels before being used to irrigate plants or used to leach salts. Visit **www.usual.usu.edu** for more information on testing secondary water sources. For more information on testing irrigation water for use in orchards, see the USU Extension fact sheet **Soil, Water, and Plant Tissue Testing in Utah Orchards**.

Some plants are more tolerant of high salinity levels than others. Therefore if high salinity levels are a concern in your area, you may want to consider growing plants with a greater tolerance to salinity. For more information on the impact of salinity on plant yield, see the USU Extension fact sheets **Water Salinity and Crop Yield** and **Salinity and Plant Tolerance**. For information on the impact of soil salinity on ornamental plants, see the USU Extension fact sheet **Soil Salinity and Ornamental Plant Selection**. Some soil amendments, like animal manures, can contain high levels of soluble salts. Compost samples can be tested for salinity levels through the USU soil testing laboratory. It is beneficial to incorporate amendments with higher salt levels into garden soil in the fall to allow winter snow pack and spring moisture to leach the soluble salts from the root-zone before the growing season. A soil test should be completed in the spring before planting to allow time for a pre-planting leaching event in case test results indicate a high salinity level in the garden soil. For more information on interpreting salinity results from a soil test, see the USU Extension fact sheet **Understanding Your Soil Test Report**. For additional information on soil salinity see the USU Extension fact sheet **Solutions to Soil Problems I. High Salinity (Soluble Salts)**.

3) SOIL COMPACTION

One of a gardener's worst enemies is soil compaction. Soil compaction refers to a situation where the soil structure is deteriorated through one or more of many causes: construction, significant foot or vehicle traffic, frequent travel patterns from animals like dogs or placement of heavy loads on an area of soil. Compacted soil lacks adequate pore space for air and water movement through the soil and acts as a barrier against plant roots exploring surrounding soil for water and nutrients. Therefore, plants typically struggle to remain healthy under compacted conditions. Clay-dominated soils and wet soils are especially susceptible to soil compaction. Therefore, it is best to avoid construction or tilling soils when the ground is wet.

Compaction can be alleviated in affected areas by multiple methods. Garden soils can be rototilled to temporarily help reintroduce water and air movement to the root zone of plants. Compaction can also be alleviated by incorporating organic matter that will separate soil particles and provide gums and waxes that form the soil into granules. Avoid placing heavy items in your garden area. It is wise to strategically place stepping stones in the garden so compaction is limited to a few pre-planned areas. Consider how people will move through the garden and design walkways or pathways to accommodate this natural flow of foot traffic. If amendment of compacted soils is impractical (for example soil clay content is 40% or higher), consider building raised beds. For more information on addressing soil compaction, see the USU Extension fact sheet **Solutions to Soil Problems IV. Soil Structure (Compaction)**.

Figure 53: *Garden furrows can serve as walkways*

ORGANIC MATTER AND SOIL AMENDMENT

INTRODUCTION

As evidenced by the number of times organic matter has been mentioned in this guide (51 times up to now), it should be clear that organic matter is the best amendment for all soil types! You may be surprised to hear that the world's soils contain about three times more carbon than all of the world's plants! Hence, organic matter is critical for a healthy soil! Unfortunately, most Utah soils do not naturally contain adequate soil organic matter for quality fruit and vegetable production. Therefore, amending garden soil with organic matter is a high priority for diligent gardeners.

Goals of this Section:

- Discover the beneficial roles of organic matter.
- Become familiar with the difference between compost and mulch.
- Learn how to amend soil with organic matter.

BENEFITS OF ORGANIC MATTER

Organic matter benefits the soil ecosystem in many ways. Some examples are increased water retention, improved soil structure, decreased soil compaction, improved soil drainage and improved soil workability. Organic matter also recycles certain nutrients back to plants and soil organisms. A beginning gardener may not understand the significance of these improvements. If this describes you, then think of organic matter this way; organic matter feeds the soil. Gardeners sometimes forget that soil is alive! Soil provides habitat for trillions of micro and macro-organisms including bacteria, fungi, nematodes, earthworms, beetles, moles, voles and even birds, like burrowing owls! All these critters reside, die, defecate and burrow through soil. These activities enhance soil qualities. Therefore, micro and macro-organisms are what transform a poor soil into a great soil! Many of these organisms, like decomposers, rely on organic matter to function. Unfortunately Utah soils are naturally relatively low in organic matter (0.25 to 1%) compared to other areas, for example, soils in some areas of the eastern United States range from 7 to 10% organic matter. Therefore, by adding organic matter to a garden soil, you are helping to bring your soil to life!

SOIL AMENDMENTS

Soil amendments describe a material added to the soil surface or incorporated into the soil in an effort to improve soil properties. Possible soil amendments include: leaves, bark, sawdust, wood shavings, peat moss, manure, straw, grass clippings, green manure crops and kitchen

TABLE 14: COMMON SOIL AMENDMENT CHARACTERISTICS

Soil Amendment	Longevity*	Water Retention	Permeability
		Organic	
Bark	Long	Low – Medium	High
Coconut fiber	Long	Low – Medium	High
Compost	Medium	Medium – High	Low – Medium
Grass clippings	Short	Low	Low
Green manure crops	Short	Medium	Low – Medium
Kitchen produce trimmings	Short	Low	Low
Leaves	Medium	Low	Medium
Manure	Short	Medium	Low – Medium
Peat moss	Medium	Very High	Low – Medium
Sawdust	Long	Low – Medium	High
Straw	Medium	Medium	High
Wood shavings	Long	Low – Medium	High
		Inorganic	
Perlite	Long	Low	High
Sand	Long	Low	High
Utelite	Long	Low	High
Vermiculite	Long	High	High

***Short:** Days to weeks **Medium:** Up to approximately six months **Long:** Several years

GARDEN MYTH #8:

It is acceptable to plant garden plants in 100% compost.

Fact: Organic matter sources, such as compost, are a wonderful amendment to garden soil, but typically gardeners experience problems when they plant in a medium of 100% compost. An ideal garden soil is made up of 25% air, 25% water, 45% minerals (from weathered rock) and 5% organic matter. Plants require a range of nutrients, some which are sourced from parent materials (weathered rock) and some which are sourced from organic matter. For this reason, it is wise to amend topsoil with organic matter to ensure your garden plants are receiving all the nutrients they require for healthy growth.

vegetable trimmings. Table 14 lists common organic and inorganic soil amendments and some of their characteristics relative to soil improvement.

A loam garden soil may grow a productive garden without added amendments for several growing seasons. However, if gardeners desire to correct soil problems associated with high clay or sand content, the addition of organic matter can be a game-changer. One of the most effective ways to improve heavy clay soils is to add coarse or woody organic matter such as composted fir bark (Soil Pep, etc.) or wood chips. When mixed with existing soil, these materials improve air and water infiltration down into the soil. Be cautious if adding sand to clay soils. The wrong proportion of clay to sand will result in low-grade concrete. It is recommended to add organic matter instead of sand. Inorganic amendments, such as perlite and vermiculite, also improve permeability and air movement into the soil. Try mixing one-third coarse organic matter (by volume) into the backfill when planting fruit trees or berry bushes. Organic matter also increases the nutrient and water holding capacities of sandy soils.

Gardeners may want to consider amending existing soil before replacing it with hauled topsoil. Replacing existing soil with high quality topsoil is often more expensive than amending the existing soil. Purchase of new soil may be necessary if the area is contaminated or if the gardener plans to raise the height of the garden. Do not add wood ashes to garden soil since they are high in salts and lime which will not improve most Utah soils. Gypsum can be used to improve soils that are very high in sodium, but it should only be applied if indicated by a soil test. For more information on soil amendments, see the USU Extension fact sheet **Solutions to Soil Problems V. Low Organic Matter**.

COMPOST VS. MULCH

Beginning gardeners are sometimes confused by differences between soil amendments. How is compost different from mulch?

1. Compost describes an organic material that has undergone the initial phase of decomposition. The composting process involves carbon, nitrogen, water, oxygen and time (see the "**Backyard Composting**" section later in this chapter for more information on composting). Therefore, compost describes a raw organic material that has broken down to a consistency that resembles soil. Compost is typically incorporated into soil to amend, or improve the soil quality. For more information on compost, see the USU Extension fact sheet **Using Compost in Utah Gardens**.

Figure 54: *Organic mulch ready to spread in the garden*

2. Mulch describes material, organic or inorganic, spread on the soil surface. Mulches benefit the soil through decreased soil moisture evaporation and an increased water in-take rate. Mulches also contribute to improved weed control, moderation of soil temperature, reduced compaction and decreased run-off and soil erosion. Mulch can also be used as an aesthetic dressing around garden plants. Mulch materials include organic materials such as bark or woodchips, and inorganic materials such as decorative rock or tumbled glass. For more information on mulch, see the USU Extension fact sheet **Using Mulches in Utah Landscapes and Gardens**.

It should be noted that the addition of organic matter to the soil is beneficial, but gardeners should not get carried away by adding too much of a good thing! USU Extension often gets calls from Utah residents trying to understand why their gardens are struggling to grow plants. Sometimes gardeners respond that they added 12 inches of woody organic matter to their garden in one application! The addition of too much organic matter in one application can throw off the ratio between carbon and nitrogen (C:N ratio) in the soil. If the C:N ratio in the soil exceeds 25:1; soil microorganisms will scour the soil in search of nitrogen. Soil microorganisms need both carbon and nitrogen to survive. Therefore, if the soil carbon content greatly exceeds the soil nitrogen content, microbes will consume soil nitrogen causing plants to become deficient in nitrogen.

It is recommended gardeners restrict organic matter applications to one inch of organic matter for every three inches of tilled soil depth per growing season. If decomposition of the organic matter is slow, gardeners may need to add nitrogen to the soil to reduce the C:N ratio below 25:1.

Nitrogen sources include organic and inorganic fertilizers. For more information on soil amendment, see the USU Extension fact sheet **Preparing and Improving Garden Soil**. Also, remember to check the salinity levels of organic amendments prior to incorporating them into the garden. Some amendments, notably amendments containing certain animal manures, can have high soluble salt levels, which adversely affect plant growth. The next section, "**Backyard Composting**" provides examples of composts with low levels of soluble salts.

GARDEN MYTH #9:

As gardeners incorporate organic matter to revive nutrient-depleted garden soils, they also need to re-introduce earthworms.

Fact: Practice the concept, "if you build it, they will come." Earthworms are fascinating and serve as a bio-indicator of ideal soil conditions for healthy plant growth. As gardeners revive depleted garden soils with organic matter, earthworms will re-populate themselves. Earthworms form a small egg sac called a cocoon. Earthworm populations can be revived through (1) the movement of soil or organic matter containing cocoons, (2) cocoons dormant over several years emerging when conditions are right, and (3) nearby adults or juveniles traveling back into more suitable areas that contain that species' preferred food, soil temperatures and soil habitat.

BACKYARD COMPOSTING

INTRODUCTION

The term composting refers to a process where raw organic matter is decomposed to a material that resembles soil. As mentioned previously, composting involves moisture, oxygen, carbon and nitrogen to proceed. However, what was not previously discussed was that these conditions are necessary for the composting process because the right balance of environmental factors support living decomposers. Compost can be described as a dark brown, humus-rich material that results from the partial decomposition of organic matter. Decomposition is aided by invertebrate organisms like worms, millipedes, centipedes, sow bugs, beetles, etc., and beneficial microorganisms like bacteria and fungi. Therefore, compost is not just a rotting pile of garbage; it's a thriving community of decomposing organisms!

Goals of this Section:

- Become familiar with benefits compost adds to the soil.
- Learn how to construct a compost pile.
- Learn how to maintain a compost pile.

Compost provides numerous benefits to the soil which include:

- Promotion of soil organism diversity.
- Optimization of soil pH and overall quality of the soil.
- Improved aeration and drainage of heavy clay soils.
- Increased water holding capacity for sandy soils.
- Bank of balanced, slowly released nutrients.
- Means of recycling kitchen and yard wastes.
- Improved soil workability.

COMPOST PILE CONSTRUCTION

Compost piles vary in size, construction and content; but certain features remain consistent from pile to pile. The minimum size for a backyard compost bin is approximately 3 feet

Figure 55: *Simple compost pile*

Figure 56: Compost bins constructed from pallets

by 3 feet by 3 feet. Smaller sized piles do not produce enough heat to kill weed seeds and pathogens; larger sized piles do not allow adequate gas diffusion into the center of the pile to support the needs of decomposing organisms unless turned more frequently. Compost piles should be located near a water source such as a garden hose. A compost pile located in full sun will require more frequent watering than a pile located in the shade. A variety of structures or bins can be made or purchased to facilitate the production of compost (**Figure 56**).

TYPES OF MATERIALS TO ADD OR AVOID ADDING TO A COMPOST PILE

Brown Materials
Dried leaves
Shredded newspaper
Sawdust
Hay
Wood and bark chips
Pine needles
Other dried plant materials

Green Materials
Grass clippings
Plant-based kitchen scraps
Coffee grounds
Tea leaves
Materials to Avoid
Weeds with seeds
Diseased plant parts
Meat or fat scraps
Feces from meat-eating animals
Other dried plant materials

COMPOST PILE ADDITIONS

Three types of materials may be added to the pile: carbon-rich brown materials nitrogen-rich green materials, and soil (optional). Brown materials are carbon-rich organic matter sources and have a higher percentage of carbon than nitrogen. For every 6 to 8 inches of brown materials, a 2 to 3 inch layer of nitrogen-rich green materials should be added to the compost pile. Items that should not be added to compost piles include weeds with seeds present, diseased plant parts, meat or fat scraps and feces from meat-eating animals. Egg shells and small pieces of citrus peels can be added.

Finally, it is optional to add a 1-inch layer of garden soil for every 8 to 14 inches of organic waste. Remember, compost is not just a rotting pile of garbage; it's a thriving community of decomposing organisms! The presence of soil microorganisms coupled with adequate moisture and aeration will facilitate rapid decomposition of organic materials. However, microorganisms will also be plentiful on some organic materials, such as leaves and grass clippings, so the addition of soil may not be necessary if these types of materials are being added to the compost pile. Finally, the decomposition rate will also be affected by the size of the organic materials. For example, sawdust will degrade more quickly than tree branch segments. For more information on the science of composting, see the USU Extension fact sheet **The Composting Process** or the University of Illinois Extension fact sheets **Composting for the Homeowner**.

COMPOST PILE MAINTENANCE

Just like our garden soils, it is important to take care of the compost piles to ensure the health and vitality of decomposing organisms. The pile should be kept moist but not soggy; the appropriate moisture level should resemble a moist sponge. Composting also requires gas diffusion throughout the pile. Aerobic (oxygen-present) decomposition occurs much more rapidly than anaerobic (oxygen-absent) decomposition. The pile can be aerated by mixing or turning the compost regularly. It is recommended

TABLE 15: COMMON COMPOSTING PROBLEMS AND SOLUTIONS*

Problem	Possible Cause	Solution
Malodorous pile	Compaction (insufficient oxygen)	Turn pile for increased air circulation
	Excess moisture	Turn pile or add dry, porous materials such as sawdust
Pile damp, but no heat	Insufficient nitrogen	Add fertilizer (see below) or green plant materials Dried blood meal (12% nitrogen – add 16 cups [≈ 1 lb] per 1 cubic yard of compost) Fish meal (10% nitrogen – add 20 cups [≈ 1 lb] per 1 cubic yard of compost)
	Compost too wet	Allow pile to dry, turn pile to dry out center, or add additional dry materials
Pile dry, but not composting	Insufficient water	Form pile so center is the lowest point (to prevent runoff) and apply water to moisten compost

Problem	Possible Cause	Solution
Ammonia odor	Too much nitrogen	Add carbon-rich material, such as sawdust, wood chips or straw, and turn pile
High pile temperature	Pile too large	Reduce pile size
	Insufficient ventilation	Turn pile
Low pile temperature	Pile too small	Make pile bigger or insulate sides
	Insufficient moisture	Add water while turning pile
	Poor aeration	Turn pile
	Lack of nitrogen	Mix in nitrogen sources such as grass clippings, manure or organic fertilizer (see example fertilizers additions above)
	Cold weather	Increase pile size, or insulate pile with an extra layer of material such as straw
Pests (rats, raccoons, insects)	Presence of meat scraps or fatty food waste	Remove meat and fatty foods from pile or cover with a layer of soil or sawdust; build an animal-proof compost bin; turn pile to increase temperature

*Table compiled from USU Extension fact sheet **Backyard Composting in Utah**.

to turn the compost pile at least once a week for rapid decomposition. Finally decomposing soil organisms produce heat as they decompose raw organic matter. The temperature of an active compost pile should rise to around 140°F after each time aerating the pile. As the composting process nears completion, the temperature will gradually drop and not rise after aerating the pile. Compost thermometers can be ordered online. For more information on composting, see the USU Extension fact sheet **Backyard Composting in Utah**. See Table 15 for common composting problems and solutions.

OTHER CONSIDERATIONS FOR COMPOSTING

Once the compost has proceeded through the decomposition process, the compost pile should be left to cure for at least 1 month before spreading in the garden. Curing allows the chemical decomposition

to stabilize and is necessary to protect plants from damage. Note that it is not recommended putting weed seeds, diseased plant parts or feces from meat-eating animals in backyard compost piles. Ideally the temperature of a backyard compost pile should reach 140° F, hot enough to cook weed seeds and kill pathogens; however, sometimes this ideal temperature is not reached. Industrial composting companies and many landfills have the necessary instruments to monitor pile temperatures and heavy machinery available to turn large piles. Leave this type of composting to the professionals and steer clear of putting non-recommended materials in your backyard compost bin. If you are unable or unwilling to water or aerate your compost pile, you always have the option of cold composting instead. Cold composting does not require pile turning or watering but materials will take about a year to fully compost; whereas, hot composting requires a little more effort, but the benefit is quicker compost.

4 ORGANIC GARDEN CARE

GARDEN SOIL FERTILITY

INTRODUCTION

Plant nutrition is oftentimes the "goldilocks" of garden decisions; what is too much, what is too little and what is just right? One important gardening tip is that plant nutrition is not a one-size fits all recommendation for garden plants; some plants, like corn, grow best with regular additions of certain nutrients while others, like grapes, prefer little or none. Therefore, gardeners should add nutrients according to the growing needs of various garden plants. A fertile soil can prevent or minimize many pest problems in the garden by producing healthy plants. Therefore it is important to understand the basics of soil fertility and follow recommended plant nutrient additions to ensure your garden plants are nourished just right.

Goals of this Section:

- Become familiar with the necessary major and micro plant nutrients.
- Understand the difference between organic and inorganic fertilizers.
- Learn how to read a fertilizer label and properly apply fertilizer.

In order to grow, plants must access 16 essential nutrients described by the mnemonic C. HOPKNS CaFe: carbon (C), hydrogen (H), oxygen (O), phosphorus (P), potassium (K), nitrogen (N), sulfur (S), calcium (Ca) and iron (Fe). Not included in the mnemonic, but still essential include the nutrients: magnesium (Mg), boron (B), manganese (Mn), copper (Cu), zinc (Zn), molybdemun (Mo) and chorine (Cl). Beginning gardeners may wonder if all these nutrients are present in purchased organic fertilizer. Typically, purchased fertilizer will not include all essential nutrients although some organic fertilizers offer a more varied analysis than most conventional fertilizers. Plants access many of these essential nutrients from weathered rock that makes up the

Figure 57: *Grapes may not require additional fertilizer*

mineral fraction of the soil: sand, silt and clay. Nutrients that plants require in larger amounts, called primary nutrients, are sometimes applied to garden soils by gardeners.

PRIMARY NUTRIENTS

Plants do not require nutrients in equal quantities. Primary nutrients describe nutrients that plants need in relatively large quantities compared to other essential micronutrients. Gardeners may need to add primary nutrients to garden soil depending on results of a soil test. Primary nutrients include nitrogen (N), phosphorus (P) and potassium (K). Other major nutrients required by plants include carbon (C), hydrogen (H) and oxygen (O). These nutrients are structural nutrients and do not need to be added to the garden soil because plants can access them via the air and soil solution. Important secondary nutrients include calcium (Ca), magnesium (Mg) and sulfur (S); of these three, sulfur is the most commonly deficient. Some purchased fertilizers contain these secondary nutrients along with one or more of NPK. The fertilizer label includes the grade or analysis which is the minimum percentages of total nutrients found in the bag. A 7-2-1 fertilizer (soybean meal) contains 7% nitrogen, 2% available phosphoric acid (P2O5) and 1% soluble potash (K2O).

Figure 58: *Bountiful harvests grow from properly nourished plants*

NITROGEN (NITRATE-N)

Nitrogen is the most likely nutrient to limit plant growth. Nitrogen is vital to almost all essential plant functions including root growth and photosynthesis. Nitrogen is almost always limited in the soil. This is why soil test results almost always recommend the addition of some nitrogen to the garden. For more information on nitrogen testing, see the USU Extension fact sheet **Diagnostic Testing for Nitrogen Soil Fertility**. Nitrogen is easily leached from the soil and can pollute groundwater supplies and adversely affect water quality in streams, lakes and estuaries if applied incorrectly (**see Figure 59**). For more information on the impact of nitrogen on water quality, see the USU Extension fact sheet **Understanding Your Watershed: Nitrogen**. Charged fractions of the soil, like organic matter and clay particles, help to retain nitrogen in the soil profile. Most soil nitrogen is found in soil organic matter; therefore the addition of organic matter increases soil nitrogen overtime. Less chemically active soil textures, like sand and silt-dominated

Figure 59: *Lake water polluted by fertilizer run-off*

soils, require more frequent nitrogen applications for adequate plant growth if soils are not amended with organic matter. High nitrogen organic fertilizers include blood meal (12-2-1), high nitrogen bat guano (10-3-1), fish meal (10-6-2) and hoof/horn meal (13-2-0).

PHOSPHORUS (P_2O_5)

Phosphorus is the second most likely nutrient to limit plant growth. Phosphorus influences photosynthesis, nitrogen fixation, flowering, fruiting, seed production and maturation. Phosphorus is considered a relatively immobile nutrient because it does not readily translocate within the soil. However, just because phosphorus is immobile in the soil does not mean it does not travel within the environment. Phosphorus can move by soil erosion to surrounding areas. It is a major pollutant of streams, lakes and estuaries. Increased phosphorus levels encourage blooms of algae, which ultimately result in reduced dissolved oxygen concentrations in bodies of water if applied incorrectly. A decreased dissolved oxygen concentration may ultimately kill aquatic life. For more information on the impact of phosphorus on water quality, see the USU Extension fact sheet **Understanding Your Watershed: Phosphorus**. For additional information on the importance of dissolved oxygen in aquatic ecosystems, see the USU Extension fact sheet **Understanding Your Watershed: Dissolved Oxygen**. Hence it is recommended to have your soil tested prior to adding additional phosphorus to determine if phosphorus levels are adequate in your garden soil. Many Utah soils contain adequate to high amounts of phosphorus. See Chapter 3 "Garden Soil" section of this guide for more information on testing soil samples. High phosphorus organic fertilizers include soft rock phosphate (colloidal phosphate), high-phosphorus bat guano and fish meal. If you regularly apply manure composts, your garden soil may test high for phosphorus in just a couple of years; therefore gardeners who frequently apply manures should have their soil tested periodically to monitor phosphorus levels.

POTASSIUM (K_2O)

Potassium is the third most likely nutrient to limit plant growth. Potassium helps protect plants against environmental stresses such as drought, winter damage, fungal disease and insect pests. Potassium has also been proven to enhance the taste and quality of fruits, vegetables and flowers. Potassium levels do not typically change rapidly in soils and excess potassium does not have a toxic effect on the environment. Many soils in Utah tend to be naturally adequate to high in potassium levels. If soil test results indicate adequate to high potassium levels, additional potassium applications are not necessary. High potash organic fertilizers include fish meal, greensand, feldspar and potassium sulfate. It is not recommended to add wood ash to Utah soils as it can be high in alkaline salts.

Figure 60: *Iron chlorosis on strawberry leaves*

MICRO-NUTRIENTS

Micro-nutrients are nutrients that plants require in trace quantities. Usually micro-nutrients are available to plants via weathered rock in the soil. Plants gradually take-up micro-nutrients via the soil solution. The nine essential micro-nutrients for plant growth include: iron, manganese, zinc, copper, boron, molybdenum, nickel, cobalt and chlorine. Gardeners only need to add micro-nutrients upon

GARDEN MYTH #10:

Treat symptoms of iron chlorosis by burying iron artifacts around garden plants.

Fact: Avoid making this hazardous gardening mistake! Do not bury iron nails or other artifacts in the soil to treat symptoms of iron chlorosis! Chelated or sequestered iron products are costly but are the only appropriate additive, other than organic matter, for treatment of iron chlorosis. Chelated iron products must be re-applied over time to maintain management of iron chlorosis. Ferric and ferrous compounds (ferrous sulfate) are allowed, albeit with restrictions, in certified organic operations. Enter "iron products" under product search at www.omri.org for a listing of accepted products. For more information on iron chlorosis, reference **What Is Iron Chlorosis and What Causes It?**, **Preventing and Treating Iron Chlorosis in Trees and Shrubs** and **Control of Iron Chlorosis in Ornamental and Crop Plants**.

evidence of a nutrient deficiency. Nutrient deficiencies can be difficult to correctly diagnose. If gardeners suspect a nutrient deficiency, it is recommended they submit a sample of the affected plant to their local USU Extension office for diagnosis. The most common micro-nutrient deficiency in Utah soils is iron chlorosis. Sufficient iron is present in Utah soils, however, due to local soil chemistries, it is tied up in a form that is unavailable for plant up-take. Treatment options for iron chlorosis include amending garden soil with organic matter and adding iron chelates or sequestered iron products (see Garden Myth # 10). Iron chlorosis symptoms may also indicate improper garden irrigation.

FERTILIZER LABELS

As mentioned previously, most fertilizers are labeled with a sequence of numbers which details the percentage of nitrogen (N), phosphate (P_2O_5) and potash (K_2O) (**see Figure 61**). For example a complete fertilizer (a fertilizer that contains percentages of all of the three nutrients) labeled 10-3-1 contains 10% N, 3% P_2O_5 and 1% K_2O. An incomplete fertilizer (a fertilizer that does not contain all of the three nutrients) labeled 12-0-0 contains 12% N, 0% P_2O_5 and 0% K_2O; this fertilizer could also be called a nitrogen fertilizer because it only contains nitrogen. Occasionally a fourth number is listed in the sequence indicating an additional nutrient such as sulfur (S). If this is the case, the additional nutrient will be identified on the package. It is wise to not assume nutrients are present in a fertilizer unless the label specifically identifies their presence. Some organic fertilizers, like seaweed products, commonly contain micro-nutrients whereas others do not. Always read the product label for information on the fertilizer contents.

Figure 61: Label on bag of organic fertilizer

INORGANIC VS. ORGANIC FERTILIZERS

Inorganic Fertilizers

Fertilizer recommendations are often given based on inorganic fertilizer sources. This is done for several reasons.

- Inorganic fertilizers tend to be inexpensive and readily available for purchase.
- Many inorganic fertilizers have a high nutrient analysis so a small amount of fertilizer will cover a large area.
- Many farmers and gardeners have traditionally used inorganic fertilizers.

Any inorganic fertilizer recommendation can be converted to an organic recommendation; however, there are

GARDEN MYTH #11:

Annual additions of manure will provide the proper amount of nutrients to garden plants.

Fact: No doubt about it, manures can be an excellent source of some nutrients. However, organic gardeners should not assume that manure alone will provide garden plants with all the nutrients they need to thrive. Depending on the source, nutrients from organic matter may not be available to garden plants in the same season it was applied. Small, annual additions of organic matter provide a "bank of nutrients" that are slowly released to plants over a long time period. Furthermore, run-off from soils with high manure loads may become a source of pollution. Have your garden soil tested periodically to determine whether the required nutrients are available in adequate amounts. If you need help interpreting results, contact your local USU Extension office.

several differences between inorganic and organic fertilizers that a gardener must take into account. Inorganic fertilizers are typically synthesized and are immediately available for plant up-take unless they are coated with a time-release coating. The release of nutrients from an inorganic fertilizer does not depend on soil microorganisms.

Organic Fertilizers

Organic fertilizers originate from a natural source; examples include plant and animal by-products and mined minerals. Many organic fertilizers release their nutrients gradually over time. Soil microorganisms help break down organic fertilizers and release nutrients. This is why release rates of organic fertilizers are typically greatest under warm and moist soil conditions. As a general rule, apply organic fertilizers when soil temperatures are above 50°F. Nutrient analysis and release rates vary greatly between types of organic fertilizers. Organic gardeners need to be knowledgeable about the product they are using to ensure they are selecting the correct fertilizer for their conditions. Allowable USDA certified organic fertilizers are listed at the **OMRI website**. For more information on organic fertilizers, see the USU Extension fact sheet **Selecting and Using Organic Fertilizers** and the Colorado State University Extension fact sheet **Organic Fertilizers**.

NUTRIENT RELEASE RATES

Rapid-release fertilizers are most beneficial when garden plants need to be fertilized immediately. Rapid-release fertilizers are often recommended for annual garden plants like tomatoes or peppers. Annual plants must complete all growth within a single growing season, so it is important to not limit plant growth by inadequate fertilization. If applied inappropriately, rapid-release fertilizers may burn plants so make sure to carefully follow the directions on the label of the product you are using. Some

Figure 62: *Perennial garden plants, like strawberries, benefit from a slow and steady release of nutrients*

nutrients, like phosphorus (P) and potassium (K), do not translocate within the soil profile readily so levels of these nutrients are not likely to change rapidly. However other nutrients, like nitrogen (N) translocate quickly through the soil profile so nitrogen levels are likely to fluctuate rapidly. Slow-release fertilizers gradually release nutrients into the soil providing plants extended access.

PERENNIAL PLANT FERTILIZATION

Perennial fruits and vegetables benefit most from slow-release fertilization. Perennial plants grow for at least three growing seasons and must balance root growth with shoot growth. Perennial garden plants, like rhubarb, strawberries and fruit trees, grow an extensive root system and therefore benefit from a consistent and gradual source of nutrients. If necessary, soils can be replenished with some nutrients by adding 1 to 3 inches of organic matter around the plants annually. Additional fertilization of perennial garden plants may not be necessary if the plants are producing well and do not show symptoms of nutrient deficiencies.

ORGANIC MATTER

Although organic matter is an excellent slow-release source of certain nutrients, it alone may not provide sufficient nutrition for adequate plant growth. It is likely that you will need to add supplemental fertilizer, especially nitrogen, to the garden during the growing season. A soil test will guide you in determining what nutrients are needed and in what quantities. See the "**Soil Testing**" section in Chapter 3 of this guide for more information on

Figure 63: *Composted animal manures provide a good source of plant nutrients*

soil testing. Some animal manures, such as steer manure, can be high in salts; therefore, do not add excessive amounts (over 2 inches per year). As fresh manure decomposes, it produces ammonia gas which can damage plant roots. USDA certified organic agriculture imposes certain restrictions on using raw non-composted manures and compost teas (see below); hence, it may be best to incorporate these materials into the garden soil in the fall.

"It [raw non-composted manure and compost tea] may only be (i) applied to land used for a crop not intended for human consumption; (ii) incorporated into the soil not less than 120 days prior to the harvest of a product whose edible portion has direct contact with the soil surface or soil particles; or (iii) incorporated into the soil not less than 90 days prior to the harvest of a product whose edible portion does not have direct contact with the soil surface or soil particles" (www.omri.org).

TABLE 16: AVERAGE NUTRIENT CONCENTRATIONS AND RATES OF AVAILABILITY FOR VARIOUS ORGANIC MATERIALS***

Material	% Nitrogen	% Posphate	% Potash	Availability*	Notes**
Composts	1-3	1-2	1-2	Moderate	Alkaline
Grass clippings	1-2	0-0.5	1-2	Moderate	
Leaves	1	0-0.5	0-0.5	Slow	
Legumes	2-4	0-0.5	2-3	Moderate	
Manures:					
Cattle	2-3	0.5-1	1-2	Moderate	Weed seed
Horse	1-2	0.5-1	1-2	Slow	Weed seed
Swine	2-3	0.5-1	1-2	Rapid	
Poultry	3-4	1-2	1-2	Rapid	
Sheep	3-4	0.5-1	2-3	Moderate	Weed seed
Pine needles	0.5	0	1	Slow	Acidic
Sawdust	0-1	0-0.5	0-1	Very slow	
Straw/corn stalks	0-0.5	0-0.5	1	Very slow	

*Approximate rate of nutrient release from the material.

**Special properties or characteristics of the material.

***Referenced from Selecting and Using Organic Fertilizers

GARDEN MYTH #12:

Garden plants prefer nutrients from organic sources over nutrients from inorganic sources.

Fact: To a garden plant, nitrogen is nitrogen. Plants do not have a preference whether nutrients originate from an organic source, like organic matter, or from an inorganic source, like inorganic fertilizer. Either way, plants take up nutrients just the same. Therefore it is gardeners, not plants, who prefer one source of nutrients over another.

SUBSTITUTING AN ORGANIC FERTILIZER FOR AN INORGANIC FERTILIZER

Organic gardeners must learn how to convert inorganic fertilization recommendations into organic recommendations. The easiest way to do this is to select an organic product with a similar analysis to the recommended inorganic fertilizer. It is often challenging to make a direct substitution because most organic fertilizers have a much lower analysis than inorganic fertilizers. Another way to substitute an organic recommendation for an inorganic recommendation is to apply more of an organic fertilizer to match the recommended inorganic nutrient addition. For example, if 1 pound of ammonium sulfate (21-0-0) per 100 square feet is recommended, an organic gardener could substitute 2 pounds of blood meal (12-2-1) per 100 square feet. Or if 0.5 pounds of a 10-10-10 all-purpose fertilizer per 100 square feet is recommended, an organic gardener could substitute 1 pound of a 5-5-5 organic fertilizer per 100 square feet. This second method is not as reliable as direct substitution (mentioned above) or by calculating out the fertilizer application (see page 145), but can be used as a quick and convenient approximation. Keep in mind that most inorganic fertilizers are fast-release, so make sure you select an organic product that is also rapid release. Even so, most rapid release organic fertilizers release nutrients less quickly than fast-release inorganic fertilizers so you may have to adjust the application timing to be sooner than that recommended for the inorganic fertilizer. See Table 17 for a list of organic fertilizers and their associated nutrient analyses and release rates.

TABLE 17: COMMONLY AVAILABLE ORGANIC FERTILIZERS*

Type	Typical Analysis (N-P-K)	Release Time	Pros	Cons	Approximate Application Rate**
Source: *Plant By-Product*					
Alfalfa meal or pellets	2-1-2	1-4 months		May contain seeds	2-5 lbs per 100 sq feet
Corn gluten meal	9-0-0	1-4 months	High nitrogen	Germination inhibitor, some are GMOs	20-40 lbs per 1,000 sq feet
Cottonseed meal	6-0.4-1.5	1-4 months	High nitrogen	Pesticide residues, most are GMOs	10 lbs per 100 sq feet
Soybean meal	7-2-1	1-4 months	High nitrogen	Some are GMOs	8 lbs per 100 sq feet
Kelp meal	Negligible	4+ months	Contains micronutrients	Insignificant N-P-K	1 lb per 100 sq feet
Kelp powder	1-0-4	Immediate to 1 month	Contains micronutrients	Insignificant N-P-K	¼ to ½ teaspoon per gallon
Liquid kelp	Negligible	Immediate to 1 month	Contains micronutrients	Insignificant N-P-K	1-2 teaspoons per gallon
Source: *Animal By-Product*					
Bat guano (high N)	10-3-1	4+ months	High nitrogen		5 lbs per 100 sq feet
Bat guano (high P)	3-10-1	4+ months	High phosphorus		5 lbs per 100 sq feet
Blood meal	12-0-0	1-4 months	High nitrogen		5-10 lbs per 100 sq feet
Bone meal	3-15-0	1-4 months	High phosphorus		10 lbs per 100 sq feet
Feather meal	Variable	4+ months		Slow release	2.5 – 5 lbs per 100 sq feet
Fish emulsion	5-2-2	1-4 months	Contains additional micronutrients	Foul smell	6 tablespoons per gallon
Enzymatically digested hydrolyzed liquid fish	4-2-2	1-4 months	More nutrients than fish emulsions		5 tablespoons per gallon

Type	Typical Analysis (N-P-K)	Release Time	Pros	Cons	Approximate Application Rate**
Fish meal	10-6-2	1-4 months	High nitrogen and phosphorus		5-10 lbs per 100 sq feet
Fish powder	12-0.25-1	Immediate to 1 month	High nitrogen and contains additional micronutrients		1-2 oz per 100 sq feet or 1 tablespoon per gallon

*Table content was referenced from Colorado State University Extension fact sheet **Organic Fertilizers**
**Have your soil tested prior to adding fertilizer and follow the directions on all fertilizer product labels.

FERTILIZATION CALCULATIONS

Fertilizer applications should be calculated based on the analysis of the product you choose to use. For example, if a soil test or recommendations indicate that 2 pounds of nitrogen should be applied to a 1,000 square foot garden area, the following calculation can be made:

(Pounds of nutrient needed)/Percent of nutrient in fertilizer] = Pounds of fertilizer to apply.

Using blood meal (12-2-1) as the fertilizer source gives the following:

2 pounds nitrogen needed/.12= 17 pounds of 12-2-1 to be applied over 1,000 sq. ft.

As mentioned previously, fertilization of garden plants is not one-size-fits-all because recommendations for fertilization rates and timing vary from one garden plant to the next. For example, some plants, like sweet corn, prefer multiple applications of nitrogen throughout the growing season whereas others, like beans, prefer nitrogen at planting only. Furthermore, inappropriate application of nitrogen can sometimes cause undesired effects in the garden. For example, frequent fertilization of tomatoes with nitrogen encourages excessive foliage growth and limits fruit production. It is recommended you adjust your fertilization schedule to reflect various preferences of the garden plants you plan to grow. See Table 18 for a summary of fertilization recommendations for common fruit and vegetable garden plants. Originally, recommendations were given based on inorganic fertilizer sources. For your convenience, an appropriate organic substitution is also included; however, the organic fertilizer chosen is one of many options. You can substitute a similar organic product of your choice; for example, if a 5-5-5 all-purpose organic fertilizer is recommended, a product with a 4-4-4 analysis will work just fine.

TABLE 18: FERTILIZATION RECOMMENDATIONS FOR VARIOUS FRUIT AND VEGETABLE GARDEN PLANTS

Garden Plant Name	Soil Preparation Suggestions*		Fertilization (Side-Dressing)**			
	Inorganic	Organic	Inorganic		Organic	
			Application Rate	Application Timing	Application Rate	Application Timing
Artichoke	½ lb complete fertilizer (16-16-8) per 100 sq ft	1.5 lb (5-5-5) organic fertilizer per 100 sq ft	2 tsp nitrogen fertilizer (21-0-0) per plant	Apply every 4 weeks after trans-planting	4 tsp organic nitrogen fertilizer (10-0-0) per plant or 8 tsp of (5-0-0)	Apply organic fertilizer slightly earlier than inorganic varieties (every 3 weeks after trans-planting)
Asparagus	½ lb high phosphate fertilizer (11-52-0) per 100 sq ft	2.25 lbs high phosphate fertilizer (0-12-1) per 100 sq ft)	1 lb complete fertilizer (16-16-8) per 100 sq ft	After harvest	3 lbs of a complete fertilizer (5-5-5) per 100 sq ft	After harvest
Basil	1/3 cup complete fertilizer (16-16-8) per 10 ft row	1 cup complete fertilizer (5-5-5) per 10 ft row.	1/3 cup liquid nitro-gen fertilizer (21-2-3) per 25 sq ft.	Every 2-3 weeks, once plants reach har-vestable age	1 1/3 cups of organic nitrogen fertilizer (5-0-0) per 25 sq ft	Every 1-2 weeks, once plants reach har-vestable age
Beans	1 lb complete fertilizer (16-16-8) per 100 sq ft	3 lbs complete fertilizer (5-5-5) per 100 sq ft	No additional fertilizer necessary			
Beet	2-4 cups complete fertilizer (16-16-8 or 10-10-10) per 100 sq ft	6-12 cups complete fertilizer in the analysis range of (5-5-5 or 3-3-3) per 100 sq ft	1/4 cup nitrogen based fertilizer (21-0-0) per 10 ft row	6 weeks after emer-gence	1/2 cup organic nitrogen fertilizer (10-0-0) per 10 ft row	Slightly earlier than inorganic to make up for release time; apply 4-5 weeks after emer-gence

Garden Plant Name	Soil Preparation Suggestions*		Fertilization (Side-Dressing)**			
	Inorganic	Organic	Inorganic		Organic	
			Application Rate	Application Timing	Application Rate	Application Timing
Broccoli	4-6 cups complete fertilizer (16-16-8 or 10-10-10) per 100 sq ft	8-14 cups organic all-purpose fertilizer (5-5-5) per 100 sq ft	1/2 cup nitrogen based fertilizer (21-0-0) per 10 ft row	4 weeks after transplanting	1 cup organic nitrogen fertilizer (10-0-0) per 10 ft row	Slightly earlier than inorganic to make up for release time; apply 3 weeks after transplanting
Brussels Sprout	4-6 cups complete fertilizer (16-16-8 or 10-10-10) per 100 sq ft	8-14 cups organic all-purpose fertilizer (5-5-5) per 100 sq ft	1/2 cup nitrogen based fertilizer (21-0-0) per 10 ft row	4-8 weeks after transplanting	1 cup organic nitrogen fertilizer (10-0-0) per 10 ft row	Slightly earlier than inorganic to make up for release time; apply 3-6 weeks after transplanting
Cabbage	4-6 cups complete fertilizer (16-16-8 or 10-10-10) per 100 sq ft	8-14 cups organic all-purpose fertilizer (5-5-5) per 100 sq ft	1/2 cup nitrogen based fertilizer (21-0-0) per 10 ft row	4 weeks after transplanting or thinning	1 cup organic nitrogen fertilizer (10-0-0) per 10 ft row	3 weeks after transplanting or thinning
Cantaloupe	4-6 cups complete fertilizer (16-16-8 or 10-10-10) per 100 sq ft	8-14 cups organic all-purpose fertilizer (5-5-5) per 100 sq ft	1 to 2 tbsp nitrogen based fertilizer (21-0-0) per plant mound	After vines develop runners	2 to 3 tbsp organic nitrogen fertilizer (10-0-0) or 4 to 8 tbsp of (5-0-0) per plant mound	After vines develop runners
Carrot	2-4 cups complete fertilizer (16-16-8 or 10-10-10) per 100 sq ft	4-8 cups organic all-purpose fertilizer (5-5-5) per 100 sq ft	1/4 cup nitrogen based fertilizer (21-0-0) per 10 ft row	6 weeks after emergence	1/2 cup of (10-0-0) organic nitrogen based fertilizer or 1 cup (5-0-0) per 10 ft row	Apply 5 weeks after emergence

Garden Plant Name	Soil Preparation Suggestions*		Fertilization (Side-Dressing)**			
	Inorganic	*Organic*	*Inorganic*		*Organic*	
			Application Rate	*Application Timing*	*Application Rate*	*Application Timing*
Cauliflower	4-6 cups complete fertilizer (16-16-8 or 10-10-10) per 100 sq ft	8-14 cups organic all-purpose fertilizer (5-5-5) per 100 sq ft	1 cup (21-0-0) per 10 ft row	4 weeks after transplanting or thinning	3 weeks after transplanting or thinning	2 cups of organic nitrogen fertilizer (10-0-0) per 10 ft row
Celery	2 lbs complete fertilizer (16-16-8) per 100 sq ft	6 lbs organic all-purpose fertilizer (5-5-5) per 100 sq ft	2 lbs complete fertilizer (16-16-8) per 100 sq ft	6 weeks after transplanting	6 lbs organic all-purpose fertilizer (5-5-5) per 100 sq feet	5 weeks after transplanting
			Additional 1/2 lbs high nitrogen fertilizer (46-0-0) per 100 sq ft	10 weeks after transplanting	Additional 2.25 lbs organic nitrogen fertilizer (10-0-0) per 100 sq ft	9 weeks after transplanting
Chive	2-3 tbsp complete fertilizer (16-16-8) per sq ft	6-9 tbsp all-purpose fertilizer (5-5-5) per sq ft	1 tsp of nitrogen fertilizer (21-0-0) per sq ft	May and July	2 tsp organic nitrogen fertilizer (10-0-0) per sq ft	Early May and early July
Cilantro			1/4 cup nitrogen based fertilizer (21-0-0) per 25 sq ft	1-2 times during growing season	1/2 cup organic nitrogen fertilizer (10-0-0) per 25 sq ft	1-2 times during the growing season
Cucumber	4-6 cups complete fertilizer (16-16-8 or 10-10-10) per 100 sq ft	8-14 cups organic all-purpose fertilizer (5-5-5) per 100 sq ft	1/4 cup nitrogen based fertilizer (21-0-0) per 10 ft of row	After vines develop runners, but before flowers develop	1/2 cup organic nitrogen fertilizer (10-0-0) per 25 sq ft	After vines develop runners, but before flowers develop

Garden Plant Name	Soil Preparation Suggestions*		Fertilization (Side-Dressing)**			
	Inorganic	Organic	Inorganic		Organic	
			Application Rate	Application Timing	Application Rate	Application Timing
Dill	1/2 tbsp complete fertilizer (16-16-8) per sq ft	1 1/2 tbsp organic all-purpose fertilizer (5-5-5) per sq ft	No additional fertilizer necessary			
Eggplant	4-6 cups complete fertilizer (16-16-8 or 10-10-10) per 100 sq ft	8-14 cups organic all-purpose fertilizer (5-5-5) per 100 sq ft	1/2 tbsp nitrogen based fertilizer (21-0-0) per plant	4-8 weeks after planting	1 tbsp organic fertilizer (10-0-0) per plant	3-6 weeks after planting
Tarragon	1/2 tbsp complete fertilizer (16-16-8) per sq ft	1 1/2 tbsp of organic all-purpose fertilizer (5-5-5) per sq ft	No additional fertilizer necessary			
Garlic	1-2 lbs complete fertilizer (16-16-8) per 100 sq ft	3-6 lbs organic all-purpose fertilizer (5-5-5) per 100 sq ft	1/2 lb nitrogen fertilizer (21-0-0) per 100 sq ft	Late April or May	1 to 1.5 lbs organic nitrogen fertilizer (10-0-0) per 100 sq ft	Mid April or early May
Horseradish	2 oz all-purpose fertilizer (16-8-8) per sq yard	6 oz organic all-purpose fertilizer such as a (5-5-5) or 10 oz of (3-3-3) per sq yard	1 tsp nitrogen fertilizer (21-0-0) per plant	Apply 4 weeks after planting and again at 8 weeks after planting	2 tsp organic nitrogen fertilizer (10-0-0) or 4 tsp of (5-0-0) per plant	First application at 3 weeks after transplanting and again at 7 weeks
Kale	4-6 cups of balanced fertilizer (16-16-8 or 10-10-10) per 100 sq ft	8-14 cups organic all-purpose fertilizer (5-5-5) per 100 sq ft	1/2 cup nitrogen based fertilizer (21-0-0) per 10 ft row	4 weeks after transplanting or thinning	1 cup organic nitrogen fertilizer (10-0-0) per 10 ft row	3 weeks after transplanting or thinning

Garden Plant Name	Soil Preparation Suggestions*		Fertilization (Side-Dressing)**			
	Inorganic	*Organic*	*Inorganic*		*Organic*	
			Application Rate	*Application Timing*	*Application Rate*	*Application Timing*
Kohlrabi	4-6 cups complete fertilizer (16-16-8 or 10-10-10) per 100 sq ft	8-14 cups organic all-purpose fertilizer (5-5-5) per 100 sq ft	1 cup nitrogen based fertilizer (21-0-0) per 10 ft row	3 weeks after transplanting or thinning	2 cups organic nitrogen fertilizer (10-0-0) or 4 cups of (5-0-0) per 10 ft row	2 weeks after transplanting or thinning
Leek			1/2 lb nitrogen fertilizer (21-0-0) per 100 sq ft	Late May and June	1 lb organic nitrogen fertilizer (10-0-0) per 100 sq ft	Mid May and June
Lettuce	4-6 cups complete fertilizer (16-16-8 or 10-10-10) per 100 sq ft	8-14 cups organic all-purpose fertilizer (5-5-5) per 100 sq ft	1/4 cup nitrogen based fertilizer (21-0-0) per 10 ft row	4 weeks after transplanting or thinning	1/2 cup (10-0-0) organic nitrogen based fertilizer or 1 cup (5-0-0) per 10 ft row	3 weeks after transplanting or thinning
Mint	1/2 tbsp complete fertilizer (16-16-8) per sq ft	1 1/2 tbsp of organic all-purpose fertilizer (5-5-5) per sq ft	1 tsp all-purpose fertilizer (16-16-8) per plant	Each spring as growth resumes	3 tsp organic all-purpose fertilizer (5-5-5) per plant	As plant growth resumes each spring
Onion	1-2 lbs complete fertilizer (16-16-8) per 100 sq ft	3-6 lbs organic all-purpose fertilizer (5-5-5) per 100 sq ft	1/2 lb nitrogen fertilizer (21-0-0) per 100 sq ft	Late May and June	1 lb organic nitrogen fertilizer (10-0-0) per 100 sq ft	Mid May and June
Parsnip	2-4 cups complete fertilizer (16-16-8 or 10-10-10) per 100 sq ft	6-12 cups complete organic fertilizer in the analysis range of (5-5-5 or 3-3-3) per 100 sq ft	1/4 cup nitrogen based fertilizer (21-0-0) per 10 ft row	6 weeks after emergence and again 4 weeks later	1/2 cup (10-0-0) organic nitrogen based fertilizer or 1 cup (5-0-0) per 10 ft row	5 weeks after emergence and again 3 weeks later

Garden Plant Name	Soil Preparation Suggestions*		Fertilization (Side-Dressing)**			
	Inorganic	*Organic*	*Inorganic*		*Organic*	
			Application Rate	*Application Timing*	*Application Rate*	*Application Timing*
Pea	1 lb of balanced fertilizer (16-16-8) per 100 sq ft	3 lbs of organic complete fertilizer (5-5-5) per 100 sq ft	No additional fertilizer necessary			
Pepper	4-6 cups of complete fertilizer (16-16-8 or 10-10-10) per 100 sq ft	12-18 cups of organic all-purpose fertilizer (5-5-5 or 3-3-3) per 100 sq ft	1/4 tsp of nitrogen based fertilzer (21-0-0) per plant	4 and 8 weeks after transplanting	1/2 tsp of organic nitrogen based fertilizer (10-0-0) or 1 tsp of (5-0-0) per plant	3 and 7 weeks after transplanting
Potato	1.5 lbs of all-purpose fertilizer (16-16-8 or 10-10-10) per 100 sq ft	4.5 lbs of organic all-purpose fertilizer (5-5-5 or 3-3-3) per 100 sq ft	1/2 lb of nitrogen fertilizer (21-0-0) per 100 sq ft	6 weeks after emergence	1 lb of organic nitrogen fertilizer (10-0-0) per 100 sq ft	5 weeks after emergence
Pumpkin	4-6 cups of balanced fertilizer (16-16-8 or 10-10-10) per 100 sq ft	12-18 cups of organic all-purpose fertilizer (5-5-5 or 3-3-3) per 100 sq ft	1-2 tbsp of nitrogen fertilizer (21-0-0) per plant mound	After vines develop runners	2-4 tbsp of organic nitrogen fertilizer (10-0-0) or 4-8 tbsp of (5-0-0) per plant mound	After vines develop runners
Radish	2-4 cups of complete fertilizer (16-16-8 or 10-10-10) per 100 sq ft	6-12 cups of organic all-purpose fertilizer (5-5-5 or 3-3-3) per 100 sq ft	1/4 cup nitrogen based fertilizer (21-0-0) per 10 ft row	After emergence	1/2 cup of (10-0-0) organic nitrogen based fertilizer or 1 cup (5-0-0) per 10 ft row	After emergence

Garden Plant Name	Soil Preparation Suggestions*		Fertilization (Side-Dressing)**			
	Inorganic	*Organic*	*Inorganic*		*Organic*	
			Application Rate	*Application Timing*	*Application Rate*	*Application Timing*
Raspberry	4-8 cups (21-0-0) fertilizer per 100 sq ft Additional phosphate may be required as indicated by soil test	8-16 cups organic nitrogen based fertilizer (10-0-0) per 100 sq ft Additional phosphate may be required	Side-dress with fertilizer as indicated by a soil test or upon evidence of a nutrrient sufficiency			
Rhubarb	2-4 inches well composted organic matter 6 inches deep into soil	2-4 inches well composted organic matter 6 inches deep into soil	1/2 cup granular all-purpose fertilizer (16-16-16) around the base of plant	Just before leaves emerge in spring; DO NOT fertilize druing first year establishment	1 1/2 cups organic all-purpose fertilizer (5-5-5) around base of plant	Just before leaves emerge in early spring; do not fertilize during first year establishment
Rutabaga	2-4 cups complete fertilizer (16-16-8 or 10-10-10) per 100 sq ft	6-12 cups complete organic fertilizer in the analysis range of (5-5-5 OR 3-3-3) per 100 sq ft	1/4 cup nitrogen based fertilizer (21-0-0) per 10 ft row	6 weeks after emergence	1/2 cup (10-0-0) organic nitrogen based fertilizer or 1 cup (5-0-0) per 10 ft row	5 weeks after emergence
Spinach	4-6 cups balanced fertilizer (16-16-8 or 10-10-10) per 100 sq feet	12-18 cups organic all-purpose fertilizer (5-5-5 or 3-3-3) per 100 sq ft	1/4 cup nitrogen based fertilizer (21-0-0) per 10 ft row	4 weeks after transplanting or thinning	1/2 cup (10-0-0) organic nitrogen based fertilizer or 1 cup (5-0-0) per 10 ft row	3 weeks after transplanting or thinning
Strawberry	1/2 to 1 lb balanced fertilizer (10-10-10) per 100 sq ft	1 to 2 lbs organic balanced fertilizer (5-5-5) per 100 sq feet	5-8 lbs balanced fertilizer (10-10-10) per 100 ft of row	At renovation	10-16 lbs organic all-purpose fertilizer (5-5-5) per 100 feet of row	At renovation

Garden Plant Name	Soil Preparation Suggestions*		Fertilization (Side-Dressing)**			
	Inorganic	*Organic*	*Inorganic*		*Organic*	
			Application Rate	*Application Timing*	*Application Rate*	*Application Timing*
Strawberry	1/2 to 1 lb balanced fertilizer (10-10-10) per 100 sq ft	1 to 2 lbs organic balanced fertilizer (5-5-5) per 100 sq feet	3 lbs (10-10-10) per 100 ft of row	In August	6 lbs organic all-purpose fertilizer (5-5-5) per 100 sq feet	In early August
			0.1 oz chelated iron per 100 ft of row	In May and September	Apply chelated iron product according to label	In May
Squash (Summer & Winter)	4-6 cups balanced fertilizer (16-16-8 or 10-10-10) per 100 sq. feet	8-14 cups organic all-purpose fertilizer (5-5-5) per 100 sq ft	1-2 tbsp nitrogen fertilizer (21-0-0) per plant mound	Once vines develop runners	2-4 tbsp organic nitrogen fertilizer (10-0-0) or 4-8 tbsp (5-0-0) per plant mound	Once vines develop runners
Sweet Corn	1-2 lbs all-purpose fertilizer (16-16-8) per 100 sq ft	3-6 lbs organic all-purpose fertilizer (5-5-5) per 100 sq ft	1/2 lbs high nitrogen fertilizer (46-0-0) per 100 sq ft	Once plants have 8-10 leaves and 1/4 lb silk first appears	1.75-2 lbs high organic nitrogen fertilizer (13-0-0) per 100 sq ft	
Sweet Potato	1-2 lbs all-purpose fertilizer (16-16-8) per 100 sq ft	3-6 lbs organic all-purpose fertilizer (5-5-5) per 100 sq ft	1/2 lb nitrogen fertilizer (21-0-0) per 100 sq ft	Early July	1 lb organic nitrogen fertilizer (10-0-0) or 2 lbs (5-0-0) per 100 sq ft	End of June
Swiss Chard	4-6 cups all-purpose fertilizer (16-16-8 or 10-10-10) per 100 sq ft	12-18 cups organic all-purpose fertilizer (5-5-5 or 3-3-3) per 100 sq ft	1/4 cup nitrogen based fertilizer (21-0-0) per 10 ft row	4 weeks after transplanting or thinning	1/2 cup (10-0-0) organic nitrogen based fertilizer or 1 cup (5-0-0) per 10 ft row	3 weeks after transplanting or thinning

Garden Plant Name	Soil Preparation Suggestions*		Fertilization (Side-Dressing)**			
	Inorganic	Organic	Inorganic		Organic	
			Application Rate	Application Timing	Application Rate	Application Timing
Tomato	4-6 cups all-purpose fertilizer (16-16-8 or 10-10-10) per 100 sq ft	12-18 cups organic all-purpose fertilizer (5-5-5 or 3-3-3) per 100 sq ft	1/2 tbsp nitrogen based fertilizer (21-0-0) per plant	At 4 weeks and 8 weeks after transplanting	1 tbsp organic fertilizer (10-0-0) per plant	At 3 weeks and 7 weeks after transplanting
Watermelon	4-6 cups all-purpose fertilizer (16-16-8 or 10-10-10) per 100 sq ft	12-18 cups organic all-purpose fertilizer (5-5-5 or 3-3-3) per 100 sq ft	1-2 tbsp nitrogen fertilizer (21-0-0) per plant mound	After vines develop runners	2-4 tbsp organic nitrogen fertilizer (10-0-0) or 4-8 tbsp (5-0-0) per plant mound	After vines develop runners

*The left side of the table lists application rate recommendations during soil preparation. It is typically recommended to also incorporate 1 to 3 inches of well-composted organic matter into the garden soil prior to planting garden plants.

**The right side of the table lists application rate and timing recommendations for subsequent side-dressing of garden plants. Side-dressing refers to the application of fertilizer to the garden soil 6 to 8 inches away from the plant.

COVER CROPS

Cover crops (CC), or green manure crops, are a great way to improve soil fertility over time. Gardeners who grow CCs over several seasons may not need to side-dress garden plants with fertilizer as often as is recommended in Table 18. Other advantages of growing CCs include the following:

- Improved soil workability
- High soil organic matter content
- Little or no soil erosion
- Suppressed weed growth
- Presence of natural enemies
- Additional soil nitrogen from legumes

CCs are usually planted in late summer or early fall and incorporated into the soil the following spring. CCs should be planted with enough time to allow seeds to germinate and establish roots prior to the winter months. Both legumes and grasses can be used as CCs. See **Cover Crops for Utah Gardens** for more details on selecting and using cover crops in Utah. Table 19 lists some commonly used CCs.

TABLE 19: COMMONLY USED COVER CROPS, THEIR GROWTH CHARACTERISTICS, AND SEEDING RATE RECOMMENDATIONS

Name	Type	Growth Characteristics	Seedling Rate
Alfalfa	Perennial	Cold tolerant, nitrogen-fixing legume. Low shade tolerance; deep rooted; drought tolerant.	½ - 1 lb / 1,000 sq ft
Hairy indigo	Perennial	Short-lived, not cold tolerant (killed by frost) legume. Low shade tolerance; drought tolerant. Slow establishment.	½ lb / 1,000 sq ft
Red clover	Perennial	Short-lived, cold tolerant, nitrogen-fixing legume. Shade and drought tolerant.	½ - 1 lb / 1,000 sq ft
Sweetclover	Annual or biennial	Short-lived, cold tolerant, nitrogen-fixing legume, strong tap root.	½ - 1 lb / 1,000 sq ft
Buckwheat	Summer annual	Cold sensitive; moderate shade and drought tolerance; rapid establishment and growth.	1 – 2 lbs / 1,000 sq ft
Garden peas	Summer annual	Cold sensitive, nitrogen-fixing legume. Low shade and traffic tolerance.	5 – 15 lbs / 1,000 sq ft
Mustard or turnips	Summer annual	Cold tolerant; tap rooted.	¼ lb / 1,000 sq ft
Spring grains	Summer annual	Includes wheat, barley, and oats. Cold tolerant; rapid growth rate. Inexpensive seed.	2 – 4 lbs / 1,000 sq ft
Annual rye grass	Winter annual	Moderately cold tolerant; rapidly establishing; extensive root system.	½ - 1 lbs / 1,000 sq ft
Austrian winter peas	Winter annual	Moderately cold and drought tolerant, nitrogen-fixing legume. Low shade and traffic tolerance.	2 – 4 lbs / 1,000 sq ft
Hairy vetch	Winter annual	Cold tolerant, nitrogen-fixing legume. Moderately shade and drought tolerant.	1 – 2 lbs / 1,000 sq ft
Winter wheat	Winter annual	Cold tolerant and rapidly establishing; inexpensive seed.	2½ lbs / 1,000 sq ft
Winter rye	Winter annual	Cold tolerant and rapidly establishing; drought and shade tolerant; inexpensive seed.	2½ lbs / 1,000 sq ft

ESTABLISHING A COVER CROP

CCs are seeded by turning over the top 2 inches of garden soil with a shovel or roto-tiller, leveling the soil with a rake and broadcasting seeds over the area. Seeds should be gently raked into the soil and buried to a depth approximately three times the diameter of the seed. Water the area immediately after seeding. Several weeks before you plant your garden, mow the CC and incorporate the plant residue into the soil using a spade or tiller. CCs can also be burned with a propane burner, although flame treatment will likely only burn the top portion of the plant. If perennial, burned plants may re-sprout from the root system.

Prevent CCs from going to seed so they do not become a new weed problem in your garden. Wait 1 to 2 weeks after destroying the plant for its residue to break down in the garden soil before planting desired garden plants. Leguminous CCs, like vetch, clover and peas, are "nitrogen-fixers" and hence have the additional appeal of transforming atmospheric nitrogen into plant-available soil nitrogen. Leguminous CCs can potentially supply up to 50-75% of nitrogen needs to certain garden plants. For more extensive information on cover crops, see the **Cover Crop in Organic Systems Western Implementation Guide**.

Figure 64: *Buckwheat cover crop in bloom; seeds will form soon*

10 COMMON ABIOTIC FRUIT AND VEGETABLE PLANT DISORDERS FOR UTAH GARDENS

Abiotic disorders describe symptoms or injuries to plants that were caused by non-living organisms. Two primary contributors of abiotic disorders include environmental factors (sometimes unavoidable) and human-caused injury (often avoidable).

TABLE 20: 10 COMMON ABIOTIC FRUIT AND VEGETABLE PLANT DISORDERS FOR UTAH GARDENS

Abiotic Disorder	Possible Symptoms	Management	
Irrigation Problems	Wilted plants. Brown leaf margins. Plant die-back.	Symptoms of over-watering look similar to those of under-watered garden plants. Gardeners may see evidence of root rot if the top few inches of garden soil does not dry out between irrigation events. Adjust irrigation schedule.	
Soil Compaction	Plants grow poorly. Soil surface cracking and crusting. Poor drainage.	Till soil when it is dry and mix in organic matter. Avoid walking on the planting bed. Strategically place stepping stones or establish pathways.	

Abiotic Disorder	Possible Symptoms	Management	
Frost damage	New growth is damaged and does not develop normally (i.e., damaged fruit buds fail to set fruit). Stunted annual garden plants (i.e., warm season vegetables exposed to spring frost). Browned or blackened tissue.	Choose varieties of garden plants appropriate for your area. Plant annual garden plants at the appropriate time to avoid spring and fall frost damage. Protect garden plants from frost injury when possible (see "**Season Extension**" section in Chapter 2 of this guide).	
Salt damage	Brown leaf margins. Plant dieback. Symptoms look similar to over- and under-watered plants.	Perform leaching events with a clean water source if soil test results indicate high salinity.	
Pesticide damage	Damage depends on the type of pesticide and the affected plant. Symptoms of herbicide injury (either from volatilization on a hot day or drift) include upturned leaf margins and contorted growth.	Apply pesticides according to the label. Do not spray pesticides during windy conditions. Avoid applying horticulture oils and soaps when temperatures exceed 85°F within 4 hours of application.	
Sunscald or winter injury	Cracking on south and west areas of thin barked tree trunks. Brown leaves in spring on perennial plants.	For the first 2 years of newly planted trees, apply light colored wrap around tree trunks in late fall and remove wrap each spring. Provide appropriate care to plants. Irrigate plants in fall before the ground freezes if the soil moisture is low.	
Iron chlorosis	Plant dieback of perennial plants. Yellow tissue between green veins on leaves. Brown leaf margins.	Mix in organic matter. Apply chelated iron product.	
Blossom end rot (tomatoes, peppers and eggplant)	Black or brown leathery decay on bottom of fruit opposite the stem caused by calcium imbalance.	Provide adequate and even watering and do not damage roots during cultivation.	

Abiotic Disorder	Possible Symptoms	Management	
Poor fruit set/ aborted or dropped fruit	Can be caused by many factors including improper irrigation, too much nitrogen fertilizer, alternate-year bearing cycle of fruit trees, normal fruit drop of fruit trees (June-drop), incorrect pruning, high temperatures, frost damage, or insufficient pollination.	Keep an updated log of garden activities (irrigation schedule, weather conditions, soil amendments, fertilizer applications, etc.) Contact your local USU Extension office for assistance with diagnosing the problem.	

ASK AN EXPERT

CHICKENS IN THE GARDEN

Dr. David Frame, *USU Extension Poultry Specialist*

Maintaining a small backyard flock of laying hens is becoming increasingly popular in urban settings. Chickens in the garden not only provide fresh home-grown eggs and enrich the soil in the process, they also enrich our lives as we enjoy watching them grow and bustle about the yard. The following basic information will help make the experience of raising chickens an enjoyable one.

Zoning

It is imperative to consult your local municipality for specific information on keeping chickens in your locale. Regulations vary depending on where you live. Generally, most places that permit the raising of chickens in urban settings will allow six to 10 hens with a minimum space requirement of 2 square feet per hen within the coop. Roosters are seldom allowed. You do not need a rooster to produce eggs; roosters are only necessary to fertilize eggs and grow chicks! Hens will lay eggs without the presence of a rooster.

Housing

There are as many workable configurations for coops as there are imaginative individuals to design them. The main requirements to consider in housing laying chickens are the following:

Figure 65: Rhode Island Red laying hen

1. Provide adequate shelter from excessively cold and hot weather.
2. Provide adequate supply of feed and fresh water.
3. Provide adequate nesting area (area where chickens lay eggs).
4. Provide adequate roost space (area where chickens sleep at night).
5. Configure the coop so that it can be easily cleaned on a regular basis.
6. Provide protection from predators (examples include dogs, raccoons, hawks and foxes) and wild birds, which may carry disease.

Feeding

Never assume your chickens are picking up all the nutrients they need just by scratching around the yard. Maturing pullets and laying hens need proper nutrient intake to sustain growth and egg production. For hens in egg production, always provide a good quality laying diet. The availability of additional free choice oyster shell or calcite grit is also advisable, especially if the hens are allowed to roam about the yard and garden. Offer treats sparingly, such as watermelon rinds, cantaloupe, garden greens and scratch (mixture of solely grains, such as wheat, milo, rye, triticale, etc.). These foods are OK in moderate amounts, but they are relatively low in nutrient value compared to a high quality commercially formulated feed. Promptly remove uneaten rinds and greens from the pen after the chickens are through eating, as the vegetable material will begin to rot and attract flies and other pests.

Health

Keeping your chickens healthy requires three things: 1) proper diet; 2) a clean, safe and hospitable environment; and 3) protection from wild birds, neighbors' poultry and wild mammals. Diet and shelter are discussed in previous sections. Protection is referred to as biosecurity. Biosecurity is the process of keeping disease away from your birds. It also encompasses the good neighbor policy of keeping any disease within your flock from spreading to other people's chickens. It is advisable to cover chicken runs with a solid roof or bird-proof wire or netting. Wild birds can carry mites and lice as well as harbor other poultry diseases. Position the feeders and waterers inside the coop or under cover. Use hanging feeders when possible to discourage mice and other varmints from getting a free meal. Mice and rats are notorious for carrying diseases that may harm your chickens. Clean up water spills immediately. Do not visit other chickens and then return to your own birds before thoroughly washing your hands and changing outer clothing including shoes. Do not allow other people to enter your chicken coop area or handle your birds.

If your chickens become listless, look "ruffled-up," or begin coughing or sneezing, consult your local veterinarian, county agent, or USU Poultry specialist. **For additional information, see the following USU Extension fact sheets:**

Keeping chickens in urban areas:
Considerations of Raising Small Populations of Backyard Poultry in Population-dense Communities

Housing:
Housing Backyard Chickens

Feeding:
Principles of Feeding Small Flocks of Chickens at Home

Health and biosecurity:
Biosecurity Principles: Protecting Your Investment

Handling Baby Poultry

Figure 66: *Slugs and snails are considered a delicacy to hungry backyard hens*

TIPS FROM MY COOP TO YOURS

Keeping backyard chickens is all the rage these days however sometimes gardeners let the romantic notion of participating in the urban farming movement cloud their vision on what is and is not a good idea. Here are a few tips to consider before taking the plunge and bringing home new baby chicks!

- Do not purchase more birds than you have room to keep, keeping in mind you may lose one or two birds. If each hen lays five eggs a week, how many birds do you need to feed your family?
- Are you comfortable harvesting your hens for meat when their egg-laying slows or do you plant to let them live-out their less productive days in your flock?
- Meat from older laying hens is not comparable in taste to chicken you purchase at the grocery store. Many chicken owners do not care for the taste of meat from old birds.
- Chicken feed is expensive; backyard chickens may not be an economical decision for your family.
- Dogs love chickens; sometimes they love to kill them too! This gardener has lost two chickens to two different playful dogs.
- Chickens should not be considered pest control in manicured landscapes. True, chickens eat insects, but they also eat plants and scratch at the ground. Free-roaming chickens could cost you hundreds of dollars in landscaping!
- Your hens will need light in their roost to lay eggs through the winter months. Prevent chickens from having to run through the snow. The roost and nesting house will need regular cleaning since hens spend more time indoors during cold weather. Rig the water source so it does not freeze over.
- You will need a bird-sitter if you plan to leave town for an extended period of time. Someone needs make sure your chickens have access to clean water and food and can collect eggs.
- Your chickens may attract rodents such as mice and rats.
- Do not address your chickens as family pets if you plan to harvest them for meat.

GARDEN IRRIGATION

Dr. Niel Allen, *USU Extension Irrigation Specialist*

ASK AN EXPERT

INTRODUCTION

One of the top contributors of plant problems in northern Utah is too much water, despite the fact that Utah is the second driest state in the United States. Utahns cannot rely on Mother Nature for adequate garden moisture and must irrigate to keep garden plants alive in our semi-arid climate. Unfortunately, many gardeners make poor judgments when determining how much and how often to water garden plants; more is not always better. A basic understanding of plant water needs will not only save your garden plants, but also lower your water bill! Now that makes "cents"!

Goals of this Section:

- Learn about factors that affect water use by garden plants.
- Learn about the benefits of using drip irrigation and discover recommended application rates and times.
- Become familiar with the basic water needs of fruit and vegetable plants at various growth stages.

PLANT WATER USE

Plant water use is related to the climate, plant type and plant growth stage. The water use of plants increases as they grow, with the peak water use being when plants are rapidly growing, blossoming and producing. Some plants, such as lettuce, spinach and chard, can begin to be harvested in about a month, while other garden plants may take several months. In Utah, average net irrigation for gardens varies from about 14 inches in communities with a high elevation to about 24 inches in Saint George, with the Wasatch Front ranging from about 17 to 20 inches.

Figure 67: *Chard growing in the garden*

GARDEN MYTH #13:

Garden plants need to be watered daily.

Fact: A gardener in Utah who irrigates garden plants daily is likely over-watering. Not only is too much water wasteful, it is also damaging to garden plants. However, if you recall garden myth #1; there are no absolute answers to gardening questions. Daily water may be necessary for garden plants growing in sand-dominated soil types with low organic matter content since these soils freely drain water down and away from the rooting zone of garden plants. A simple way to tell how well your soil drains water is to dig a hole and fill it with water. If the water is gone in seconds, you will need to irrigate frequently. If the water drains after several minutes, your soil both drains and retains moisture; good news! If water stagnates in the hole for many hours, you have drainage issues that need to be addressed before you plant your garden.

Monthly water use is highest in June and July and then decreases as some vegetables mature and come out of production. Weekly water use rates range from about 1 inch to 2 inches depending on the time of year and plant growth stage. Peak daily water use of some garden vegetables is about 0.25 to 0.3 inches per day.

When vegetables are rapidly growing or producing, an irrigation of 1 inch can be applied every 3 or 4 days. Irrigation interval can be adjusted when the precipitation is more than 0.20 inches. Estimated monthly water use for a garden with a mixture of leafy vegetables, carrots, beans, squash, corn and tomatoes for locations in Utah can be found in the USU Extension publication **Garden Water Use in Utah**.

SOILS AND IRRIGATION

Soils include solids and voids. The solids are mostly minerals with a smaller amount being organics. The voids are filled with air and water which are both necessary for plant health. Good garden soils have 40 to 45 percent voids; thus saturated soil would have about 5 inches of water per foot of soil; after drainage by gravity the soil would have about 3 inches of water per foot of soil with about 2 inches of water per foot of soil that is available to plants. However, before plants utilize all the available water they begin to stress and their yield and quality are reduced; thus for gardens it is best to manage about 1 inch of water per foot of soil in all but

Figure 68: *Drip irrigation system tested and garden row ready to plant*

very sandy soils where ½ inch per foot would be more appropriate. For shallow and medium rooted garden plants such as onions, potatoes, beans, lettuce, chard, peas, and strawberries, an irrigation of 1 inch can be applied after the depletion from the soil of an inch of water by the plants and from soil evaporation. For deep rooted garden plants like corn, tomatoes and winter squash, the irrigation events can be 2 or more inches after depletion of 2 or more inches of water. If both shallow and deep rooted garden plants are irrigated together, the shallow irrigation of 1 inch works well, especially when using a drip irrigation system.

IRRIGATION SYSTEMS

An irrigation system applies water to the soil when precipitation is insufficient for plant needs. While sprinkler and flood irrigation systems can be used to irrigate a garden; a drip system offers several advantages which include:

- Good irrigation application uniformity,
- High irrigation efficiencies,
- Control of irrigation on individual rows,
- No irrigation between rows,
- Reduced evaporation from wet soil,
- Ability to irrigate tall plants such as corn,
- Low flow requirements.

With a drip system, individual rows can be shut off when the vegetables no longer need water; some vegetables have a short season (e.g., lettuce and spinach), others have a medium growing season (e.g., beans and corn), and some a long growing

Figure 69: *Drip irrigation layout*

season (e.g., tomatoes, peppers, melons and winter squash).

The following table can be used to determine the set time for common drip irrigation. For example, with an emitter spacing of 12 inches and an emitter flow rate of 0.5 gallon per hour (i.e., 0.5 gallon per hour per foot), the application rate is 0.32 inch per hour for a 30 inch row or drip tubing spacing; therefore, it takes 3 hours to apply an inch of water. Drip tubing with an emitter spacing of 1 foot with a flow rate of 0.5 or 0.6 gallon per hour works very well for most soils and garden plants and does not result in runoff. Drip irrigation equipment with pressure compensating (PC) emitters applies water more uniformly than non-pressure compensating emitters. Irrigation efficiencies of about 85 percent are common for well operated drip systems.

Flood irrigation can be used, but is often limited due to water supply, slopes and un-level ground in a garden. Flood or furrow irrigation is suited for garden plants with deep roots because typically irrigation water saturates the top several inches of garden soil.

The irrigation efficiency for a well-designed and managed sprinkler

TABLE 21: IRRIGATION SET TIME RECOMMENDATIONS FOR COMMON DRIP IRRIGATION

Irrigation Application Rates and Time		Drip Tubing/Tape Emitter Flow Rate (gallon per hour per foot)				
		0.2	0.5	0.6	0.9	1
		Application Rate (Inches/hour)				
Drip Tubing Spacing (inches)	12	0.32	0.80	0.96	1.44	1.60
	18	0.21	0.53	0.64	0.96	1.07
	24	0.16	0.40	0.48	0.72	0.80
	30	0.13	0.32	0.38	0.58	0.64
	36	0.11	0.27	0.32	0.48	0.53
		Minutes to Apply 1 Inch				
	12	187	75	62	42	37
	18	281	112	94	62	56
	24	374	150	125	83	75
	30	468	187	156	104	94
	36	561	224	187	125	112

Figure 70: *Irrigating the orchard*

system is about 75 percent, which is lower than drip due to evaporation during irrigation and the non-uniformity of the application. Sprinkler systems require nearly head-to-head coverage for good irrigation efficiencies. Setting out cans to catch irrigation water is a good way to determine irrigation application rates.

IRRIGATION MANAGEMENT

The following table provides some irrigation management guidelines for various plant growth stages and specific plants. The guidelines along with visually monitoring the plants and checking soil moisture can help determine the proper irrigation amount at the proper time.

TABLE 22: IRRIGATION GUIDELINES FOR VARIOUS GARDEN PLANTS AND GROWTH STAGES

Plant or Stage	Irrigation Practice
Seeds	All seeds need to be in good contact with the soil to receive the moisture required for germination. For good germination, seeds need to be planted in a fine-textured seedbed with adequate moisture and good contact between the soil and seeds. Small seeds (such as carrots, lettuce, spinach, dill, etc.) are planted shallow and need frequent (at least daily) irrigation until they germinate. The irrigation interval can be decreased if fine mulch is used to reduce the evaporation from the soil. Larger seeds (such as corn, beans, large squash, etc.) are planted deeper and require less frequent irrigation than small seeds, and often one irrigation is sufficient. If planted in moist soil, these seeds may not need irrigation for germination. Too frequent irrigation can keep the soil temperatures low which increases the time required for germination and can cause the seed to rot or be eaten by pests.
Transplants	Transplant vegetables (tomatoes, peppers, cabbage, broccoli, cauliflower, etc.) and flowers require a thorough irrigation immediately after planting and then irrigation every couple of days until the root system is well established. The irrigations can be light and only need to maintain moist, but not saturated soils.
Potatoes, tubers and bulbs	Spring potatoes, dahlia tubers, gladiolus bulbs, lily bulbs and similar plants are generally planted several inches deep. They need moist soils, but need one or no irrigation before they emerge from the soil. It is always good to dig down in the soil to make sure that it is moist. Fall planted bulbs such as some lilies and tulips generally do not require irrigation until spring growth, provided the soil is moist when planted in the fall.
Early growth and vegetation periods	The period of early growth and vegetation has a significant influence on production later in the year. As the plants grow, their root systems become larger providing greater access to soil and water resources. An irrigation interval of 3 to 5 days works well for most garden plants during this period.
Flowering and production period	The water uses of vegetables are highest when they are near full growth, are flowering and producing fruit. Maintaining adequate soil moisture by irrigation every 3 to 5 days (depending on application amounts) is important for vegetable quantity and quality.
Raspberries	Raspberries require consistent irrigation through the entire growing season. In the late fall as the leaves begin to turn and drop, irrigations can be discontinued as the plants prepare for winter dormancy.
Fruit trees*	Established fruit trees have an extensive root system and require deep irrigations (about 3 to 4 inches every couple of weeks). After harvest, the irrigations can be decreased and then discontinued as the trees go into winter dormancy.

Plant or Stage	Irrigation Practice
Evergreens*	Irrigation of evergreens after establishment can be every 2 to 3 weeks (depending on temperature and season) with an irrigation of approximately 3 to 4 inches. Evergreen trees and shrubs have some water use all year long, even during the winter. It is important to have moist soil going into winter. In some areas of the state during dry winters, monthly irrigations are needed to maintain tree health.
Strawberries	Strawberry production is sensitive to water availability, and adequate soil moisture should be available through final harvest of berries. Drip irrigation works well on strawberries because of the good control of soil moisture. Strawberries have a rooting depth of 1 to 1.5 feet, so an irrigation of 1 inch every 3 to 5 days works well (could be every 2 days with a light irrigation from a drip system). See the USU Extension fact sheet **Strawberry Irrigation**.
Grapes	Irrigate with 2 inches of water every 10 days through grape initiation. Full irrigation is often used from bud break through fruit set to ensure good canopy development, fertile pollen and adequate flower pollination. Shortly after fruit set, many viticulturists decrease irrigation to less than potential until harvest to limit further canopy and improve the quality of the grapes. After harvest, the irrigation can be decreased or discontinued as the vines go into dormancy for the winter. See the Washington State University Extension publication **Irrigation Basics of Eastern Washington Vineyards**
Ornamental shrubs and trees*	Shrubs and trees generally have deep roots and roots that can extend horizontally well beyond the canopy. After establishment irrigations can be deep and less frequent than shallow rooted plants. Trees that are planted in lawns may need deep watering, approximately every month, beyond that received from the turf irrigation.
Annual flowers	Annual flowers can be irrigated similarly to vegetables.
Perennial flowers	Perennial flowers generally have larger root systems than annual flowers and many vegetables. Many perennial flowers begin growth earlier than annuals and may require water prior to seeding or planting of annual flowers. If they are mixed with the annual plants, the irrigation of annual plants provides adequate water for perennial flowers. It is also important that the soil is moist in the late fall as the flowers head into dormancy.

*Deeply irrigate fruit trees around the dripline (**Figure 71**). Spread 2-4 inches of mulch under the tree canopy, but keep mulch from touching the tree trunk.

For more information on irrigation of small plots, go to: **extension.usu.edu/irrigation**

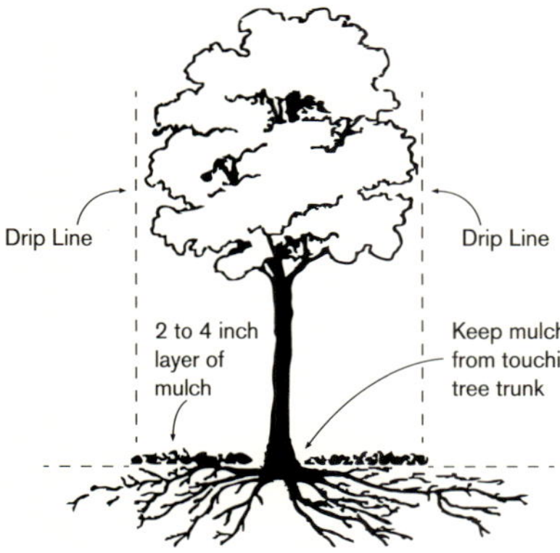

Figure 71: *Drip line of tree*

Helpful information can be obtained at the following websites.

Fruit: **USU Extension Fruit Fact Sheets**

Vegetables: **USU Extension Vegetable Fact Sheets**

Turf: **USU Extension Turf Fact Sheets**

Summaries of climate data from 235 weather stations in Utah. **Western Regional Climate Center**

BACKYARD BEEKEEPING

James Barnhill, *USU Extension Agriculture Faculty (Weber and Morgan Counties)*

Beekeeping can be an immensely rewarding activity. There is a thrill in being closely associated with the fascinating world of honey bees as they work together to build wax comb, collect food resources and reproduce. The pollination service provided by bees is essential for the production of many vegetable and fruit crops. Honey, pollen and wax are some of the valuable products produced by these industrious insects.

Bee Biology

The primary food sources for honey bees are honey for energy and pollen for protein.

There are three types of individuals in a honey bee colony: workers and queens, which are females, and drones, which are males. The life of a honey bee begins as an egg in the bottom of a six-sided wax cell. The egg hatches into a larva that is fed and cared for by the worker bees. The primary food of the worker and drone bee larva is beebread, made from a mixture of honey and pollen. When the larva is fully grown, its cell is caped with wax, it pupates and then emerges as a mature bee.

Figure 72: *Queen surrounded by workers*

The workers and queens develop from fertilized eggs. The fate of the female larvae, whether they develop into a worker or a queen, is determined by what they are fed. If it is royal jelly, beebread mixed with a gland secretion from the nurse bee's head, the larva will develop into a queen bee with functioning ovaries. Drones develop from non-fertilized eggs. Their only function in honeybee society is to mate with newly emerged queens.

Figure 73: *Langstroth hive*

Beekeeping Equipment

The basic equipment needed for keeping bees is a hive to keep the bees in, a smoker to calm the bees, a hive tool to pry the hive boxes and frames apart and a veil to protect the beekeeper from stings.

There are numerous hive types. The most common is the Langstroth hive, with 10 removable frames per box. The critical factor in all modern hives is to recognize that honey bees naturally build their combs one-fourth to three-eighths inches apart. Spaces smaller than this do not give the bees room to work and the bees often fill wider spaces with cross comb, making it difficult to remove individual combs. Hives generally consist of a bottom board, one or two Brood hive boxes (that are considered the permanent residence of the colony), one or more supers (temporary boxes where the honey to be harvested is collected) and a top board. Some beekeepers use a queen excluder to keep the queen out of the supers from which they plan to harvest honey. An inner cover, placed just under the top board, is another optional hive component. It is also important to have some type of feeder to allow syrup to be accessed during times of the year when honey or nectar are not available.

Obtaining Bees

The most common method of starting a honey bee colony is to purchase a package of bees. A package contains 3 ½ pounds of workers and a mated queen. The queen cage is removed from the shipping box, the cork removed and, if candy is not plugging the hole, a marshmallow is inserted. The cage is then hung between two frames in the box and the worker bees are dumped in with her. The bees will eat through the candy and release the queen. This slow release allows the workers to become accustomed to the new queen.

Figure 74: *Package of honey bees*

Bee Management

Spring – On a day when temperatures are above 50°F, open the hive and ensure that adequate honey and pollen are available to feed the colony until natural nectar and pollen sources become available. If honey supplies are short, begin feeding sugar syrup (one part sugar and one part water) or stored honey to the bees. Pollen substitutes are also available.

Summer – As the nectar flow starts, check the hives weekly and when the top box has two-thirds of its frames full of brood or honey; add another box.

Fall – Leave 60 pounds (one full box) of honey for the colony to feed on through the winter and harvest the excess.

General management – Reduce the size of the hive entrance during cold months or when hives are weak to make it easier for guard bees to keep intruders out. Because queens are less productive as they age, most are replaced every 1 to 2 years. Strengthen weak colonies by adding capped brood frames from strong colonies.

Pests of Bees

Honey bees have many pests. The most serious is the varroa mite. These mites attach themselves to larva or adult bees and feed on their body juices. A few organic approaches to controlling this pest includes:

- Use queens that have been bred for hygienic behavior; they are better at cleaning mites off.

Figure 75: Beekeeper tending hive

- Use screened bottom boards; mites that are knocked off of bees fall through the screen to the ground where they are eaten by ground-dwelling insect predators.

- Dust the bees with powdered sugar; mites are dislodged from bees by other bees in the colony that clean the sugar off them.

Harvesting Honey

If honey cells have been capped with wax, they are at a moisture level that will not ferment and will store well over a long period of time. Only those frames where a predominant portion of the honey cells have been capped are ready to be harvested.

Harvest generally takes place in late August, while it is still hot enough that the honey flows easily. Harvest can be as simple as scraping the honey-filled combs onto a screen filter and letting the honey drain out. The disadvantage of this method is that the wax combs are destroyed and the bees will need to expend energy to rebuild them.

Most honey is harvested by uncapping the comb with a knife and then spinning the honey out of the frame using an extractor. The honey is then filtered and put into containers for use.

Figure 76: *Honey-filled comb ready for harvest*

Figure 77: *Extracted and filtered honey*

Bee Stings

The stinger of the worker bee is barbed, so it remains in the skin of the victim and results in the death of the stinging bee. The stinger continues to pump venom for some time, so it is important to remove it as soon as possible. Use a fingernail, knife edge or credit card to scrape the stinger out without squeezing it. Squeezing the stinger forces more venom into the victim. Some people are allergic to bee stings. For them, a sting can be life threatening and they will need medical attention immediately. Those who are not allergic will have localized swelling that can last for several days. Benadryl® will make this reaction less severe.

To avoid stings, do not confine pets and livestock close to the bee-yard. Avoid agitating bees more than is necessary and position the hives so that the bee flight path is faced away from heavy traffic areas.

PESTICIDE APPLICATION

INTRODUCTION

If you mention the word "pesticide" to a group of gardeners, you are likely to receive varying reactions. Some gardeners praise pesticides for their help in controlling garden pests while others dislike their use for various reasons, such as their effect on the environment or perceived health risks. Some gardeners think pesticide use in moderation is acceptable while others feel absolutely no pesticides should be used on or around edible garden plants. Whatever your preference, this section covers a few facts about pesticides that may help you separate fact from fiction. It is USU Extension's goal to help you better understand your gardening choices, and leave you to decide what you feel comfortable using on your garden plants.

Goals of this Section:

- Better understand the meaning of the term pesticide.
- Learn about organic pesticides.
- Better understand common risk factors associated with pesticide use.

Contrary to popular belief, organic foods are not always grown pesticide-free. Pesticide is an umbrella term for chemicals used to control insects (insecticide), weeds (herbicide), fungus (fungicide), mites (miticide), bacteria (bactericide), mollusk (molluscicide) and nematodes

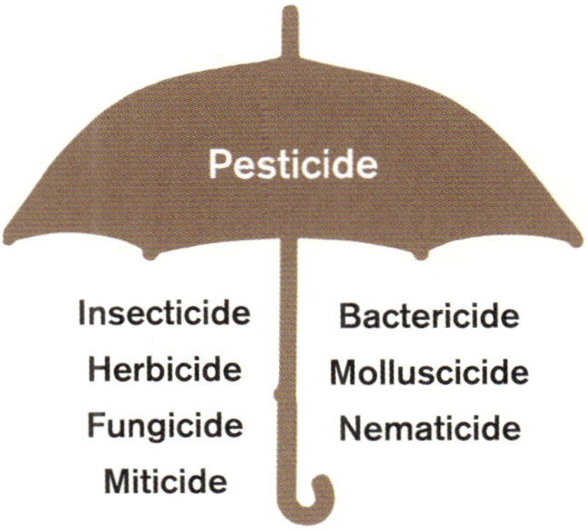

Figure 78: *Illustration of pesticide umbrella concept*

(nematicide). Therefore, common organic gardening products used to control pests, like neem oil, insecticidal soaps and vinegar, are all pesticides. Organic pesticides are derived from naturally occurring botanical or mineral sources.

All pesticides allowed for use in USDA certified organic agriculture are listed at www.omri.org. Just because a pesticide is organic does not mean it is automatically safe to use around natural enemies and other beneficial insects. Some organic pesticides are highly toxic to our tiny garden heroes; while others can harm other forms of life such as aquatic organisms. Pesticides should be used in conjunction with other cultural, mechanical and biological controls;

GARDEN MYTH #14:

Organic production restricts the use of pesticides.

Fact: Many organic pesticides are approved for use in USDA certified organic agriculture. Gardeners can visit the Organic Material Review Institute website at **www.omri.org** to view pesticides accepted for use on certified organic foods. If you prefer to not use any pesticides, it is important to use all other available control techniques to prevent pest infestations. See the "**Integrated Pest Management**" section in Chapter 5 of this guide for detailed discussion on mechanical, cultural and biological control tactics. For more information on organic pesticides for vegetable and fruit plants, see Chapter 5 "**Garden Pest Control**" section of this guide.

Integrated Pest Management does not restrict the use of pesticides; however, chemical control should be used as a last resort. Use of multiple control strategies typically results in the most effective pest control. It is important to take action to prevent pest problems if you plan to grow fruit and vegetable garden plants. Untreated plants can harbor garden pests which become problematic for neighbors and nearby commercial producers. Be a good neighbor and do your part to control garden pests. If you do not have time to care for your plants, remove them and purchase fruits and vegetables from local growers instead.

Figure 79: *Take precautions to protect bees and other beneficial insects*

Pesticides should be applied with diligence. Wear appropriate personal protective equipment when applying pesticides and always wash your hands immediately after application. Store all pesticides appropriately; read and follow storage directions on the product label. Apply herbicides close to the ground and on days with low wind. Show caution to spray insecticides when bee activity is low. Try not to spray insecticides directly on insects or on plants that are in bloom. See the USU Extension fact sheet **Reducing Pesticide Poisoning of Bees** for more information on protecting bees. Avoid using pesticides toxic to aquatic life around water sources. Avoid use of insecticidal soaps and horticultural oils if temperatures are projected to reach 85°F within 4 hours of application. The most important factor to consider before pesticide application is to thoroughly read the label. The label provides detailed application directions. The labels are important to protect both the safety of the user and the environment. Remember to follow the label; the label is the law!

FALL GARDEN CARE

INTRODUCTION

After a long successful growing season, most gardeners are anxious to prop their feet up and take a much deserved break, but fall is a great time to get your garden ready for next spring. A little time spent in the garden in the fall can save work and frustration the following growing season. Furthermore, more and more gardeners are taking advantage of season extension techniques and extending their harvest into the winter months. With the lure of garden fresh winter produce on the brain, it is easy to see why fall is almost as important a season for gardening as spring!

Figure 80: *Plan on taking a much deserved break – after completing fall garden chores!*

Goals of this Section:

- Discover the advantages of amending garden soil in the fall.
- Learn about important fall garden maintenance chores.
- Discover what to plant in the fall.

Fall is the ideal season to add organic matter to the soil. Incorporating organic matter into the soil in the fall will allow time for materials to break down into "black gold" by the following spring. Gardeners with clay-dominated soils should take advantage of dry soil conditions present in the fall months to incorporate organic matter into the soil. Avoid tilling clay soils when they are saturated with water; wet clay soils form clods when tilled. If you add high-carbon organic materials, such as dried leaves or wood shavings, make sure to chop them up and add a nitrogen source to expedite the decomposition rate (see the "**Backyard Composting**" section in Chapter 3 of this guide).

Fall is also a great time to plant a cover crop (see the following pull-out section on "**Winter Cover Crops**"). Diseased plants or weeds that have gone to seed should not be added to your backyard compost bin. It is also a good idea to check your irrigation system to make sure it is functioning properly. Do not forget to drain your irrigation lines before freezing temperatures set in. For more

Figure 81: *Some garden vegetables, like carrots, can be mulched-over with leaves or straw and harvested late into the fall*

information on irrigation maintenance, see the USU Extension fact sheet **Irrigation System Maintenance**. Finally, remember to wrap the trunks of newly planted fruit trees with light colored tree wrap to prevent southwest winter injury. For more information on southwest winter injury, see the USU Extension fact sheet **Sunscald Injury or Southwest Winter Injury on Deciduous Trees**.

If the fall weather has been dry and soil moisture levels are low, it is a good idea to deeply water trees, shrubs and perennials before the ground freezes. Schedule an appointment with a certified arborist to have your fruit trees pruned in the late winter or early spring before bud break. If you plan to prune your own trees, note a reminder on your calendar for around early Spring.

Lastly, remember fall is a great time to plant! Sprinkle native wildflower seeds in adjacent garden beds or plant other perennial flowers attractive to pollinators and beneficial insects. Some Utah native wildflowers require a cold treatment to germinate so fall seeding is ideal for spring germination. And, of course, do not forget to plant this gardener's favorite bulb – garlic!

Figure 82: *Plan to prune fruit trees early spring before bud break*

Figure 83: *Fall pumpkin field*

ASK AN EXPERT

WINTER COVER CROPS FOR PLANT AND SOIL HEALTH

Marion Murray, *USU Extension IPM Project Leader*

Avoid lugging manure or compost to the garden or field and save money on fertilizer by using winter cover crops instead. A cover crop, also known as green manure, is easy to grow if the right crop is chosen, and it is planted and killed at the right time.

Winter cover crops will not take any space out of production and should only be used in beds that will be planted with warm season crops (tomato, pepper, summer squash, etc.) so that spring crops won't be delayed in planting. Ideally they should be seeded between mid-August and early October, depending on location. If the cover crop is planted late, the seedling rate should be increased. Most crops need about 30 to 40 days to germinate and grow before a killing frost.

Figure 84: *Winter cover crop planted in raised bed*

Hairy vetch (Vicia villosa) is a hardy, viney, moderately drought tolerant legume that fixes nitrogen. Vetch will survive winter temperatures to -20°F. It should be planted in early September at a rate of 1 to 2 lbs/1,000 ft^2. The seed requires inoculation by Rhizobium bacteria, which comes as a dry peat-based powder and is shaken with the seeds just before sowing.

Vetch will begin to grow in the fall, with the majority of growth in the spring. The longer it is allowed to grow, the more nitrogen it adds to the soil. Hairy vetch residues decompose rapidly and release nitrogen more quickly than most other cover crops.

The downside of vetch is that it may be difficult to remove or till. Its heavy growth may clog a rototiller. Several low mowings or cutting the tops off at the crown with a sharp hoe or machete can also kill the vetch. It must be killed before it seeds or it will become weedy.

Austrian winter pea Pisum sativum subsp. arvense, also known as field pea or Canadian field pea, is an annual that is only hardy to 10°F, and may die in winter in northern Utah. This plant will establish quickly (planted at 2 to 4 lbs/1,000 ft^2) in fall, and produce a significant amount of residue before winter. The stems will grow up and over other plants, so it is best to combine it with an upright winter grain. In spring, if the plants have not been winter-killed, pull them up when they are about 2 feet high and compost or turn under.

Winter rye Secale sp. is an annual grain that is cold hardy and vigorous. Rye seeds are cheaper than legumes and tolerate a later planting at 2.5 lbs/1000 ft^2. Rye germinates quickly and grows later into the fall and begins growth earlier in spring than other grains.

Rye's deep and fibrous rooting system helps to build soil organic matter and is excellent for breaking up soil particles and preventing compaction. It also has excellent weed preventing benefits. The decomposing mulch not only smothers weeds, but also chemically suppresses weed seeds through allelopathy. Vegetable seeds can be planted within 3 weeks, and transplants are not affected by the allelopathic chemicals.

In spring, rye should be killed via removal or top-kill herbicide when it is about 6 to 8 inches tall or killed with mowing at flowering. Do not let it go to seed or it will become a weed. To kill by mowing, wait until the anthers are extended and pollen falls from the flower heads when shaken. The residues are high in nitrogen and can be left on the ground or composted.

Some gardeners will mix rye with a legume to get the properties from both crops. The grain will provide an upright support, allowing for better growth of the legume and easier killing by mowing in the spring. If the crops are to be mixed, a little trial and error may be necessary to optimize the seed ratio to prevent the grain from out-competing the legume. In general, rye should be seeded at about 40% of full rate and the legume should be closer to 80% of the full rate.

Pacific gold mustard, rapeseed (canola), forage radish and other brassicas have received much attention due to some species' having biofumigant properties. These biofumigants can suppress soil borne pathogens and plant-parasitic nematodes. Results in research trials have been inconsistent, and more research is needed to clarify under what conditions the plants' chemical compounds work. Most brassicas are probably best utilized in a long rotation to get the full effects, rather than as a winter cover crop.

Forage radish is one brassica that some are trying as a winter cover crop. It will die in northern Utah winters, but it grows quickly in the fall, trapping soil nutrients for release the following spring, thus preventing nutrient leaching and adding soil organic matter. Because the radish dies back, there is no worry about killing it in the spring, or waiting for it to decompose. In addition, its long taproot breaks through compacted earth, leaving the soil in friable condition and improving water and root penetration for the next crop.

Killing the Cover Crop

Although herbicides or tillage are often used to kill cover crops before planting the main crop, a well-timed mowing is just as effective. Backyard gardeners may instead choose to remove the plants entirely and compost them or use them as mulch. Another option for cover crop removal that some farmers have used is to pen chickens in the field to feed on the crop until it is gone. (Note that seeds of hairy vetch are poisonous to chickens.) Unless the plants are pulled out, wait 3 weeks before planting the vegetable seed or transplant crop to lessen problems of nitrogen immobilization and allelopathic effects.

Pest Suppression

There have been many research reports on the effects of cover crops on pests. Most pest management benefits have been documented from the use of long rotation cover crops rather than a seasonal winter rotation. Much information about pest management benefits from winter cover cropping is anecdotal and often difficult to replicate.

In general, the primary pest benefit is against weeds. A heavy surface residue suppresses perennial weeds, and the allelopathic effect of some crops suppresses weed seeds. An indirect effect of winter cover crops is the increased health of the soil (increased organic matter, nitrogen and friability) leading to improved growth and vigor of crop plants.

Winter cover cropping is not for every farmer or field, but in the right situation, can be an important tool in nutrient management, and indirectly, pest management. First timers should start small to determine the crop that works best and to prevent possible pitfalls such as generating an unintended weed problem if the cover crop is allowed to go to seed.

5 GARDEN PEST CONTROL

INTEGRATED PEST MANAGEMENT

Dr. Diane Alston, *USU Extension Entomologist and IPM Coordinator*

ASK AN EXPERT

WHAT IS IPM?

Regardless of our best efforts, no garden is without insect, disease or weed pests. Pest control is a constant chore for any gardener and one of the most difficult aspects of gardening to master. Although it may be easier to reach for synthetic chemicals to control pests, an organic gardener can control pests with limited or no application of broad spectrum chemicals by using Integrated Pest Management (IPM).

Goals of this Section:

- Better understand IPM and how it fits into an organic gardening approach.
- Learn about the key components of an IPM approach.
- Discover the benefits of IPM.

IPM is comprehensive approaches to pest control that:

- uses a combination of methods to reduce pest populations;
- increases tolerance of plants to pests;
- avoids harm to human and environmental health;
- improves sustainability (economic, environmental, social).

IPM evolved from the concept of "Integrated Control," first defined in the late 1950s by a team of entomologists at the University of California. Integrated Control emphasized the selective use of chemicals so that natural enemies, such as beneficial insects and soil microbes, were conserved. During the post-World War II era, discontent with pest control strategies that had shifted to heavy reliance on pesticides started the push to search for a more balanced and sustainable approach to pest management. Many aspects of IPM have been practiced since plants were first cultivated by humans. The strategy of maintaining healthy plants so that they are better able to resist pests and other stresses is a well-known approach.

How does IPM fit into an organic gardening approach? If fits perfectly. While IPM does not prohibit the use of all chemicals, neither does organic production. Organic approaches limit the types of chemicals to those that are organically certified. IPM advocates the use of non-chemical approaches first, with the intent of

Figure 85: *Bumblebee visiting sunflower*

reducing the likelihood that an organic chemical treatment will be necessary. By using cultural, mechanical and biological methods first, and emphasizing maintenance of strong, healthy plants, many pest problems can be effectively managed without pesticides (organic or otherwise).

KEY COMPONENTS OF AN IPM APPROACH

1. Identify the primary plant health problems in your garden.
2. Decide the threshold of unacceptable pest damage.
3. Consider all available pest management practices, especially preventive ones.
4. Conduct pest controls during "windows of opportunity," when the pest is most susceptible to control and before plant damage is excessive.

IPM FOUNDATION - KNOW YOUR GARDEN AND PEST BIOLOGY!

IPM relies on knowledge and information of the plants and pests. An information-intensive foundation is what sets IPM apart from a pesticide-centric approach. While a pesticide application, organic or conventional, may be viewed as an easy or simple approach to a pest problem, in reality the situation is more complex. There is a misconception that organic pesticides will not harm pollinators or beneficial insects. This is false. All pesticides have off-target effects. More selective, or "soft," pesticides are less toxic than broad-spectrum pesticides, but there can still be undesirable side effects. By applying a pesticide to the garden, whether it is selective or not, a gardener makes the garden system less balanced and more susceptible to future pest outbreaks. Sustainable practices such as increasing plant diversity and beneficial insect populations, and keeping plants healthy and able to resist pest problems, are all part of an IPM approach.

The foundation for the building blocks of garden IPM is based on information about the plants and pests. A savvy gardener will already have a good foundation on plant biology, but may not be as well versed in pest biology. This guide and other organic gardening pest management resources can be utilized to help the organic gardener develop a balanced and sustainable IPM program for his or her own garden site and situation.

KNOW YOUR RESOURCES

Before deciding to take any pest control action, be sure you have correctly identified the pest (insect, mite, disease, weed, vertebrate, etc.). USU Extension has many resources to help you identify pests and their damage:

1. Visit out online resources.
   a. The Utah Pests website (**utahpests.usu.edu**) includes:
      i. an image gallery of common insect, disease and abiotic disorders for fruit, vegetable and ornamental plants
      ii. more than 200 fact sheets to help you identify and manage common pests
      iii. video fact sheets that highlight identification and management of common insects and diseases in Utah, including pest monitoring techniques
      iv. more than 100 slideshows on management of pests in many situations, including the garden, turf, ornamentals, greenhouses, and human health-related problems
2. Contact your local county Extension agent (**extension.usu.edu**) for assistance.
3. Learn about pests that are currently active from the Utah IPM Pest Advisories for fruits, vegetables, landscape and turf (**ipm.usu.edu**).
4. Submit specimens and damage samples to the Utah Plant Pest Diagnostic Lab (**uppdl.usu.edu**) at 5305 Old Main Hill, Logan, UT 84322. The fee is $7. A submission form available on the website must accompany the sample.

WHAT TO KNOW ABOUT PLANT AND PEST BIOLOGY:

- Seasonal cycles
  - When is the plant most attractive and susceptible to pest attack?
    - Plants in the seedling stage can be highly susceptible to certain pests, such as damping off fungi, cutworms and flea beetles. Another highly susceptible time period is during the fruiting stage when pests are attracted to feed on the nutrient-rich fruits and seeds. Anticipating and preventing pest problems at critical points in the seasonal cycle will reduce harvest loss to pests.

- Pest life-cycle
  - Which pest life stages cause the most harm, and are easiest to control?
    - For example, squash bug adults overwinter in protected sites in

and near the garden and lay eggs on the leaves of young plants in the early summer. Adults are difficult to kill; however, the eggs can be mechanically smashed or removed with sticky tape, and the early nymphs that hatch from the eggs are the most susceptible to organic insecticides, such as kaolin clay, pyrethrin, insecticidal soap and horticultural mineral oil.

- Pest behavior
  - Which attractants or repellents can be used to trap or deter pests from the plant?
    - The European earwig is attracted to smelly baits, such as tuna juice, bacon grease and soy sauce. These odiferous baits can be added to vegetable oil in a closed plastic container (yogurt cup) with holes punched at the top of the sides to allow for earwig entry, and buried slightly in soil near plants with earwig injury. Empty the cups when the bait is filled with earwigs, then replenish and replace.

Figure 86: *Earwig trap*

- Pest population dynamics
  - When are pest populations most abundant, and when is intervention needed to prevent them from causing unacceptable damage?
    - The population size of many garden pest peaks in mid- to late summer, and intervention is often needed before then to prevent severe plant loss. For example, grasshoppers are often not noticed as a garden pest until later in the summer when older nymphs and adults feed voraciously on plants; however, the optimal time to reduce grasshopper populations is when they are young nymphs. Early intervention with the organic bait containing Nosema locustae, a natural pathogen of grasshoppers, can prevent grasshopper populations from reaching peak numbers.

- Interactions
  - Interactions among pests and their environment can affect pest management
    - For example, leaves coated with dust are more attractive to spider mites; they hide under the dry dust particles from predatory mites and moisture. Use of ground covers, mulches, and windbreaks can reduce dusty conditions, and thus spider mites. Likewise, spider mites prefer leaves with powdery mildew, a white powdery fungus, for the same reasons they prefer dusty leaves. Good management of powdery mildew can reduce spider mite outbreaks.

Toolbox of Management Tactics:

Biological Controls, Cultural Controls, Mechanical Controls, Chemical Controls

Decision-making Aids:

Proper Pest Identification, Pest Monitoring Methods, Environmental Monitoring	Use of Degree-day Models, Economic Injury Levels, Action Thresholds

Knowledge of Pest/Host/Ecosystem Biology:

Life Cycle	Behavior	Seasonal Cycle	Population Dynamics	Interactions

Figure 87: *Diagram of IPM building blocks*

As you ponder how to go about using an IPM approach, ask yourself these questions:

- Do you know which pests are present and which pests commonly occur on different garden plants?
- Do you know where and how to look for pests in the garden?
- Do you know how many pests are present and how many it takes to cause real harm to the plant?
- If you use an organic pesticide, how do you determine when to apply it at the optimal timing to have the most impact on reducing pest populations while conserving beneficial insects, spiders and other natural enemies?
- If you use an organic pesticide, will the repercussions outweigh the benefits due to the potential loss of pollination and natural biological control?
- Could non-chemical practices have been used first, and if successful, prevented the need for chemical intervention?

PEST MONITORING

Monitoring for pests and plant injury symptoms on a regular basis is essential for effective pest management. Regular monitoring provides information on:

- early warning of potential pest problems
- which pest life stage is active
- presence or absence of natural enemies
- when to implement control measures
- follow-up on whether pest control actions were effective

How often to monitor: From spring through early summer, monitor weekly, and then at least every 2 weeks thereafter through late summer.

Figure 88: *Squash bugs on pumpkin*

Where to monitor: Look in the places where pests commonly occur – undersides of leaves, on stems, on and inside fruits, on roots in the soil, under bark, etc. Look across the garden for symptoms of poor plant growth, stress, changes in topography or soil type, and focus pest monitoring in these locations. Also, inspect border rows, as immigrating pests often show up on edge plants first. Become informed about which pests are most common on the plants that you grow (see online resources under Pest Identification or enroll in a USU Extension Master Gardener or other gardening course), and look for these pests as you scout.

How to monitor: First, visually inspect the overall health of plants and look for insect and disease activity. On leaves, look for chewing injury, skeletonizing, spots, changes in color or stippling (tiny spots without chlorophyll). On fruit, look for discolored spots, bumps, indentations and rot. On the stems and root collar, look for discoloration, oozing sap, cracking and holes. Over- or under-watering are the most common plant problems in Utah. Check lower stem and roots for signs of decay (over-watering) or drought.

Use a hand lens (10-30× magnification) to magnify small pests and plant structures. To focus on a small object, hold the lens approximately 1 to 2 inches above the specimen. You can either look down through the hand lens from above, or lower your eye to the hand lens.

To dislodge insects for easier viewing, vigorously shake a leaf or branch over a light-colored piece of paper or cloth. To monitor insects and mites in fruit trees, construct a beating tray from window screen frame and white fabric (see Utah Pests video fact sheets at **utahpests.usu.edu/htm/video-fact-sheets** for instructions on how to make a beating tray), and use a padded stick to strike the tree limbs.

Sticky traps with attractive colors can be used to lure target insects to the trap for observation and counting. In the home garden, yellow and blue

Figure 89: *Demonstrating use of a hand lens*

sticky traps will attract aphids, thrips (especially blue), leafhoppers, psyllids and other small insect pests. They will also attract non-target insects such as flies, parasitoid wasps and bees. Avoid white sticky traps as they are especially attractive to bees. Inspect sticky traps with a hand lens to identify pest insects.

Traps with an attractive odor, such as a pheromone or food source, are available, but are generally more suitable for larger gardens and small farms. For example, a pheromone trap that has the specific sex pheromone for the codling moth, peach twig borer or greater peachtree borer is available, but it may be adequate to find out about activity of these orchard insect pests in your location through the Utah Tree Fruit IPM advisory (ipm.usu.edu) rather than trapping for them yourself. Pheromone traps will not provide control of orchard insect pests. However, it may be appropriate to use Pherocon AM yellow sticky traps with a yeast attractant incorporated into the adhesive in cherry trees so you will know when the fruit fly is active in your specific location. Also, commercially available traps for yellow jacket, or homemade traps for European paper wasp, earwig and codling moth can be effective in the home garden. View the Utah Pests video fact sheets (utahpests.usu.edu/htm/video-fact-sheets) to learn more about traps that are suitable for use in your garden.

Retailers of monitoring supplies: Local, well-stocked garden supply retailers may carry some pest monitoring tools. The following retailers are examples of some that sell pest monitoring tools and products online:

Figure 90: *Pherocon AM yellow sticky trap for monitoring cherry fruit fly*

Alpha Scents
West Linn, OR
503-342-8611
alphascents.com

Great Lakes IPM
Vestaburg, MI
800-235-0285
greatlakesipm.com

Gardens Alive
Lawrenceburg, IN
513-354-1482
gardensalive.com

Peaceful Valley
Grass Valley, CA
888-784-1722
groworganic.com

Gempler's
Mt. Horeb, WI
800-382-8473
gemplers.com

Suterra
Bend, OR
866-326-6737
suterra.com

TREATMENT THRESHOLDS

Each organic gardener should develop a set of personal guidelines to decide when a pest has exceeded an acceptable level of injury. These treatment thresholds will vary with the gardener and situation. A low level of pest injury may be ignored if the loss will not justify the cost or labor for control. The economic and aesthetic values of the garden plant should be considered, and will likely be the primary drivers of pest control decisions. Other considerations may be the environmental costs of pest control options, such as soil contamination and reduction of pollinators. Activity of natural enemies should also be considered when determining whether to treat. For pests like aphids and spider mites, natural enemies can potentially keep these pest populations below economic injury levels.

Beyond your own garden, a consideration in selecting treatment thresholds is how pests moving out of your garden could affect other gardens, or, more importantly, nearby commercial farms. High pest pressure in home gardens can be a problem for commercial producers. There are export quarantines for some pests such as apple maggot and plum curculio in fruit crops. New invasive insects, such as spotted wing drosophila and brown marmorated stink bug have now made their way into Utah, and home gardens could be sources of these pests. Commercial growers may need to treat their crops more than would be otherwise necessary because of high populations of pests coming from poorly managed gardens and landscapes. Be aware of these concerns, and take action to prevent your garden from being a nuisance to neighboring farmers.

Using degree-day information: Degree-days (DD) are a measurement of heat units over time, calculated from daily maximum and minimum

County	Location	*Option A*		*Option B*
		Apply Oil	**Apply First Spray**	**Apply First Spray**
Box Elder	Perry	May 25	June 7	May 27
	Tremonton	No data yet	No data yet	No data yet
Cache, Carbon, Davis, Iron, Uintah, Wasatch	All locations	No data yet	No data yet	No data yet
Salt Lake	All locations	May 23	June 3	May 25
Tooele	Tooele	May 23	June 4	May 25
Utah	Alpine	No data yet	No data yet	No data yet
	American Fork	No data yet	No data yet	No data yet
	Genola	May 24	June 6	May 26
	Lincoln Point	No data yet	No data yet	No data yet
	Orem	May 20	May 31	May 22
	Payson	May 24	June 4	May 26
	Santaquin	May 25	June 6	May 27
Weber	Pleasant View	May 21	June 2	May 23

Figure 91: *May 10, 2013, pest advisory of spray application timing for codling moth control*

temperatures. DDs are used to predict insect life cycles, and in turn, time control treatments for susceptible life stages. Insects are cold-blooded and their body temperature and growth are affected by their surrounding temperature. Every insect requires a consistent amount of heat accumulation to reach certain life stages, such as egg hatch or adult flight. DDs can be used to determine optimal timing of insect control activities.

Where to get degree-days: There are a variety of ways to acquire DDs, such as a personal max-min thermometer, but the easiest access is through USU Extension online resources:

1. USU Extension IPM pest advisory newsletters are e-mailed to subscribers – advisories provide forecasted DDs for numerous pests in many locations in Utah. To sign up for a free subscription to one or all of the IPM advisories (tree fruit, vegetable and small fruit, landscape ornamental and turf), go to **ipm.usu.edu**.

2. Utah TRAPs (Timing Resource and Alert for Pests, **climate.usurf.usu.edu/traps.php**) is an online degree-day calculator for a variety of pests and locations in Utah.

IPM TACTICS

The easiest, lowest-cost, and often the most reliable way to avoid many pest problems is to provide a healthy garden environment that discourages pest activity and reduces the plant's susceptibility to damage. Preventive methods can promote stable and balanced pest suppression over the longer-term. For pests that directly attack essential or yield-producing structures of the plant, such as fruits, seeds, flowers, stems and trunks, short-term tactics such as organic pesticides may be necessary. A combination of long- and short-term tactics is often the best approach.

Short-term vs. Long-term Tactics	
Short-term	**Long-term**
Chemicals	Cultural
Mechanical	Habitat Modifications
Biological	Salt Lake

Figure 92: *Table of short- and long-term pest management tactics*

CULTURAL CONTROLS

Effects of cultural controls can be variable and depend upon the situation and target pests. Beyond the brief introduction presented here, learn more about the suitability of specific cultural practices through additional resources such as fact sheets and pest advisory newsletters.

Garden diversification: Avoid large plantings of monocultures (the same plant). Smaller plantings dispersed among other types of plants in a garden will be hidden from their specific pests. A diversity of plants in an area will diversify populations of beneficial insects, spiders and other organisms. Plant diversity in time and space, such as plants blooming at different times and in multiple locations within a garden, will attract pollinators and beneficial insects.

Ground covers and mulches: Certain ground cover plants can attract beneficial insects, such as blooming alyssum that will attract tiny wasps that parasitize aphids. Mulches of straw or bark and ground covers can reduce dust on plants which can exacerbate spider mite populations. Another benefit from ground covers and mulches is water conservation; however, covers and mulches can provide both benefits and detriments for management of some pests. For example, mulches are attractive daytime hiding places for the European earwig that emerges at dark to feed on plants, but ground covers can also increase populations of beneficial ground beetles that are predators of ground-dwelling garden pests.

Intercrops and trap crops: Some plants can deter certain pests. For intercrops like marigold and garlic, the greatest benefit comes after tillage of their residues into the soil. As the "green manure" breaks down it increases beneficial soil microbes that reduce plant-feeding nematodes and other soil pests. A trap crop is grown to attract insect pests. For example, yellow squash is more attractive to squash bugs than zucchini and many winter squash varieties; however, to be effective, squash bug populations must be intensively reduced on the trap crop plants.

Resistant and tolerant plant cultivars: Select pest resistant plant species and cultivars whenever they are available. For perennial plants, select species and cultivars that are cold hardy for northern and high elevation locations. A winter-damaged plant will be more susceptible to pest attack.

Soils and nutrition: Although you cannot change the soil type in your garden, there are steps you can take to improve soil health. Amend soil with organic matter and compost (see Chapter 2, '**Garden Soil**') to improve plant health and decrease susceptibility to pests; however, be aware that an excess of organic matter can increase some pest problems such as phytophthora root rot and sowbugs.

Figure 93: *Alyssum used as a ground cover*

Water management: Avoid over- or under-watering to minimize plant stress and decrease susceptibility to pests. Flood irrigation can exacerbate iron chlorosis and blossom end rot due to excessive and highly variable moisture levels. Overhead irrigation can increase some fungal disease infections on foliage, but it can reduce spider mites and thrips that prefer dry leaves.

MECHANICAL CONTROLS

Sanitation: Removal of plants, plant structures and debris that can harbor pests can be a highly effective preventive pest control tactic. Hand-pull or mow weeds before they produce seeds. Smash squash bug and Mexican bean beetle eggs masses, and mow or chop dropped fruit to destroy pests such as codling moth larvae in apples and pears and overwintering powdery mildew spores on cherry leaves in the fall. Prune-out diseased and injured fruit tree limbs and the tips of raspberry canes infested with raspberry horntail. Corral chickens or other fowl just outside the garden to eat insects, snails and slugs.

Traps: Attractive traps can be used to mass trap and remove pests from the garden or to monitor their activity so that control actions can be appropriately timed (see the previous section on "**Pest Monitoring**"). Traps are primarily used for insect and vertebrate pests. Attractive traps use visual cues (color, shape) and/or odors (pheromones, food baits) to lure pests to them. Passive traps may be placed in areas of common pest activity, or use wind currents to catch pests. Corrugated cardboard strips placed around apple tree trunks will attract codling moth larvae ready to pupate and earwigs looking for a daytime hiding spot.

Figure 94: *Corrugated cardboard strip with codling moth cocoon and pupa*

Exclusion barriers: Sticky bands placed on trunks and stems (e.g., a band of duct tape coated with Tangletrap™) can prevent earwigs and spider mites from crawling into trees. Diatomaceous earth sprinkled around seedling plants can deter cutworms, slugs, earwigs and other pests. Floating row cover fabric placed over cruciferous crops, such as cabbage and broccoli, will prevent egg-laying by the cabbage butterfly and cabbage looper moth, and will deter grasshoppers from feeding on vegetable plants later in the summer. Fruit bags placed over apple and pear fruits after they reach a one-half inch in diameter will exclude codling moth. Remove bags about a week before fruit maturity so skin color will develop.

BIOLOGICAL CONTROLS

Conserving and augmenting biological control organisms is an important component of an IPM program. A well-balanced pest management program that includes sound cultural practices will enhance the populations of beneficial insects, fungi and nematodes. The most important steps you can take to encourage activities of natural biological control agents include:

- Avoid the use of toxic and broad-spectrum pesticides. Only use selective pesticides when necessary, and target them to spots in the garden with problem pests.
- Provide a garden habitat that is favorable for natural enemies (see "**Garden Diversification**" under Cultural Controls) with a diversity of plants in time and space that supply nectar, pollen, alternate feeding sites and shelter.
- Add organic matter to the soil to ensure good habitat for soil microbes that control a variety of pests, particularly soil fungal pathogens and root-feeding nematodes.

Refer to the "**Beneficial Insects**" section of this chapter for more information on this topic.

Figure 95: *Syrphid fly adult feeding at a flower*

CHEMICAL CONTROLS

Pesticide – *"any substance applied to control a pest; pests include weeds, and plant-feeding insects, mites, fungi, bacteria, nematodes and vertebrates."*

Organic pesticides can be divided into categories based on their origination:

- Animal products
    - Fatty acids used in insecticidal soaps are derived from animal fats.

GARDEN MYTH #15:

It is always safe to spray organic insecticides around bees and other beneficial insects.

Fact: There is a misconception that organic pesticides will not harm pollinators or beneficial insects. This is false. All pesticides have off-target effects. Many organic pesticides are less toxic than broad-spectrum pesticides, but there can still be undesirable side effects.

Figure 96: *Bacillus thuringiensis (Bt) is an organically certified chemical control option for tomato hornworm*

- Botanical products
  - Acetic acid, capsaicin, citrus oils, neem, pyrethrum, rotenone, ryania, sabadilla and sucrose octanoate ester
- Microbial organisms
  - Living microbes and toxins derived from fermentation of microbial organisms.
    - Bacteria - *Bacillus thuringiensis and spinosyn*
    - Fungi – *Beaveria bassiana, Metarhizium anisopliae*
    - Nematodes – *Heterorhabditis and Steinernema*
    - Virus – *codling moth granulosis virus*
- Mineral sources
  - Boric acid, copper, diatomaceous earth, iron phosphate, kaolin clay, lime, and sulfur
- Petroleum sources
  - Dormant and horticultural mineral oils

Using pesticides safely: Use of a pesticide can provide benefits in pest control, but all pesticides (including organic products), have risks. Not all organic pesticides are registered with the U.S. Environmental Protection Agency. Some are classified as minimum risk and exempted from registration. Many plant oils and some minerals are exempted from registration. For registered products, using a pesticide in any means

Figure 97: *Home gardener applying an organic pesticide with a hand-pump sprayer wearing personal protective equipment*

other than that registered by the manufacturer is a violation of the law. A label is included with all registered pesticides. Thoroughly read the label before using the product. The label provides information on:

- Which plants it may be used on.
- The rate at which it should be applied.
- How to apply and what protective clothing to wear.
- Incompatibilities of the product with other chemicals.
- What to do in an emergency.
- How to store it properly.
- How long to wait before re-entering the treated area.
- How long to wait between application and harvest of the produce.
- How many applications allowed per growing season.

Keep the label with the product so that this information is always on hand.

RECORD-KEEPING AND ASSESSMENT OF TREATMENT RESULTS

Keep a garden journal or notebook to document your gardening successes and challenges. Record pest observations, such as which garden plants and varieties had the most pests and the timing of pest activity in relation to plant growth stages and calendar dates. Record all pest management actions that you undertake, including cultural, mechanical, biological and chemical treatments. Take notes on the outcomes of the treatments so you can assess their effectiveness to guide your pest management program in the future.

BENEFITS OF IPM

There are numerous benefits to maintaining a balanced and sustainable garden. Each garden and gardener will vary in what are the most important pest problems. The important thing is for each gardener to be willing to experiment and determine which IPM practices work best in their own garden. Some of the tangible benefits to a well-balanced IPM program include:

- Optimal and sustainable garden production from year to year.
- Reduction in costly inputs, such as pesticides.
- Enhanced natural enemy populations encouraged by a diverse garden habitat and minimal use of pesticides.
- Improved crop pollination due to protection of bees and other pollinators.
- No pesticide resistance problems where pests no longer respond to pesticides due to over-use.
- Reduced pest resurgence and secondary pest outbreaks associated with reductions in natural enemies due to pesticide use (e.g., aphids, spider mites).
- Enhanced food safety and quality due to reduced pesticide residues on garden produce.
- A healthy environment for the gardener and all who visit the garden.
- A successful and sustainable organic garden!

TABLE 23: IDENTIFICATION AND CONTROL OF COMMON INSECT PESTS ON VEGETABLES

Plant Family	Insect Name	Identification	Affected Plant Name(s)	Control
Composite (artichoke, chicory, lettuce, tarragon)	Aphid	Green or black soft-bodied, sucking insects that feed on underside of leaves and reduce yield and plant vigor. Leaves become crinkled and curled.	Chicory, Artichoke	Lady beetle adults and larvae. Aluminum foil mulch. Insecticidal soap. Strong water stream.
	Spider Mite	Piercing type pest that feeds on plants cell contents causing tiny yellow or white speckling. Problem mostly on indoor plants.	Lettuce	Use insecticidal soaps or spray plant with a forceful jet of water to dislodge.
	Worms and Loopers	Light to dark green insects that chew holes and hide in leaves. Adult loopers are gray or brown moths while cabbage worms are white butterflies.	Chicory	Hand pick loopers. Control worms with Bt or labeled organic insecticides.
Goosefoot (beets, spinach, swiss chard)	Aphid	Green or black soft-bodied insects that feed on underside of leaves. Leaves become crinkled and curled.	Spinach, Swiss Chard	Lady beetle adults and larvae. Aluminum foil mulch. Insecticidal soap. Strong water stream.
	Flea Beatles	Small black beetles that feed on seedlings. Adults chew tiny holes in cotyledons and leaves. Beetles can reduce plant stands or may kill seedlings.	Beets, Spinach, Swiss Chard	Clean up garden in the fall. Rototill in the fall. Protective coverings on plants.

Plant Family	Insect Name	Identification	Affected Plant Name(s)	Control
Goosefoot (beets, spinach, swiss chard)	Leaf Miners	Small white maggots that burrow and feed in the leaves. Leave a lacy trail. Do not significantly affect yield, but make the leaves less usable.	Beets	Cover plants. Hand remove damaged leaves. Plant early or late.
	Slugs	Soft-bodied or shelled mollusks that chew holes in leaves.	Spinach, Swiss Chard	Thin plants, reduce water and trap under flat objects. Clean up debris, remove excess mulch. Cottage cheese containers as traps or bait station. Avoid moist that favor these pests.
Gourd (cantaloupe, cucumber, pumpkin, summer and winter squash, watermelon)	Aphids	Green or black soft-bodied insects that feed on underside of leaves. Leaves become crinkled and curled. May transmit virus diseases. Secreted honeydew makes plants appear shiny, wet or sticky.	Cantaloupe, Cucumber, Pumpkin, Summer and Winter Squash, Watermelon	Lady beetle adults and larvae. Aluminum foil mulch. Insecticidal soap. Strong water stream.
	Cucumber Beetle	Adults have stripes or spots and feed on leaves and vines which reduce vigor. May transmit bacterial disease. Larvae bore into roots and stems causing plants to wilt and die.	Cantaloupe, Cucumber, Pumpkin, Summer and Winter Squash, Watermelon	Plant more crops than needed and then thin out infected plants.

Plant Family	Insect Name	Identification	Affected Plant Name(s)	Control
Gourd (cantaloupe, cucumber, pumpkin, summer and winter squash, watermelon)	Squash Bugs	Adults are gray or brown and 5/8 inch long. Adults and immature forms suck the sap from leaves, leaving them speckled before they wither and die.	Pumpkin, Summer and Winter Squash	Trap adults under boards, check each morning and kill pests. Pick adults, immatures and eggs off of the leaves. Clean up garden in the fall.
Grass (popcorn, sweet corn)	Aphids	Green or black soft-bodied insects that feed on leaves, tassels and ears. Plants become crinkled, curled and growth is stunted when plants are small. Honeydew makes plants and ears sticky.	Popcorn, Sweet Corn	Lady beetle adults and larvae. Aluminum foil mulch. Insecticidal soap. Strong water stream. Aphids cause cosmetic damage to the ears.
	European Earwig	Feed on leaves, flowers and corn silk.	Popcorn, Sweet Corn	Clean up garden area. Newspaper or board traps. Use cooking oil in traps. Do not overwater.
	Corn Earworms	Larvae feed on silks and ears of corn. Damage symptoms include holes in ear tips, loss of silks and damp excrement near silk.	Popcorn, Sweet Corn	Spray with Bt or labeled organic insecticides. Regular applications are necessary to protect the plants. Apply mineral oil to silks. Cut off damaged part of ear at harvest.
	Corn Sap Beetle	Enter corn ear at the tip and feed on kernels.	Popcorn, Sweet Corn	Beetles enter ears through earworm damage areas. Control earworms. (see above)

Plant Family	Insect Name	Identification	Affected Plant Name(s)	Control
Grass (popcorn, sweet corn)	Corn Rootworm	Larvae feed on corn roots causing stunting, lodging or death.	Popcorn, Sweet Corn	Rotate planting location yearly.
	Cutworms or Army Worms	Larvae feed near the soil surface and sever the plants close to the ground. Most damage done at night.	Popcorn, Sweet Corn	Use barriers or collars around plants. Keep organic mulches way from young plants. Aluminum barriers. Hand pick.
Legume (beans, peas)	Cutworms and Army Worms	These are green, reddish or black caterpillars up to 2 inches long. Army worms will climb the plants and feed on leaves and stems. Cutworms do most of their feeding near the soil surface.	Beans, Peas	Control weeds and debris in the garden that provide cover for worms. Use aluminum barriers. Hand pick. Provide plant collars.
	Leafhoppers	Small green wedge-shaped sucking insects that feed on leaf juices. Leaves curl and dry out.	Beans, Peas	Difficult to control as insects are very mobile. Maintain healthy plants.
	Mexican Bean Beetle and Leaf Beetle	These beetles are round, copper or tan colored with black spots on their wings. Beetles look like lady beetles. Larvae feed on roots, leaves and pods, doing the most damage when plants are small. Look for yellow eggs under leaves.	Beans	Late planting (after June 15). Large, flowering plants can withstand feeding pressure with minimal loss in production.

Plant Family	Insect Name	Identification	Affected Plant Name(s)	Control
Legume (beans, peas)	Pea Aphids	The pea aphid is a large green to pinkish species. It forms large colonies on the undersides of leaves near the tips of new growth. This insect transmits the Pea Enation Virus, which causes curling, mottling and deformation of the leaves.	Peas	Plant virus resistant peas. Wash aphids from plants with a strong stream of water. Destroy infested plants after harvest. Excess nitrogen increases aphid populations. Treat plants with appropriate insecticides.
	Pea Weevil	The pea weevil is a brown flecked beetle with a short, broad snout. Adult females lay eggs on pea pods and the larvae enter the pod and feed on the seed.	Peas	Early planting and harvest minimizes exposure. Pick off adults when found. Plant fresh seed and clean up debris in the fall.
Lily (asparagus, chive, garlic, leek, onion)	Asparagus Aphid	Green plant sucking insects that stunt fern and reduce yield and plant vigor.	Asparagus	Use insecticidal soaps or labeled organic insecticides.
	Asparagus Beetle	Beetles are black or orange and have 6 or 12 spots on their wings. Larvae feed on fern, which reduces leaf area and plant vigor. Adults feed on emerging spears in spring.	Asparagus	Destroy fern and debris in the fall. Use insecticidal soap.

Plant Family	Insect Name	Identification	Affected Plant Name(s)	Control
Lily (asparagus, chive, garlic, leek, onion)	Onion Maggot	White worm that feeds on seedlings, roots or bulbs.	Garlic, Leek, Onion	Use crop rotation. Destroy cull onions. Rototill deeply in spring and delay planting. Avoid excessive amounts of organic matter.
	Thrips	Tiny, slender insects that feed on leaves. Leaves turn silver or gray, and may twist and die. Thrips hide near where the leaf and bulb meet.	Chive, Garlic, Leek, Onion	Strong stream of water. Aluminum foil mulch.
	Wireworm	Larvae of chick beetle. Dark brown to yellowish, jointed hard-shelled and cylindrical. Feeds on roots, seeds and underground stems.	Leek	Use crop rotation, avoid excessive amounts of organic matter. Rototill in the fall. Flood soil. Rotenone or wood ashes also provide some control.
Mustard (broccoli, Brussels sprouts, cabbage, cauliflower, horseradish, kale, kohlrabi, mustard, radish, turnip)	Aphids	Green or black, soft-bodied insects that feed on underside of leaves. Leaves become crinkled and curled.	Broccoli, Brussels Sprouts, Cabbage, Cauliflower, Kale, Kohlrabi, Mustard, Radish	Lady beetle adults and larvae. Aluminum foil mulch. Insecticidal soap. Strong water stream.

Plant Family	Insect Name	Identification	Affected Plant Name(s)	Control
	Imported Cabbage Worm	Soft, velvety, green with faint yellow stripes. Adults are white butterfly with black spots. Feed on foliage.	Cabbage	Early planting. Plant red cabbage varieties. Avoid mulching cabbage plantings. Control with Bt or labeled organic insecticides.
	Cabbage Worm and Loopers	Worms and loopers are light to dark green. Adult loopers are gray or brown moths while cabbage worms are white butterflies. Worms and loopers chew holes in leaves and hide in cauliflower heads.	Broccoli, Brussels Sprouts, Cabbage, Cauliflower, Kale, Kohlrabi, Mustard	Hand pick worms off plants. Control with Bt or labeled organic insecticides.
Mustard (broccoli, Brussels sprouts, cabbage, cauliflower, horseradish, kale, kohlrabi, mustard, radish, turnip)	Flea Beetles	Small black beetles that feed on seedlings. Adults chew tiny holes in cotyledons and leaves. Beetles can reduce plant stands or may kill seedlings.	Broccoli, Brussels Sprouts, Cabbage, Cauliflower, Kale, Kohlrabi, Mustard, Radish	Clean up garden in the fall. Rototill in the fall. Protective coverings on plants.
	Slugs	Soft-bodied or shelled mollusks that chew holes in leaves.	Mustard	Thin plants, reduce water and trap under flat objects. Clean up debris, remove excess mulch. Cottage cheese containers as traps or bait station. Avoid moist conditions that favor these pests.
	Root Maggots	Small white maggots that burrow into the root and bulb. Lowers yield and quality.	Radish	Clean up debris, remove excess mulch.

Plant Family	Insect Name	Identification	Affected Plant Name(s)	Control
Mint (basil, mint)	Aphids	Green or black soft-bodied insects that feed on leaves. Foliage curls, puckers, yellows or becomes stunted.	Mint	Lady beetle adults and larvae. Aluminum foil mulch. Insecticidal soaps. Strong water stream.
	Flea Beetle	Small, shiny black beetles that chew tiny holes in leaves.	Mint	Clean up garden in the fall. Rototill in the fall. Protective coverings on plants.
	Cutworms	Larvae feed at or below ground level and sever stems of seedlings or transplants.	Mint	Protect individual plants with a collar or trap, use Bt or other labeled organic insecticides.
	Japanese Beetles and Grasshoppers	Holes eaten in the leaves.	Basil	Clean up vacant lots. For adults, cover plants with garden fabric. Bait area with Nosema locustae.
	Slugs	Soft-bodied or shelled mollusks that chew holes in leaves.	Basil	Thin plants, reduce water, and trap under flat objects. Clean up debris, remove excess mulch. Cottage cheese containers as traps or bait station. Avoid moist conditions that favor these pests.

Plant Family	Insect Name	Identification	Affected Plant Name(s)	Control
Nightshade (eggplant, peppers, potatoes, tomatoes)	Aphids	Green or black soft-bodied insects that feed on underside of leaves. Aphids transmit virus diseases that affect the plant growth. Leaves become crinkled and curled.	Pepper, Potato, Tomato	Lady beetle adults and larvae. Aluminum foil mulch. Insecticidal soaps. Strong water stream.
	Colorado Potato Beetle	Yellow and black striped beetle, about ½-inch long and ¼-inch wide. Larvae are reddish orange, with rows of black spots on each side. Yellow egg clusters are found on the undersides of leaves. Larval feeding defoliates the plants.	Potato, Eggplant, Tomato	Hand pick adults from the plants and rub out egg masses as they appear. Plant potatoes early. Plant hairy-leaved eggplants.
	Flea Beetles	Small, shiny black beetles that feed on seedlings. Adults chew tiny holes in leaves of young plants. Beetle feeding reduces plant vigor and decreases yield.	Eggplant, Pepper, Potato, Tomato	Clean up garden in the fall. Rototill in the fall. Protective coverings on plants.
	Hornworms and Fruit Worms	Larvae feed on leaves and fruits, causing defoliation and fruit damage. Look for bare areas and black fecal matter.	Pepper, Tomato	Hand removal is an easy control method. Clean up debris in fall. Rototill in fall.
Parsley (carrot, celery, cilantro/ coriander, parsnip)	Aphids	Green or black soft-bodied insects that feed on underside of leaves. Leaves become crinkled and curled.	Celery	Lady beetle adults and larvae. Aluminum foil mulch. Insecticidal soaps. Strong water stream.

Plant Family	Insect Name	Identification	Affected Plant Name(s)	Control
Parsley (carrot, celery, cilantro/ coriander, parsnip)	Carrot Fly	Small white maggots that feed on and burrow into the developing root.	Carrot	Cover young emerging seedlings with fabric row covers to exclude egg-laying adults.
	Leafhopper	Damage done includes piercing plant tissue to feed on sap. May transmit Aster's yellows.	Cilantro/Coriander	Maintain healthy plants.
	Parsnip Fly	Small white maggots that feed on and burrow into the developing root.	Parsnip	Cover young emerging seedlings with fabric row covers to exclude egg-laying adults.

GARDENING FOR THE "GOOD GUYS"

Attracting pollinators and natural enemies to your garden is both easy and fun! Try the following tips and be on the look out for pollinators, natural enemies and other beneficial organisms taking up residence in your garden.

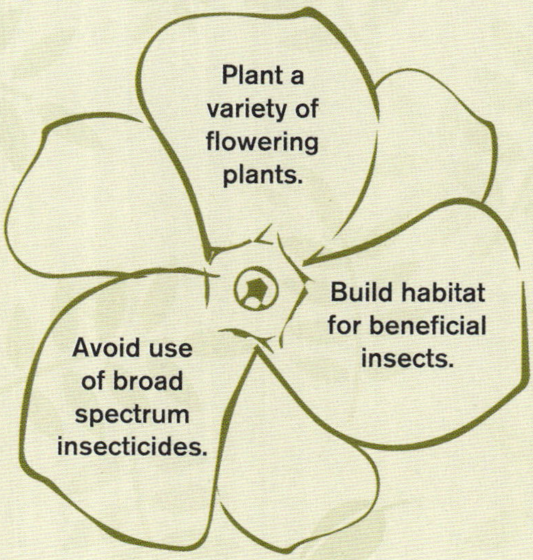

1. Plant a variety of herbs, fruit and vegetable plants and other flowering plants.

- Plant native plants! Native plants provide an excellent source of pollen and nectar ideal for many types of pollinators and natural enemies. See the USU Extension fact sheet **Gardening for Native Bees in Utah and Beyond** for a listing of local "pollinator friendly" plants. For gardeners outside of Utah, visit the Xerces Society website (**www.xerces.org**) for regional pollinator plant lists.
- Remember to diversify bloom color, bloom time and flower shapes to attract a variety of garden visitors.
- One good tip is to plant a few more herb plants than you intend to consume and allow them to flower to draw-in the good guys.
- Another tip is to plant a native flower garden near your vegetable garden (perhaps adjacent or bordering it) to attract hungry predators.

2. Avoid the use of broad spectrum insecticides toxic to beneficial insects whenever possible.

- Alternatively, practice cultural, mechanical and biological integrated pest management controls to maintain garden insect pest populations at a tolerable level.
- If it is necessary to spray insecticides harmful to beneficial insects, avoid spraying garden plants when they are in bloom or during daylight hours when bees are most active.
- Always read and follow the product label before applying pesticides.

3. Build and protect habitat for beneficial insects whenever possible.

- If you notice tiny ground-nesting bees hovering over exposed soil, avoid tilling the ground or spreading mulch on the soil surface.
- Consider planting pollinator friendly plants in under-utilized areas of your yard, like parking strips or side yards.
- Leave tree snags and brush piles if they do not present a hazard in the landscape and you are not trying to maintain optimal plant health.
- Provide a clean water source in a shallow vessel with gently sloped sides or maintain buffer strips along exposed surface water sources.
- When asked by family or neighbors for gardening advice, suggest they plant pollinator friendly plants.

BENEFICIAL ORGANISMS

Dr. Ricardo Ramirez, *USU Extension Entomology Specialist*

ASK AN EXPERT

INTRODUCTION

A component of organic pest management is the use of biological control or bio-control, a tactic to maintain or apply beneficial organisms, or natural enemies, that aid in pest suppression. The interest in organic pest control, namely bio-control, has intrigued many in part due to having alternative options for pest management that are relatively safe for human and environmental health. Natural enemies provide a service of natural pest control; however, an understanding of the biology, use, and care of these beneficial organisms is critical for effective bio-control success. Have you ever been discouraged after purchasing lady beetles, feeling happy when you released them onto aphid-infested plants only to see the majority of them fly away? The following will outline the general biology of natural enemies, concepts in biological control of arthropods and maintenance and application of these natural enemies.

Goals of this Section:

- Learn about different types of predators, parasitoids and insect pathogens.
- Learn about natural enemies "for hire."
- Learn about biological control strategies.

WHO ARE THE GOOD GUYS?

Predators

Natural enemies vary in size, in how they feed and in their feeding behavior. Predators attack and kill their prey immediately and feed on multiple prey to complete their development. Think of a lady beetle that walks up to its prey, like an aphid, and with its chewing mouthparts kills the aphid and feeds on multiple

Figure 98: *Praying mantis*

aphids to maintain its diet, develop and survive. Although there are some predators that may prefer certain prey, many are generalist predators which means they will feed on any prey item whether pest or beneficial. A praying mantis, for example, eats many species of prey and if you have ever collected their egg case and kept it in a jar to see them emerge, shortly after their emergence you may see them eventually start eating each other. This is perhaps one of the more extreme cases.

Predators forage in different ways. Some are sit-and-wait predators that ambush their prey. The praying mantis is a good example of a sit-and-wait predator that attacks prey as it passes by and does not necessarily seek out its prey. Predators that use this strategy may be most effective against actively moving prey. Some predators are active foragers that are constantly on the move and seek out their prey. Other predators have a combination of these foraging strategies. Spiders, a group of predators, can have an additional trapping strategy because of their web-building ability.

There are a number of predator species. Here we highlight the most common and abundant predators that are naturally occurring. Some of these predators are commercially available and are indicated below. Be aware that there are other naturally occurring predators you may come across that may not be mentioned here.

Predatory true bugs: These include but are not limited to the damsel bug, big-eyed bug, and minute pirate bug. Predatory bugs have piercing-sucking mouthparts that are used to penetrate their prey and suck out the body contents. Some predatory bugs supplement their diet by feeding on plants, but do not harm plants. The nymph and adult stages are predatory and look similar to each other but vary in size and wing development. They feed on different prey items from pest moth eggs, to caterpillars, mites, aphids and other prey. Minute pirate bugs are very small (2 to 5 mm), feed on smaller prey items and are commercially available.

Predatory beetles: Lady beetles, predatory ground beetles, rove beetles and collops beetles all have complete metamorphosis, meaning they have an egg, larva, pupa and adult stage. It is important to know this because the adult and larval

***Figure 99**: Lady beetle larva, pupa, and adult*

stages are predatory but look nothing alike. These predators have chewing mouthparts and tend to be active foragers. They feed on a variety or prey including insect eggs, caterpillars, aphids, mites, mealy bugs, etc.

The lady beetles are perhaps the most recognized predators in this group. Be on the lookout for naturally occurring lady beetle egg stages which are yellow, football-shaped and found in clutches. Predatory larvae will emerge from these eggs and are impressive predators that also do not fly. Therefore they stay in the immediate area. Lady beetles are commercially available and sold in the adult stage, however, purchasing lady beetles is generally not recommended and encouragement of resident populations is favored. Many of the lady beetle species for purchase are caught from the wild (e.g., convergent lady beetle and Asian lady beetle) and only a few are commercially raised. Those coming from wild populations may have a certain percentage with parasites and the possibility exists to introduce these parasites to resident lady beetle populations. Some species, such as the Asian lady beetle, are exotic species, capable of out competing native lady beetle populations and becoming a nuisance pest in homes. Because the adult beetles fly, their application may be limited to enclosed settings such as a greenhouse, high tunnel, etc.

Lacewings: You may have seen naturally occurring adult lacewings around outdoor lighting in the evenings. Green and brown lacewings have membranous wings (translucent and vein-like). These predators have

Figure 100: *Green lacewing adult*

complete metamorphosis and the larval stage is predatory. Although most adult green lacewings feed on pollen and nectar, the adult brown lacewing is predatory. Some call the larval stage aphid-lions because of their affinity to eat aphids with their curved mandibles that puncture prey. The larvae look alligator-like and the eggs are unique in that they are often attached to a silken stalk. Lacewing larvae will eat a wide variety of prey including insect eggs, mites and caterpillars. Lacewings are typically sold as eggs in a bran-type carrier, as larvae in a corrugated cardboard frame or as egg laying adults. Things to consider with the adults are that they can fly and eggs that are deposited will take time to develop before the predatory larvae emerge.

Mantids: Next to lady beetles, praying mantids are commonly highly regarded as good natural enemies to have around. However, because of their high cannibalistic manner, the fact that they often hang around flowers to capture pollinators, and have no discrimination of what prey they eat, they are not recommended for strict pest suppression. They have chewing mouthparts and adults and nymphs are predatory. The egg case resembles the texture of expanding foam from which several nymphs emerge.

Predatory flies: Several fly species are predatory including the Dolichopodid flies and predaceous fly larvae. Dolichopodid flies are long-legged, metallic green, red or blue flies with a tapered abdomen. The adults are predatory and commonly found feeding on aphids, leaf hoppers and mites. The larval stages are assumed to be predatory but not much is known about them. Several species of flies have predaceous larvae such the syrphid fly and predaceous midge. The adult syrphid fly or hover fly resembles a bee but cannot sting and feeds on pollen and nectar, while the larva is green in color with no distinct head and a white line running down the length of its back. The predaceous midge larva (3 mm in size), Aphidoletes aphidimyza, is commercially available and is primarily used in greenhouse settings with high humidity for aphid management. Many of these predatory fly larvae feed on aphids, mealybugs, scales and other soft-bodied insects.

Predatory mites: These tiny predators are arachnids. Predatory mites have piercing-sucking mouthparts and feed on a number of small prey including pest mites, arthropod eggs, whitefly nymphs and thrips. Predatory mites tend to be fast moving compared to pest mites and supplement their diet with pollen. There are a number of predaceous mite species that are naturally occurring and commercially available. Typically mites are sold in a shaker bottle with a granular carrier such as vermiculite or bran.

Spiders: These arachnids are all predatory. Some are active foragers (e.g., wolf spiders), some are ambushers (e.g., jumping spiders), and others build webs for capturing prey (e.g., orb-weaver and common garden spiders). Spiders feed on a wide range of prey and their foraging strategy dictates the kind of prey they may capture (i.e., flying insects and active prey caught in spider webs). There is not a lot of research on how to manipulate spiders to be more efficient predators, but some work shows that naturally occurring spiders help to suppress insect pests.

TABLE 24: QUICK GUIDE TO NATURALLY OCCURRING BENEFICIAL PREDATORS

Predator	Commercially available	Foraging strategy*	Prey Type	Comments
Damsel Bug	No	S+A	Aphids, mites, thrips, insect eggs and larvae	Associated with low-growing plants and shrubs.

Predator	Commercially available	Foraging strategy*	Prey Type	Comments
Big-eyed Bug	No	A	Small prey, aphids, insect eggs, mites	Fast runner, hides well, scurries around soil surface but found in plant canopy.
Minute pirate bug	Yes	A	Aphids, mites, thrips, insect eggs, whitefly nymphs	Primarily purchased for greenhouse settings; enhancement of naturally occurring populations is encouraged.
Lady beetles	Yes	A	Aphids, insect eggs, small larvae	Buying is not encouraged; useful in greenhouse situations; larvae are great predators.
Predatory mites	Yes	A	Mites, thrips, small insects and eggs	Species vary in prey preference and environmental conditions.
Praying Mantis	Yes	S	Large and small prey	Purchase is not recommended.
Lacewing	Yes	A	Aphids, mites, small larvae and nymphs, and eggs	A good alternative to purchasing lady beetles.
Spiders	No	A+S+T	Large and small prey	Different modes of capturing prey depending on the species.

* S=sit and wait A=active T=trapping

PARASITOIDS

These natural enemies differ from predators in that parasitoids are insects that parasitize and kill their prey. The majority of parasitoids used for biological control are parasitic wasps. Here, the adult stage parasitoid is free living and often smaller than their prey. The adult parasitoid will deposit an egg in or on its prey host where then the juvenile stage parasitoid will emerge and develop on/in this single prey individual. Think of the late 70s film Alien and life-cycle of the aliens. Parasitoids are specialists in that they attack a single group or species of prey. Several are naturally occurring and they are commercially available. These wasps are often very small and are generally not capable of stinging because the stinger has been modified as an egg depositing structure known as an ovipositor. This also means that the female wasp is the one parasitizing the prey. Depending on the parasitoid, some wasps parasitize by depositing a single egg while others deposit multiple eggs in a single host. The parasitoid may attack a specific host life-stage, for example, there are egg parasitoids and parasitoids that attack only the caterpillar stage.

Be on the lookout for parasitism. Often naturally occurring parasitoids are overlooked because hosts can be alive while parasitized and the cryptic nature of the parasitoid is less familiar to many. When evaluating parasitism, recognize that a parasitized host may have a different color from a healthy host. Parasitized aphids called mummies, for example, will be dead and gold or black in color compared to the yellow or green color of some healthy aphid species. Sometimes the developing parasitoid is visible in or on the host. Some larval parasitoids pupate on the outside of the caterpillar and are visible as white cocoons attached to the host. The host may be mummified such that the outer host skin or exoskeleton is hardened and maintains the shape of the host. This is commonly seen with aphid mummies. Check for emergence holes of parasitoids that have left their dead host. These holes tend to be round and have smooth edges. Seeing these signs is a good indication parasitoids are helping to suppress pests or that a release of purchased parasitoids are effective.

When purchasing parasitoids, they will often be shipped as loose parasitic wasp pupae, parasitic wasp pupae or parasitized eggs attach to cardstock,

Figure 101: *White cocoons attached to a host caterpillar*

or live adult wasps in vials with a food source. The pieces of cardstock are placed next to pest-infested plants. Sometimes the cardstock is cut so that the card can hang on a branch or plant stem. Loose wasp pupae or adults are sprinkled around. Be sure to follow the supplier instructions for care and application.

INSECT PATHOGENS

There are several disease-causing parasites (e.g., bacteria, fungi, viruses) that can be used to weaken and kill insects and that are specific to insects and will not harm humans or plants. These parasites are microscopic or nearly microscopic and live in or on a larger prey host. Insect pathogens (aka entomopathogens) are commercially available as a bio-pesticide or microbial insecticide. Take note that some of these pathogens are also naturally occurring and it would not be surprising to come across pests infected with one of these pathogens. Insect pathogens

TABLE 25: QUICK GUIDE TO COMMERCIALLY AVAILABLE PARASITOIDS

Parasitoid	Stage attacked	Prey Type	Comments
Trichogramma wasps	Egg	Moth and many other insect eggs	Species vary in habitat preference (tree canopy vs. ground cover)
Aphid parasitoids	Nymph and adult	Aphids	Aphidius species, Diaereriella species, Aphelinus species
Whitefly parasitoids	Nymph	Whitefly nymphs	Encarsia species, Eretmocerus species
Scale parasitoids	Nymphs	Soft and armored scales	Encarsia species, Metaphycus species, and Aphytis species
Cotesia wasps	Larva	Armyworms, loopers, other caterpillars	Multiple white cocoons found on the outside of host. Availability is variable.

formulated as a bio-pesticide are registered and labeled under the restrictions seen with chemical pesticides, with the exception of insect pathogenic nematodes (entomopathogenic nematodes).

Bacteria: These are single-celled organisms of which some species are known to infect insects. Bacillus species bacteria are the most widely used for pest control. Bacillus thuringiensis or Bt is perhaps the most well-known species and commercially available bacteria with several subspecies that infect and kill specific groups of pests. These bacteria are associated with a Bt protein crystal, an endotoxin, that deteriorates the insect gut. Therefore the insect has to ingest the bacteria and upon disruption of the gut, bacterial spores will spread throughout the insect host, eventually killing it. In general, infection is most effective against younger pest life-stages, caterpillars or larvae. Infected insects will stop feeding and be slow moving compared to healthy insect hosts. Be on the lookout for dead and decomposing hosts that usually turn black in color and will eventually ooze body contents.

Entomopathogenic Fungi: Insect pathogenic fungi are multi-celled organisms that have a spore stage associated with dispersal and attachment to a host. Naturally occurring fungal spores can be spread by wind, water and other modes. Formulations as a bio-pesticide contain the spores that would be applied to the insect host. Spores that contact an insect cuticle will attach and germinate, much in the way a small root germinates from a plant seed into the soil. The fungus

Figure 102: *Larvae infected with nematodes*

will penetrate into the insect and will eventually spread by developing fine threads called hyphae that form into a mass called mycelium. The insect will die and eventually the fungus will produce spores for dispersal. Spores for these pathogens do not need to be ingested for an insect to be infected. High humidity tends to allow pathogenic fungi to be effective and persist in the environment. Entomopathogenic fungi have broad-spectrum activity and can be a better option for pests with piercing-sucking insects that may not ingest bacteria given their feeding strategy. Infected insects will stop feeding, be slow moving and may be found at the top of the plant canopy. Dead insects may be found drooped over or insects may be covered in spores or a fuzzy mass of mycelium that vary in color depending on the fungus. White insect pathogenic fungi may belong to the commercially available Beauveria bassiana that is seen naturally occurring.

Entomopathogenic nematodes: These are clear, nearly microscopic roundworms that enter the insect host through body openings, such as the mouth. They are associated with a bacterium they release that kills the insect within a couple of days and allows the nematodes to develop and reproduce. Nematodes are soil dwelling and perform best against insect pests, in particular larval stages, associated with a moist soil environment. Entomopathogenic nematodes are resident in soil and do not harm plants but are often found at low levels. Many insect pathogenic species are commercially available. Foliar applications of nematodes have been less successful and are not generally recommended, but may be used in greenhouses and against leafminers and thrips on ornamentals. Species vary in their behavior, specificity to attack particular insects and tolerance to various environmental conditions. These characteristics should be used to select the appropriate species. Be on the lookout for resident infection by nematodes or the success of a nematode application. About 2 to 3 days after an application, nematode infected larvae are dead and tan to brown in color for Steinernema species or reddish to orange for Heterorhabditis species compared to healthy larvae that are cream to white in color.

TABLE 26: QUICK GUIDE TO ENTOMOPATHOGENS

Pathogen	Pathogen Type	Stage attacked	Prey Type	Comments
Beauveria bassiana	Fungus	Larva and adult stages	Broad activity to many insects	Botanigard; Mycotrol
Bacillus thuringiensis	Bacteria	Primarily larva	Depends on subspecies: israelensis- flies tenebrionis- beetles kurstaki- moths	Thuricide; Dipel
Entomo-pathogenic nematodes	Nematode	Primarily larva	Depends on nematode species: Armyworm, cutworm, weevil grubs, white grubs, fungus gnats	Steinernema carpocapsae; S. feltiae; Heterorhabditis bacteriophora; trade names include Nemasys; Millenium; NemaShield

WHAT ARE THE STRATEGIES?

There are a number of factors that can lead to increases in a pest population and it is clear that high numbers of a pest can damage plants. When using bio-control, the hope is that natural enemies can kill pests faster than the pest can reproduce or migrate into an area and that this will result in low pest numbers, reduced plant damage and loss, and a benefit to the end-user economically and environmentally. Many potential pests are often kept in check; that is below damaging levels, by natural enemies that are resident in the local environment. Are natural enemies working for you? If not, some adjustments may be needed to enhance their presence and effectiveness. Depending on the local environment or the situation (e.g., greenhouse) resident natural enemies may not always be the option. It is possible, however, to supplement with various biological control strategies.

Conservation Biological Control:
The contribution of biological control is often overlooked until natural enemies are disrupted by factors such as a pesticide application or unfavorable weather. Here a plant feeding insect then escapes from being eaten by natural enemies, increases in number and reaches pest status. Often, secondary outbreaks of pests (such as aphids and mites) result from the mortality of their natural enemies following a pesticide application. Therefore, conservation and enhancement of these natural enemies is important for pest suppression. One approach

in conserving natural enemies is reducing and if possible eliminating the use of pesticides that harm beneficial organisms. Unfortunately, many insecticides, even organic products, have broad activity and kill pests and harm beneficial organisms. Some insecticides have lower toxicity, such as insecticidal soaps, kaolin clay, azadiractin and microbial pesticides. Another approach would be to simply monitor pest populations and start with washing small soft bodied pests from plants with water (and insecticidal soaps could be a component) that can help reduce a starting pest population and allow the natural enemies to persist.

Figure 103: *Diverse garden planting*

Modifications to the local environment can also help to conserve and enhance natural enemies. One way this is achieved is by increasing plant diversity, which in general appears to be more attractive to natural enemies than a large area of a single plant species (monoculture). Natural enemies often require shelter, alternative food sources, reproduction and overwintering sites, and other conditions that may not be provided with a monoculture. An area with diverse plants will ensure different (1) flowering times when nectar and pollen is a supplementary food source for a natural enemy, (2) leaf and stem types that provide varied shade (microclimates), places to deposit egg-stage natural enemies, and hiding places from enemies of natural enemies, and (3) prey that is available at any one time so that natural enemies stay in the local environment. Plant diversity can encourage a diverse community of natural enemies that also vary in the times, places and sizes of prey they feed on. It is thought that having this diversity of natural enemies is more efficient at suppressing pests than a single natural enemy on its own.

Augmentation Biological Control: The augmentative strategy supplements resident natural enemies with releases of purchased laboratory-raised or field collected natural enemies. Here, natural enemies are released using an inoculative or inundative approach. In an inoculative release, natural enemy populations are added earlier in the season than usual or to establish them where they are not present. It would be expected that the natural enemy would reproduce and increase its population on its own. The inundative release is different in that natural enemies are released periodically and they are not expected to reproduce and increase in number. Therefore, the natural enemy released is expected to help reduce the current pest population and additional releases (applications) may be required.

Some bio-control practitioners have been manipulating the habitat to maintain their released natural enemies. Banker plants, for example, are plants used to host prey that will not move to other plants that are of interest so that predators have an alternative food source. As an example, some growing greenhouse plants have planted barley to host bird cherry oat aphid which does not infest broadleaf vegetables or herbs but acts as a perfect host for various predators or parasitoids. Similar practices used in conservation bio-control will also work here, such as utilizing flowering plants to provide pollen, nectar and other food sources for released predators and parasitoids.

Purchasing beneficial organisms: Natural enemies vary in their behavior, specificity to attack particular pests, their habitat and tolerance to various environmental conditions. These characteristics, often provided by the supplier, should be used to select the appropriate species for the pest being targeted. Additional considerations such as garden preparation may also be required, for example, irrigating before and after nematode applications or avoiding UV exposure with microbial pesticides. Often these purchased beneficial organisms will not adapt to the local environment and may not survive over the winter, so applications the following season may be required.

There are several reputable garden centers and online suppliers dedicated to selling predators, parasitoids and microbial pesticides. Keep in mind that these beneficial organisms are living organisms so they should be handled with care. When natural enemies are shipped from a supplier, the container should have ice packs to keep them cool in transport and they should not be heated. At a garden center, natural enemies should be kept refrigerated and similarly kept out of the heat, otherwise they may not be alive. It is best to apply natural enemies immediately after

Figure 104: *Cilantro flowers are attractive to many natural enemies*

they arrive, otherwise, refrigerate and avoid freezing them. Some natural enemies may be more sensitive to certain temperatures (hot or cold), and supplier instructions should be followed to minimize harm.

Not all naturally occurring beneficial organisms are endemic, or native to a certain area. Over the years some have been accidentally introduced and have now become established. It is important to note that commercially available natural enemies may be exotic species and care should be taken so that these beneficial organisms do not out-compete native species or become a pest themselves. Asian lady beetles are one example where this has occurred.

Figure 105: *Asian lady beetle*

Bio-control compatibility: Generally pesticides are not compatible with natural enemies. Some of the microbial pesticides, however, can be used in combination with other insecticides, although these should not be mixed with fertilizer solutions. In some cases, pesticides have been used to first bring down a pest population, then this is followed by a predator or parasitoid release after the insecticide has diminished. For aphids and mites, a plant wash of water (sometimes with insecticidal soap) has been effective to suppress pest populations to a low level and allow predators to build their population and sustain the low pest population.

Be aware that there are other management strategies and natural factors that may be working against a natural enemy release. For example, some strategies used to reduce plant parasitic nematodes in the soil, such as mustard green manures, may decrease the effectiveness of beneficial nematodes used for insect management. Ants are involved in another interaction that has been seen when predators or parasitoids are released for aphids and other honeydew producing insects. Some species of ants will tend aphids, keeping them alive to harvest the honeydew produced by aphids, and they will protect this pest from natural enemies. Recognizing these types of complex interactions will help in determining whether an application will be a good approach or if other adjustments need to be made before proceeding with a release.

Bio-control is one aspect of a pest management program, and an integrated pest management approach should be used to ensure effective pest suppression. Knowledge of the complex interactions and trial and error of what works and what does not will need to be recorded and used to improve the use of biological control in your garden. Being aware of the natural

Figure 106: Ant protecting aphids

enemies both naturally occurring and commercially available and the situation in which they can be effective will help improve your pest management program.

For more information on bio-control, see the following resources:

- Flint, M.L., and S.H. Dreistadt. 1998, Natural Enemies Handbook: The Illustrated Guide to Biological Pest Control. University of California Press, Berkeley, CA.
- Association of Natural Biocontrol Producers http://anbp.org/index.php/members-products
- Utah State University Fact Sheets: Insects-Beneficial Section at www.utahpests.usu.edu

ASK AN EXPERT

BIRDS AND BATS FOR ALTERNATIVE PEST MANAGEMENT

Marion Murray, *USU Extension IPM Project Leader*

Some bird and bat species can be useful allies in running a successful IPM program. They are motivated, efficient and cost-effective pest predators. Foraging by birds or bats alone will not completely prevent pest injury, but in a healthy landscape or farm, they can play an important role. There are ways to manage or manipulate your garden or farm to attract the best and hungriest workhorses.

Birds Of Prey

Birds of prey feed on small mammals (mice, gophers), birds and large insects. The kestrel (Figure 107) is a small hawk that has long been used in some Utah fruit orchards for seasonal mice control. The McMullin Orchard in Santaquin has maintained kestrel boxes for more than 10 years. They find that kestrels return year after year to the boxes, but are highly territorial, so the McMullins only use about 6 to 8 boxes per 400 acres. The McMullins monitor the boxes for starlings and remove their nests. Claude Rowley of Cherry Hill Farms built and installed a box in the summer of 2009 on his 250-acre Goshen farm. The box remained empty until mid-summer, when he decided to add some nesting material of dried sticks and twigs. Five days later, a pair of kestrels moved in that eventually fledged four young. Rowley is impressed with the mouse control, and says that so far, the only place they can find mice is in the highest pressure area, although he has yet to see the full effects until after they mow in fall. He will be adding more boxes in Goshen as well as on other family farms.

Figure 107: *Kestrel feeding on prey*

Figure 108: *Barn owl nesting in tree cavity*

Barn owls (found in limited numbers in Utah) feed on large rodents and birds, and their number one choice of prey is gophers (**Figure 108**). They can be of great value in all agricultural situations, but their population is dwindling due to lack of nesting sites.

To attract birds of prey:

- *Kestrels:* Screw nesting boxes to power poles or trees 10 to 20 feet above ground, away from human activity. Install up to 1 box per 5 acres to increase chances of nesting, but note that a pair may defend up to 250 acres. Adding a bit of nesting material (twigs, wood shavings) can help attract the birds. Monitor each box weekly and remove starling nests. Watch for starlings moving in and out of the box.

A starling nest will fill the cavity floor with a deep bowl in the back and material up the sides. Eggs are blue like robin eggs.) Clean the boxes each year.

- *Barn owls:* To attract/keep birds on the farm, do not destroy old wooden barns; barn owls will not nest in metal barns. Nest boxes can be used in place of cavity trees or abandoned buildings. Owls may patrol up to 200 acres per nesting site.
- Install hawk perches at least 8 feet off the ground; one grower in Utah attached posts to his irrigation risers and they are often used by hawks.

Small Insectivorous Birds

Some of the most common and hard-working are:

- *Bluebirds* – eat large numbers of a variety of insects including grasshoppers; nest in boxes or cavities
- *Chickadees* - eat more insects per bird (up to 900/day) than any other, including scale, aphid, leafhoppers; nest in boxes or cavities
- *Robins* – primarily eat insects in spring when raising young; nest in trees
- *Swallows* – eat flying insects including mosquitoes; variety of nesting sites
- *Woodpeckers* – eat borers, bark beetles and overwintering codling moths; feed by extending their long tongue into tight crevices; cavity nester
- *Wrens* - eat grasshoppers, slugs, others; nest in a variety of places

Figure 109: *Robin perched on handle*

In orchards (particularly organic), birds such as juncos, flycatchers, swallows and sparrows have been shown to help regulate codling moth densities by feeding on diapausing larvae. A study of a California apple orchard showed up to 83% predation of codling moth larvae by birds during the winter (Baumgartner 2000). Insectivorous birds are most successful in organic orchards. To attract and keep birds in larger orchards, maintain diverse habitats (border planting mixes, alternate row plantings), leave a few older apple trees or large dead limbs for cavity nesters and provide water and nesting boxes.

Cropland bordering woodland, shelterbelts or riparian areas will also see benefits of bird predation, as birds will feed far into the field when prey is available (Puckett et al., 2009). In research conducted in Ohio, red-winged blackbirds were shown to consume large quantities of corn earworm and other corn pests (Bollinger and Caslick, 1985).

To attract insectivorous birds to your property:

- Place birdhouses and nesting boxes throughout; monitor all boxes weekly during the nesting season and remove competitive nests such as starlings or house sparrows, and leave bluebirds, house wrens, chickadees and tree swallows; clean out the boxes each year.

- Provide nesting materials including small pieces of string, dryer lint, twigs and shavings at various locations
- Keep at least two sources of water filled throughout the year, one raised and one that sits on the ground
- Plant a variety of trees and shrubs including those that provide nuts, berries and seeds

Poultry

Poultry in the farm or garden has many benefits beyond providing food. They eat insects, snakes and rodents and provide fertilizer.

Guinea fowl work best within a vegetable garden because they can be trained to eat only insects or other creatures and avoid the produce. They have keen eyesight, easily spotting prey from a distance. They are not suitable for small neighborhood lots because they have a very loud, distinctive call against intruders or other alarms. For farms, though, they are tough, disease-free birds, continuously on the move in search of food. They will also eat weed seeds, and their droppings make excellent fertilizer.

Layer chickens are quieter and more suited for smaller farms. They eat voraciously, including grasshoppers, flies, ants, grubs and weeds, providing good fertilizer. They are not compatible with a vegetable garden, especially with young plants and when food is nearing harvest. They scratch the earth endlessly, and will peck at plants and produce. But they are useful in neutral areas, or for cleaning up a garden after harvest, tilling the garden in spring, or fertilizing/weeding fallow beds. Some organic farmers use poultry and geese in their orchards to keep insect and weed populations at tolerable levels.

Figure 110: *Bat hanging on tree bark*

Bats

Bats can be an important component of an IPM program because they are the only night flying predator that targets moths. Not all bats can be attracted to the farm. Of the Utah bat species, the big brown bat is the most common that is adaptable to farmland or cities. An established colony feeds by the millions on larger insects. The little brown bat (locally abundant) also adapts to farmland, and feeds on flies (including mosquitoes), moths, mayflies, beetles and leafhoppers. A single little brown bat can catch 600 mosquitoes per hour.

The Natural Resources Conservation Service runs an environmental quality incentives program (EQIP), and has provided funds to establish bat colonies. According to the program, an organic farmer in western Oregon was able to establish several bat colonies, and as a result, reduced his pesticide use for corn earworm from 13 to 2 applications per season.

There is research underway looking at the use of bats to manage codling moths. A UC-Davis farm advisor is trapping bats in orchards and using DNA testing of the guano for evaluation of codling moth presence. Bats are generalist feeders, but where pest populations are high, they are likely to target that insect. Previous UC-Davis studies showed that moths comprise up to 70% of the diet of bats (Long, 1996).

References:

Baumgartner, JoAnn. 2001. Birds, Spiders Naturally Control Codling Moths. Tree Fruit Magazine, April 2001. pp 5-7.

Bollinger, E.K, and Caslick, J.W. 1985. Red-wing blackbird predation on northern corn rootworm beetles in field corn. J. Appl. Ecol. 22: 39-48.

Long, Rachel. 1996. Bats for Insect Biocontrol in Agriculture. The IPM Practitioner: 18 (9): 1-6.

Puckett, H.L., et al. 2009. Avian foraging patterns in crop field edges adjacent to woody habitat. Agriculture, Ecosystems & Environment 131 (1): 15

ORGANIC FRUIT PEST CONTROL

Marion Murray, *USU Extension IPM Project Leader*

ASK AN EXPERT

ORGANIC FRUIT INSECT CONTROL

Imagine growing your favorite summertime fruit only to find insects got to it first! Most fruits are easy to grow at home, but unfortunately, some insects love to eat them. Insects can feed on fruit or deteriorate the health of the plant. But with the right knowledge, gardeners can learn how to protect fruit trees from our tiny foes and enjoy the favorites – like worm-free organic apples and pears.

Goals of this Section:

- Learn about common insect pests of fruit.
- Discover how to identify symptoms of insect damage.
- Learn how to manage insect pests using organic controls.

In Utah, pest-free apples and peaches can sometimes be difficult to grow, even with regular spraying. Some insect pests, such as codling moth and peach twig borer, feed inside the fruits, presenting obstacles to organic production. In most cases, picture-perfect fruit may not be consistently possible, but with proper management and a healthy soil, a decent crop can be produced organically.

The information provided below covers the primary pests of fruit trees in Utah. There are many secondary pests that we occasionally encounter, and concerns about pests not covered here should be addressed with your local USU Extension office.

INSECT PESTS THAT AFFECT ALL FRUIT PLANTS

Aphids

Aphids are small, soft-bodied insects that often occur in clustered colonies. They suck sap from leaves and excrete sticky honeydew. Dark-colored fungi called "sooty mold" grow on the honeydew. Heavy feeding may reduce tree vigor. Most aphids leave the fruit tree and migrate to alternate hosts for the summer, returning to the fruit tree in fall to lay eggs for the winter.

Symptoms: Curled leaves; yellowed leaves; sticky honeydew; leaf drop; dark substance on leaves, bark, fruit.

Management: Numerous beneficial insects (lady beetle adults and larvae, lacewing larvae, syrphid fly larvae, and minute pirate bug) help suppress aphid populations, so conserve and protect these natural enemies. Most aphid infestations can be ignored unless the populations are extremely high, growth of young trees is being stunted or black sooty mold is staining the fruit. Apply horticultural oil at a rate of 2% in early spring (at bud break) to kill eggs. During the growing season, insecticidal soap or horticultural oil (at 1% rate) can suppress aphids. Other options include neem or other plant oils (rosemary, peppermint, thyme, clove), garlic extract or pyrethrin.

Figure 111: *Aphids on cabbage plant*

Spider mites

Mites are very small arthropods that are more closely related to ticks than insects. The two-spotted spider mite is the most common in Utah. It overwinters as adults at the base of plants and crawls up the stems in early summer. They may become a problem during hot, dry conditions in mid and late summer when they are reproducing rapidly. As they feed,

Figure 112: *Spider mite damage*

they remove chlorophyll from leaves, causing tiny yellow spots, also known as stippling.

Symptoms: Stippled leaves; scorching (burning) of leaves in high populations; leaf yellowing; leaf drop; fine silk webbing on leaves and fruit in high populations.

Management: Low populations of spider mites can be ignored and are often kept in check by predatory mites. Conserve predatory mites by avoiding use of pyrethrin in spring. If mite damage becomes apparent, apply insecticidal soap or horticultural oil (0.5-1%) every 5 to 7 days until mite population declines.

APPLE AND PEAR PESTS

Codling Moth

Codling moths are the adults of the common worms that infest apples. These moths start flying in spring and lay their eggs on and near developing fruits. Larvae feed for about 7 to 10 days inside the fruit and then exit out to pupate on the ground or in the tree. There are up to three generations from spring to late summer. (One generation is a cycle of moth, egg, larva in fruit and pupa.)

Symptoms: Frass (sawdust-like excrement) on the outside of the fruit; small holes in fruit; white larva in fruit (if still present); fruit drop; rot associated with feeding sites.

Management: In most areas of Utah, with no management of this pest, at least 60% of fruit on the tree will be infested. There are several predators of codling moth that should be conserved (birds and bats, spiders, beetles, earwigs, parasitic wasps and others) but their work alone is not enough to result in a clean crop. Other ways to reduce the codling moth population are to conduct good sanitation (remove and destroy all fallen fruit immediately or allow chickens to eat them, remove unmanaged or unwanted apple or crabapple trees, strip fruit after harvest), and practice trunk banding. Trunk banding involves wrapping a 3 to 5 inch wide strip of corrugated cardboard around the trunk and/or scaffold limbs. After codling moth larvae leave the fruit, they seek out cracks and crevices in which to pupate. Bands should be up by early June (corrugated side of the cardboard toward the tree), removed and destroyed by early July, and repeated from mid-July to October.

A pristine apple crop can be produced without spraying by bagging the fruit (do not bag pears). This option is highly labor intensive (about 30 apples/hour), but excludes the larvae from the apples. Fruit should be bagged at the same time as thinning–about 2 to 3 weeks after petal fall. There are various bag options, including Japanese 2-ply apple bags, Ziploc sandwich bags, white or tan paper sacks (remove 2 weeks before harvest to allow fruit to color) or disposable nylon foot socks dipped in Surround (kaolin clay).

If you do not bag your fruit, spraying may be necessary, and options include spinosad, horticultural oil (1%), Bacillus thuringiensis plus oil, codling moth virus, garlic extract and pyrethrin.

The key to success with spraying is to target egg hatch. Codling moth activity (like all insects) is regulated by temperature, and egg hatch for each generation varies from year to year. To find out when codling moth is active in your area of the state, contact your local county Extension agent, or go online to the Utah Pests website (**ipm.usu.edu**) and sign up for periodic pest alert emails (**IPM pest advisories**).

Figure 113: *Codling moth damage to apple*

Woolly Apple Aphid (apple only)

The woolly apple aphids are different from other aphids in that they feed on succulent roots and twigs rather than leaves. These cotton-looking aphids overwinter on roots or in protected areas of the canopy (primarily pruning cuts and other small wounds). Starting in late May, colonies in the tree start multiplying, creating large, cottony masses. Their feeding on twigs and roots causes galls.

Symptoms: Galls on roots and twigs that sometimes crack; cottony masses on twigs and bark wounds; honeydew; curled, yellowed leaves.

Management: The primary natural enemies of woolly apple aphid are syrphid fly larvae, lacewing larvae, lady beetles, earwigs and parasitoid wasps. If this aphid is a problem, apply horticultural oil (2% rate) at bud break in the following season to kill overwintering adults. Toward mid-June, watch for colonies forming at wounds or pruning cuts. If they are visible, an additional spray of 1% oil plus insecticidal soap may be warranted. Apply with good coverage and pressure to penetrate the waxy aphid colonies.

Figure 114: *Woolly apple aphid*

San Jose Scale (primarily apple)

San Jose scale is a mostly immobile insect that feeds by sucking sap from bark and fruit. The soft body of the insect is hidden underneath an armored shield. On fruit, they resemble small white to gray pimples with a red halo. In mid-June, crawlers emerge from under the mother scale and move around to find a location to settle to feed for the rest of their lives. If heavy infestations are not controlled, a tree can be killed.

Symptoms: Peppery-looking flakes on apple fruit; limbs encrusted with small, circular, black and gray armored scales; small red halos with white centers on apple; limb dieback; loss of yield; small fruit.

Management: Several parasitoid wasps help to keep the scale population in check. In addition, a 2% oil application applied when leaves are ½-inch long will kill immature scales, but not the adults that give rise to crawlers. To kill crawlers, apply horticultural oil (1%) or insecticidal soap in mid to late June. To find out when crawlers are active in your area, contact your local county Extension agent, or go online to the Utah Pests website (ipm.usu.edu) to sign up for periodic pest alert emails.

Blister Mites

Blister mites are microscopic mites that cause small, blister-like galls. They spend the winter within buds. As leaves enlarge in spring,

Figure 115: *San Jose scale*

the mites become active and start feeding under the lower surface of leaves. Each small blister provides protection for hundreds of mites. Very high populations can reduce photosynthesis and tree vigor. Trees easily tolerate lower populations.

Symptoms: "Blisters" on leaves that start green and turn brown as they age.

Management: Treat large infestations in early fall, before leaf drop, when mites are migrating from leaves to buds, by spraying trees with sulfur or horticultural oil (1.5%).

Figure 116: *Blister mites*

Pear Psylla (pear only)

Pear psylla is an insect whose feeding can cause a dramatic scorching (browning) of the foliage. Pear psylla adults fly to pear trees in the early spring to lay eggs on buds and twigs. Nymphs hatch in spring and feed sap from the undersides of leaves. As they feed on leaves and fruit, they secrete copious honeydew which can serve as a substrate on which sooty mold fungi grow.

Symptoms: Sticky honeydew on leaves and fruit; black sooty mold; random, scorched appearance to leaves; leaf drop and decreased fruit yields.

Figure 117: *Pear psylla damage*

Management: The best control is achieved with a horticultural oil spray (2% solution) just before buds start to swell (early spring) to kill newly laid eggs. If further control is needed during the growing season, use either a 1% oil spray or insecticidal soap.

PEACH, NECTARINE, APRICOT, PLUM PESTS

Greater Peachtree Borer (rarely on plum)

This insect, also known as trunk, or crown borer, has the potential to kill young trees, and is very common in Utah. It is a moth whose larvae tunnel in the cambium (just below the bark) at or just below the soil-line of the trunk. An infestation is characterized by amber sap oozing from the base of the tree, mixed with frass (sawdust-like excrement). In northern Utah, egg-laying by adult moths occurs from late June through late September. Young trees and old or drought-stressed trees are most vulnerable.

Symptoms: Slowed growth; small leaves and early fall color; dead twigs or branches; oozing at soil-line.

Management: Non-spray options focus on tactics to prevent infestation. Painting the bark from the ground to the first scaffold limbs with a 1:1 dilution of latex paint and water can not only help prevent wounding from sunscald but also smooth out cracks and crevices where adults like to lay eggs. In addition, keep trees healthy with optimal watering and fertilization, and keep grass, weeds and mulch away from the base of the tree.

Where this pest may be an issue, young peach trees should be protected from early July to August with weekly preventive trunk sprays until the peach bark becomes thick and furrowed, using a product containing Bacillus thuringiensis or pyrethrin. In addition, the insect-parasitic nematode Steinernema sp. could be applied as a lower-trunk drench in late April, although its efficacy has not been tested in Utah. It should be used at a rate of 500 nematodes per square inch of bark surface as well as drenching the soil. Nematodes and the soil must remain moist to work.

To deal with an existing infestation, remove soil from around the base of the tree to find the origin of the ooze, and to see if any additional holes exist. Use a flexible wire to probe through the ooze and into the hole in the tree to kill the larva inside. Be careful not to further injure the tree.

Figure 118: *Greater peachtree borer*

Peach twig borer

Despite its name, peach twig borer is primarily a pest of the fruit, although it does not attack fruit until later in the season. In the spring, the chocolate brown larvae prefer to tunnel into succulent shoot tips. In summer, a second generation of these worms enters fruit when succulent shoot growth has ceased. Larvae typically enter fruit near the stem end.

Depending on your location in Utah, injury may not be severe enough to require treatment every year.

Symptoms: Wilting of outer 2 to 3 leaves of twigs in early summer; holes in fruit with sawdust-like frass; rot associated with entry/exit holes.

Management: Over 30 natural enemies have been found to target peach twig borer larvae and adults such as birds and bats, spiders, parasitoid wasps and predators. Many of them can be attracted to the area using habitat plantings. Keep in mind that by themselves, natural enemies cannot reduce twig borer populations below economically damaging levels in areas of high population.

Peach twig borers can usually be managed with two well-timed treatments. The first is when the leaves just start emerging from the buds, using a product containing spinosad, mixed with horticultural oil (2%). At this timing, larvae are still coming out of dormancy in the tree canopy. The second timing is during bloom, using a product containing spinosad or Bacillus thuringiensis. Treat twice, once at the beginning of bloom and again 7 to 10 days later. During bloom, larvae are exposed and feeding on new leaves, flower petals, etc., before shoot elongation. Although Bt is an organically accepted product targeted to caterpillar larvae, apply after dusk when bees are less active.

In areas of high populations, one or two additional sprays during the growing season may be necessary. Products to choose from include horticultural oil (1%), spinosad, or Bt. To find out when peach twig borer is active in your area of the state and for when to spray, contact your local county Extension agent or go online to the Utah Pests website (ipm.usu.edu) to sign up for periodic pest alert emails.

Western Flower Thrips (on Nectarine)

Thrips are minute, thin insects that cause damage when they feed within the flowers and on young fruit. They are primarily a problem of nectarines, and only during bloom. Their feeding damages the fruit and scars form as fruit matures.

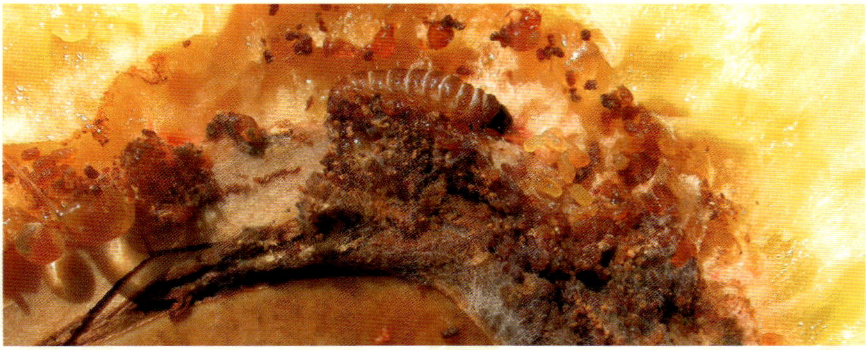

Figure 119: *Peach twig borer*

Symptoms: Fruit scarring/russeting; clear gumming from scarred areas; deformed fruit.

Management: Injury is not noticed until months after feeding has occurred. Fruit is still edible, but not marketable. For this pest, only an insecticide treatment will prevent injury, and treatment is only recommended if injury occurred the previous year. Spinosad or pyrethrin should be applied close to petal fall (end bloom), at dawn or dusk (when bees are not flying).

Figure 120: *Thrips damage*

European Paper Wasp

The European paper wasp is attracted to overripe fruit or fruit with exposed flesh. This insect builds umbrella-shaped nests with open cells in protected sites. (Yellow jackets build nests underground). Keep in mind that this insect is also a predator of caterpillars such as peach twig borer.

Symptoms: Oozing from holes in fruit

Management: Clean up rotting fruit on the ground and regularly pick ripe fruit. To help keep populations down, start trapping European paper wasps

Figure 121: *European paper wasp*

in late June and continue through the summer. Homemade traps are made by cutting off the top third of a soda bottle and inverting it into the bottom portion. Punch holes along the top edges and insert wires for hanging. Fill the bottle with 1 part fruit juice, 10 parts water, and 1 teaspoon detergent. Hang the trap where wasp activity is seen, and later in the season, hang them in peach trees just before the fruit starts to ripen.

CHERRY PESTS

Western Cherry Fruit Fly

Western cherry fruit fly is a common pest of sweet and tart cherries throughout Utah. Every cherry on a single tree can be infested by a fly maggot if populations are high. Adults are identified by a distinct banding pattern on the wings. They lay eggs by piercing through the fruit, about the time when the fruit begins to turn a salmon blush color.

Symptoms: White maggots in fruit; small holes in fruit; blackened or collapsed of fruit.

Management: Cherry fruit fly is a serious pest for commercial growers–

Figure 122: *Adult Western cherry fruit fly on coloring fruit*

if a single fruit from their crop is infested, the entire crop is rejected by the packing plant. Therefore, it is important that all non-commercial trees are treated (or removed) to help reduce the population. There are no natural enemies that can keep the population levels down. To prevent egg-laying in fruits, start treatment when fruits develop a salmon-blush color. The only organic option is products containing spinosad. Mixing molasses and yeast with the spinosad spray may improve effectiveness.

Other steps to help reduce the fly population is to not leave any fruit on the tree, remove all fallen fruit, and prevent flies from pupating in the soil by laying a tarp under the trees from late July until all fruit are gone (destroy tarp contents). Chicken and other fowl will eat fly larvae and may scratch pupae out of soil.

PESTS OF SMALL FRUITS

Raspberry Horntail

This pest is a wood wasp, and has become the most common cane-boring pest of raspberries in Utah. In early May (in northern Utah), adult females insert their eggs within emerging raspberry canes, just under the epidermis in the upper portion of the cane. Larvae then feed up and down the cane, resulting in wilting and dieback of the top part of the cane.

Symptoms: Wilting of leaves at top of cane; center of cane packed with brown frass.

Management: There are several parasitoid wasps that attack and feed on horntail larvae inside the cane; attract them to the garden with small-flowered, pollen-producing plants including those in the carrot, aster, mustard and legume families. The horntail population and subsequent damage can be reduced by immediately pruning out the tops

Figure 123: *Western cherry fruit fly larva in cherry*

Figure 124: *Raspberry horntail*

of canes (with the larva inside) just as they start to wilt. Start monitoring for wilt in mid-to-late June (in northern Utah), and continue until August.

Raspberry Crown Borer

This insect is a serious pest of raspberries, and can be difficult to control. When plants are infested, individual canes will die back during the growing season and are killed during the winter. Canes that are easily pulled out of the ground are indicative of crown borer. Raspberry crown borer larvae will spend 2 years inside the plant before emerging as an adult moth. Young larvae will bore into the lower portion of the canes during the first spring and summer, and in the crown and roots in the second summer. Adult moths emerge in July and August (in northern Utah). Evidence of crown borer damage cannot be ignored, as the pest population can increase rapidly.

Symptoms: Spindly canes; dying foliage on canes; poor bud break in spring; dead canes in summer; canes that are easily pulled out of the ground.

Management: Monitor for crown borer by examining lower canes and crown area for swelling caused by larval feeding. Try to pull up any canes that are weak or dying; if they pull out easily, suspect crown borer. Prevent infestation by using clean planting stock and removing wild or unmanaged blackberries. There are no organic insecticides for this pest.

Figure 125: *Raspberry crown borer*

Figure 126: *Rose stem girdler*

Rose Stem Girdler

The rose stem girdler is a flatheaded beetle whose larvae (worms) feed within raspberry, blackberry, currant and gooseberry canes. The shiny, bronze-colored adult beetles lay eggs on the canes from early June to mid-July. Larvae feed in a spiral pattern around the cambium (under the bark) and then move to feed in the center of the cane. The larvae spend the winter inside the canes.

Symptoms: Swollen, gall-like area at feeding site; entire or top half of cane dies back; canes break off easily; buds do not emerge in spring.

Management: The best way to minimize this pest is to remove and destroy infested canes late in the season and over the winter. If a crop becomes infested, cut all canes (healthy and symptomatic) to the ground in the fall. An insecticide spray of pyrethrin will help only minimally, and should be applied starting in early June, every 7 days, until mid-July.

Root Weevil

The strawberry and lilac root weevils feed on foliage (adults) and roots (grubs) of strawberries and other fruit plants. Root weevils spend the winter primarily as larvae, although some adults survive the winter. Egg-laying begins in late spring and the majority of grubs have hatched starting in late July (in northern Utah).

Symptoms: Tiny half-circles cut from leaf edges; weak, spindly plants; plant wilting starting in mid-summer; dying plant easily removed from soil due to root feeding.

Management: Infestations may be prevented through proper site selection, applying organic matter to the soil, providing optimal irrigation and fertilization, and rouging out plants when beds become crowded. Lightly infested sites can be treated with nematodes (Steinernema spp., Bacteriophora spp.) applied to the soil, any time from early summer to early fall. Keep soil moist after application. Severely infested sites should be brought out of production (bare soil) for at least 1 year.

Figure 127: *Root weevil damage*

TABLE 27: QUICK GUIDE TO ENTOMOPATHOGENS

Growth Stage	Host	Target Insect Pest	Cultural Practices	Insecticide
Dormant (just before buds swell)	Pear	Pear psylla eggs	---	Insecticidal soap; pyrethrin; horticultural oil (2%); neem oil
Delayed dormant (bud swell to beginning of leaf emergence)	all	Aphid eggs, overwintering scale	---	Insecticidal soap; pyrethrin; horticultural oil (2%); neem oil

Growth Stage	Host	Target Insect Pest	Cultural Practices	Insecticide
Dormant (just before buds swell)	Apple, pear	Blister mites emerging from buds	---	horticultural oil (2%) or sulfur
Delayed dormant (bud swell to beginning of leaf emergence)	Peach, nectarine, apricot	Peach twig borer overwintering larvae	---	Insecticidal soap; pyrethrin; horticultural oil (2%); neem oil
Bloom to petal fall (as dead flowers drop)	Peach, nectarine, apricot	Peach twig borer overwintering larvae	---	Spinosad; Bt – 2 sprays 7 days apart
Bloom to petal fall (as dead flowers drop)	Apricot	Western flower thrips adults in flowers	---	Spinosad; pyrethrin
Fruit present (late spring to early summer)	Apple, cherry, peach, plum, pear	San Jose scale crawlers	Monitor existing scale colony with hand lens to determine crawler hatch	Horticultural or plant-based oil (1%); insecticidal soap
Fruit present (late spring to early summer)	Cherry (when fruit turns salmon blush color)	Western cherry fruit fly adults	---	Neem oil, Pyrethrin
Fruit present (summer)	All	Aphids	Spray foliage with water; ignore small populations; promote natural enemies	Horticultural or plant-based oil (1%); insecticidal soap
Fruit present (summer)	All	Spider mites on undersides of foliage	Ignore small populations; promote natural enemies	Horticultural or plant-based oil (1%); insecticidal soap
Fruit present (mid spring through late summer)	Apple, pear	Codling moth eggs on fruit	Bag apples; cardboard bands on trunk	Bt; spinosad; codling moth virus, horticultural or plant-based oil (1%)

Growth Stage		Target Insect Pest	Cultural Practices	Insecticide
Fruit present (early through late summer)	Peach, nectarine, apricot	Peach twig borer eggs on twigs and fruit	Ignore small populations	Bt; spinosad; horticultural or plant-based oil (1%)
Fruit present (mid-summer through Sept.)	Peach, nectarine, apricot	Greater peachtree borer eggs on trunk	Prevent grass, weeds, or mulch from touching trunk; use wire to kill larvae inside tree	Bt, pyrethrin to lower 18" of trunk and exposed roots every 14 days; nematodes

*Organized by growth stage of tree, from early spring to late summer.

TABLE 28: INSECTICIDES FOR ORGANIC FRUIT PRODUCTION

Type	Name	Application Notes* and Toxicity Information**
Microbial – Virus	Cyd – X	Microbial insecticide containing the virus that infects only codling moths. Must be purchased online to get small quantity (expensive).
Microbial – Bacteria	Bacillus thuringiensis (Bt) - various subspecies	Bt is a bacterium that contains a toxin that paralyzes the insect's stomach. It is only toxic to caterpillars, and works best when the larvae are less than ½ inch. Only effective for 4 to 6 days. Practically non-toxic to birds and mammals. Low toxicity to aquatic life, natural enemies and honey bees.
Microbial – Bacteria	Spinosad	Metabolite of naturally occurring soil bacterium. Effective against codling moth, cherry fruit fly, earwigs, thrips and caterpillars. Slightly toxic to mammals, low to moderate toxicity to natural predators. Moderate toxicity to honey bees.
Microbial – Fungi	Beauveria, Entomophthora, & Metarrhizium spp.	See "Beneficial Organisms" section of this guide.

	Name	Application Notes* and Toxicity Information**
Microbial – Nematode	Steinernema sp. Heterorhabditis sp.	See "**Beneficial Organisms**" section of this guide.
Botanical	Pyrethrin	Extracted from Chrysanthemum cinaeriofolium flowers. Breaks down rapidly so only effective 1 to 3 days. Must come in contact with the pest, and can be used for most fruit pests except spider mites. Low toxicity to mammals and birds. Moderate toxicity to honeybees and other beneficial insects. Highly toxic to aquatic life.
Botanical	Neem Oil	Extracted from Azadirachta and Melia species. Lasts 2 to 4 days. Especially effective against soft-bodied insects. (Although listed on product labels, not highly effective for powdery mildew.) Practically non-toxic to birds and mammals. Low toxicity to aquatic life and natural enemies. Moderate toxicity to honey bees.
Botanical	Rotenone, Sabadilla, Ryania, Citronella, Pennyroyal	Not proven effective as insecticides. Rotenone moderately toxic to mammals and honey bees, highly toxic to aquatic life, and low to highly toxic to natural enemies. Citronella non-toxic to birds, slightly toxic to aquatic life, low toxicity to mammals, honey bees and other natural enemies.
Insecticidal soap		Insecticidal soaps are "salts of fatty acids" that kill insects by disrupting membranes. Works only against those insects that are contacted by the spray including aphids, mites, scale, and other soft bodied insects. Do not use when temperatures are higher than 85°F. Practically non-toxic to mammals and birds. Low toxicity to natural enemies and honey bees.

Type	Name	Application Notes* and Toxicity Information**
Oils	Petroleum or Plant-derived Oils	Oils work by smothering insect eggs and soft-bodied insects. When used as a dormant spray, use at a 2% concentration in water and at temperatures of at least 45°F and never within 48 hours of a frost. During the growing season, use a lighter rate (1% solution), and only when temperatures are below 85°F for at least 4 hours to prevent plant injury. Oil must contact pest to be effective. Practically non-toxic to mammals. Low toxicity to natural enemies. Moderately toxic to honey bees.
Abrasive	Kaolin Clay (Surround)	Kaolin clay is naturally occurring mineral clay used for making many of our day-to-day products (porcelain, paper, paint). When used on plants, it provides protection from stink bugs, lygus bugs, leafhopper and more. To apply, it must cover the entire plant and be reapplied after rain. Purchase in small quantity online or locally in larger quantity.
Elemental Compound	Sulfur	Effective against mites (miticide) and powdery mildew (fungicide). Practically non-toxic to mammals. Low toxicity to aquatic life and honey bees. Low to high toxicity to natural enemies.
Elemental Compound	Iron phosphate	Effective against slugs and snails when eaten (molluscicide). Very low toxicity to mammals. Low toxicity to natural enemies and honey bees.

*Insecticides should always be applied in accordance with the product label. Do not use an insecticide on any pest not listed on the product label. Always wear appropriate personal protective clothing when applying pesticides.

Toxicity information referenced from **UC Davis IPM Online Pesticide Active Ingredients Database and **National Pesticide Information Center Active Ingredient Fact Sheets**.

INTEGRATED WEED MANAGEMENT

Dr. Mark Williams, *University of Kentucky Extension Landscape Horticulture and Weed Management Specialist*

ASK AN EXPERT

INTEGRATED WEED MANAGEMENT

Weeds are one of the most challenging parts of pest management for organic farmers and gardeners. Although a weed is commonly defined as a plant growing where it is not wanted, from a management perspective, it is more helpful to think of weeds as plants that are well-adapted to growing in conditions of soil disturbance and more efficient at using nutrients to out-compete desired garden plants. Organic gardeners work hard to develop fertile soils, with optimal workability and high organic matter, and then disturb these soils through routine tillage to grow primarily annual vegetables. These conditions create ideal environments for weeds to flourish. By using integrated weed management techniques, gardeners can gain the upper hand on weeds and, over time, reduce the time they spend controlling them.

Goals of this Section:

- Become familiar with the impact of weeds on the garden and how a deeper understanding of weeds can guide the development of a sustainable management system.
- Become familiar with control practices to reduce the weed seed bank and prevent weed seeds from germinating.
- Become familiar with techniques to suppress weeds growing at the seedling stage or larger.

INTRODUCTION TO WEED MANAGEMENT

Weeds negatively impact the garden in many ways. They compete for resources such as light, nutrients, water and space and often grow much faster than desired garden plants. Weeds return every growing season because they are not host specific like many other pests. They may be alternative hosts for insects that prey on desired garden plants, such as pigweed and beet armyworms, or insects that vector disease, such as chickweed and thrips (carrier of tomato spotted wilt virus). Additionally, many weeds are very heavy seeders – one pigweed can produce up to 50,000 seeds - such that it only takes a few plants reaching maturity to perpetuate or increase the weed pressure in subsequent years.

Although they usually present a problem in the garden, certain weeds can be useful if they are not allowed to get out of control or propagate themselves, because they can act as indicator species of underlying soil conditions. For instance clover tends to grow on low nitrogen soils, plantains and wild strawberries prefer acidic soils and pigweed can indicate good soil fertility. A great source for weed indicator information is the book "Weeds and What They Tell Us" by Ehrenfried Pfeiffer, Floris Books. Certainly indicator weeds should not be viewed as a substitute for a good soil test; however, developing a deeper understanding of why weeds grow where they do can help guide the correction of underlying problems that encourage their growth.

Figure 128: *Clover growing next to a vegetable garden at the USU Botanical Center*

WEED IDENTIFICATION AND BIOLOGY

As in all pest management, the first step in developing a weed control strategy is to be able to correctly identify weeds in the garden. This knowledge can help target weeds at the most critical or vulnerable points in their life-cycle to more efficiently prevent and remove them from the garden. Annual weeds complete their life-cycle in 1 year and either germinate in the fall and set seed the following late spring or early summer (winter annuals, such as henbit), or they germinate in the summer and set seed before winter (summer annuals, such as lambsquarters). These plants typically produce many seeds to spread the risk of death from disturbance, but the seeds tend to be small, with limited stored nutrient resources. This is important because these seeds tend to germinate from the top 1 to 2 inches of soil, and the young seedlings are very susceptible to being killed by cultivation. It is essential to control annual weeds before they produce viable seeds. Biennials (such as mullein, or wild carrot) complete their life cycle in 2 years, typically producing an overwintering basal rosette in the first year, and then setting seed in the second. Biennials are usually not a problem in annual production systems because the ground is tilled at least once a year, preventing them from setting seed. Perennial weeds (such as johnsongrass) live for more than 2 years and can reproduce by seed or underground root structures. Other weeds, such as field bindweed, have underground stem structures equipped with nodes, or growing points. Often the stem structure is brittle at the node so when a gardener tries to pull the weed, the stem will break easily and generate new growth at the node. This category of weeds is particularly important to be able to identify because the weeds can be very aggressive, and can easily colonize an area if the root or buried stem systems are chopped-up and allowed to re-grow. Methods for controlling perennials often rely on depleting the energy reserves of these underground structures.

Figure 129: *Field bindweed is a common and troublesome perennial weed in Utah*

INTRODUCTION TO WEED CONTROL

In the organic garden, weed control techniques can be grouped into two main categories: cultural and mechanical techniques. Regardless of the technique used, the overarching goal of organic weed control is not to just control weeds in a single season, but to reduce the cumulative population of weed seeds in the soil, known as the weed seed bank. Up to 50% of the weed seed bank is deposited from the preceding year, therefore a focus on not letting weeds, particularly annuals, go to seed can significantly reduce weed pressure – and the labor required to control weeds – over time.

Although there are a number of herbicides labeled for use in organic production systems, their effectiveness may be limited, especially on mature weeds or perennials. These products are typically made from clove extracts, citric acid, or acetic acid. Vinegar can be used and may be somewhat effective depending on the species and life stage of the weed. Instead of relying on any of these products. it is advisable to develop a system whereby weeds are controlled through cultural and mechanical techniques working in concert to eliminate or reduce the weed pressure to acceptable levels.

CULTURAL WEED CONTROL TECHNIQUES

Cultural practices prevent weed seeds from germinating and suppress young weed seedlings from maturing. They are the principle way in which organic growers can reduce their reliance on cultivation, which disturbs and aerates the soil, thereby reducing organic matter levels.

Cover Crops

Using cover crops is one of the most powerful ways for the organic grower to provide short- and long-term weed control. Cover crops compete with weeds for resources and can effectively weaken the root structures of perennial crops. Many of the grass cover crops, such as cereal rye, secrete chemicals from their root systems that act as herbicides to prevent seeds from germinating. This attribute, termed allelopathy, is a very effective technique to prevent annual weed seeds from germinating, depleting the weed seed bank over time. In addition, when these plants are mixed with legumes, such as hairy vetch, they have the added benefit of increasing soil nitrogen levels. Cover crops can be planted throughout the year based on crop rotation. Fall planted mixtures could consist of rye and vetch, oats and winter peas, or wheat and crimson clover. Common summer cover crops are sorghum-Sudan grass, which is strongly allelopathic, buckwheat, which is an excellent attractant for pollinators and beneficial insects, or foxtail millet, which can be mixed with legumes such as clover. An excellent resource for information on cover crops is the book "Managing Cover Crops Profitably, 3rd Edition," by Andy Clark, Sustainable Agriculture Research and Education (SARE) program handbook series.

Figure 130: *Buckwheat cover crop at Salt Lake County Jail garden*

Mulching

Covering the soil with organic materials such as leaf or grass clippings, or straw or hay, can be an effective way to prevent weed seed germination. It is important that the material is deep enough to provide weed control because if weeds do break through the mulch, then cultivation is usually not possible and hand weeding must be done. Mulches, especially those that have a high carbon to nitrogen (C:N) ratio, can tie up nitrogen and may require additional fertilizer applications if applied too heavily. A critical aspect of using organic materials for mulch is to insure that they are not contaminated with weed seeds. This is especially true for straw and hay, but should be a general consideration for any inputs into the garden, such as compost or manure.

A highly effective mulching technique is to use black polyethylene plastic to cover the ground around the plants. This technique is common in commercial vegetable production but can also be used by the home gardener. In addition to weed control, the mulch moderates soil moisture when irrigation line is installed beneath it, heats the soil up earlier in the spring, and helps to keep vegetables cleaner by reducing soil contact. There are other materials such as landscape fabric that can be used in place of the plastic mulch. Although more expensive, this material is usually much more durable and can be used for multiple growing seasons.

***Figure 131:** Black plastic mulch*

Additional Cultural Practices

From a preventative perspective, it is important to make sure that awareness of weeds extends beyond just the garden area, and holistically manage the areas around the garden and yard. If weeds in the vicinity of the garden are allowed to set and disperse seed, this will continuously add to the seed bank, and limit the ability to reduce weed pressure.

Another powerful cultural practice is to restrict the placement of resources in the garden to just the desired garden plants. This is true for watering, such as with drip irrigation, and with placement of fertilizer. Anything done to deprive weeds of the resources they need to flourish can help to reduce their populations.

MECHANICAL WEED CONTROL TECHNIQUES

Mechanical weed control is sometimes referred to as physical weed control, and typically includes hand pulling, cultivation or some other technique to remove or suppress weeds after they have germinated. Mechanical techniques vary in their aggressiveness and ways in which they effectively kill weeds. The goal of all of these techniques is to use them at the proper time and to limit the degree of soil disturbance.

Stale Seed Bedding

This is a powerful technique that involves preparing a bed for planting a crop, then allowing weeds to just germinate and emerge from the soil so that they can be killed by shallow (1 to 2 inches) cultivation. If this can be done multiple times prior to

***Figure 132:** Shallow cultivation of garden weeds*

planting garden plants, the weed seed bank in the top part of the soil can be effectively depleted for that growing season. The reason this technique works so well is because most annual seeds can only germinate from near the soil surface; therefore, if only shallow cultivation is used no additional viable seeds will be brought up where they can germinate. Sometimes in dry periods irrigation may be required to promote weed seed germination.

Cultivation

There are multiple ways to kill a weed through cultivation, such as cutting it into pieces, burying it, exposing it to the soil surface to die from desiccation or crushing it. Organic growers commonly use cultivation tools which are designed to kill weeds in different ways. It is a good idea for the organic gardener to become familiar with the strengths and limitations of the various available tools, so they can be matched to the weed and soil conditions. Although there are many tools on the market they can be grouped based on their degree of aggressiveness or depth of cultivation.

One of the best tools for shallow cultivation is the stirrup hoe (**Figure 133**). This tool has a blade consisting of a piece of thin steel in a bracket that resembles a stirrup, and is mounted on a long wooden handle. The tool comes in several blade widths and is pushed back and forth just under the soil surface in a scuffle motion to kill weeds. A version of this tool for larger scale gardeners is called the wheel hoe (**Figure 134**). This tool has two long wooden handles attached to a frame that is connected to a wheel and the stirrup hoe blade. This configuration substantially increases the efficiency of cultivation. A discussion of the merits and uses of these tools can be found in the book "The New Organic Grower," By Elliot Coleman, Chelsea Green Publishing. Both of these tools are most effective when weeds are small in size.

When weeds become too large for shallow cultivation, tools such as grubbing or chopping hoes can be used (**Figure 135**). Although these tools are effective they should be viewed as a last line of defense and

Figure 133: *Stirrup hoe*

Figure 134: *Wheel hoe*

Figure 135: *Grubbing hoe*

not the primary tool of choice for organic weed control. In addition to being labor intensive, these tools can be so aggressive that they can expose viable seeds from deeper in the soil, perpetuating the weed problem.

For weeding very close to desired garden plants there are several tools to consider, but one of the most versatile is the soil knife. This tool can be used for precise removal of small- to medium-sized weeds and can cut out larger weeds with its serrated edge. Additionally this tool can be used to dig transplanting holes, divide plants and other functions typically done by a knife.

Flame Weeding

One additional technique that can be used for post-emergent weed control is flame weeding. Although it has recently gained popularity with home gardeners, this technique has been used in agriculture since the mid-1800s. Flame weeding uses propane gas from a tank equipped with a special nozzle that focuses the flame for a controlled application. You can find smaller hand held systems or those that are carried by backpack. The intense heat of the flame boils the water in the sap of the plant cells and causes the cells to be severely damaged. Once this happens, the leaves wilt, water movement in the plant stops and the plant dies. It is important to note that it only takes a few seconds to initiate this process, especially in small weeds. This technique works best on annuals and broadleaf weeds, but can be effective on perennials and grasses with repeat applications.

Flame weeding can be a particularly effective tool to control weeds in areas of the garden not amenable to cultivation, such as around sidewalks or gravel paths. If flaming is used close to established plantings, it is advisable to protect the plants from the intensity of the flame. You can do this by using a shovel to shield desired garden plants. Since the flame used with this technique is very hot you should check with local governing agencies on open flame restrictions and always practice appropriate precautions, especially around wood structures or during dry weather conditions. Never risk starting a fire for controlling weeds in the garden!

PREVENTION AND MANAGEMENT OF COMMON GARDEN DISEASES

Dr. Claudia Nischwitz, *USU Extension Plant Pathology Specialist*

ASK AN EXPERT

INTRODUCTION

Disease can be a gardener's worst nightmare; soon after plants are established and growing, disease hits and weakens them. Diseases of garden plants are also tricky to control because often the best management strategy is prevention. As with other pests, it is wise to learn about garden plant susceptibilities to different diseases and life-cycle biology of pathogens to prevent disease from ruining your garden harvest. This section will discuss 10 common garden diseases and organic controls.

Figure 136: *Shepard's Crook – Characteristic symptom of fire blight*

Goals of this Section:

- Learn how to identify common diseases of fruit and vegetable garden plants.
- Learn about the life-cycle of common garden diseases.
- Learn how to manage common garden diseases.

FIRE BLIGHT

Disease cycle

Fire blight is caused by the bacterium Erwinia amylovora. The bacteria infect members in the family Rosaceae including apple, crabapple, pear, ornamental pear, firethorns and other ornamentals. The first symptom is a dieback of new shoots from the tip down. The tip of the shoot is often bent downward which is characteristic for fire blight (**Figure 136**). If the bacteria can move through the vascular tissue in the shoot to larger branches and eventually the trunk, they cause cankers (**Figure 137**) (large wounds on the branch) from which bacteria ooze. Cankers reaching the trunk can kill the tree. The bacteria are spread by insects such as honey bees when they pollinate the flowers. Bees are attracted to cankers oozing bacteria because they smell sweet. When they land on the canker bacteria stick to them, which they then leave behind

Figure 137: *Apple branch with fire blight canker*

when visiting flowers. The bacteria can also be spread by water from sprinkler irrigation or rain splashing on oozing cankers. Occasionally fruit gets infected as well (**Figure 138**).

Figure 138: *Bacteria oozing from infected apple*

Management

Cultural control

To control fire blight in infected trees, it is very important to prune out infected shoots as soon as possible. The sooner infected branches are removed, the less the chances are for the disease to progress and kill the tree. Infected shoots should be cut off 8 to 12 inches beyond where the symptoms are visible. For example, if 6 inches of a branch are brown and dead, cut 14 to 18 inches of the branch off to stop the infection. This is necessary because the bacteria have already moved beyond the point where symptoms are seen. After removing an infected branch, wipe the blades of pruning tools thoroughly with disinfecting wipes or dip the blades in a 70% alcohol solution to disinfect them before you cut the next branch. Fire blight can be spread by pruning tools contaminated with E. amylovora.

Chemical control

Chemical control options are limited. There are copper-based products available, but they often have limited success in controlling the disease and if applied too late in the season can cause russeting of sensitive apple varieties. Copper products are used during the dormant season on overwintering fire blight cankers from which bacteria could ooze the following spring. Products such as Bordeaux mixture can be applied as a dormant treatment before bud break. Cueva (Certis USA) can be applied from the silver tip stage and bud break to petal fall following the label instructions. See the USU Extension fact sheet **Critical Temperatures for Frost Damage on Fruit Trees** for pictures of fruit tree bud stages.

Resistant varieties

Resistant varieties are a good option. However, none of these varieties are 100% resistant and in years with heavy fire blight pressure some shoots may still become infected and need to be pruned. Resistant apple varieties available include: Jonafree, Melrose, Northwestern Greening, Nova EasyGro, Prima, Priscilla, Quinte, RedFree, Sir Prize, Turley, Wellington and Winesap. Resistant pear varieties include: Honeysweet, Kieffer, LaConte, Magness, Moonglow, Old Home, Tyson and Waite. For more fireblight, see the USU Extension fact sheet **Fire Blight** and for more information on resistant varieties, see the Purdue University Extension fact sheet **Fire Blight on Fruit Trees in the Home Orchard**.

POWDERY MILDEW

Powdery mildews are caused by a group of fungi. Except for conifers like pine, spruce and fir, every plant species can get infected by at least one powdery mildew. Some powdery mildew fungi are host specific and others infect many different plants. For example, powdery mildew on grass will only infect other grasses or small grains but not ornamentals or vegetables. In contrast, Podosphaera pannosa (syn. Sphaerotheca pannosa) frequently found on roses can also infect peaches and some ornamentals.

Disease cycle

Powdery mildews produce two types of spores. Conidia, which are produced in the summer time for mass dispersal, and ascospores that are produced in fruiting structures (**Figure 139**) and can survive winter and other adverse conditions. In the spring when humidity is high and temperatures warm up, plants leaf out and ascospores are released and are washed or blown by wind onto the new leaves. The spores germinate and penetrate green plant tissue. Once established, the fungus grows across the leaf surface and starts producing conidia. The conidia give the leaves the appearance that they are covered in powder. The fungus starts producing conidia within 6 days after infection. The conidia are blown by wind to neighboring leaves or plants where they cause new infections. Conidia can also be spread by humans when spores get attached to clothes after walking past infected plants and are then deposited on healthy plants. In contrast to many other fungi, powdery mildews do not like free water such as water drops on leaves. High humidity is all they need for infection.

Figure 139: *Black fruiting structures, chasmothecia, on powdery mildew on maple leaf*

Management

Cultural control

When available, resistant varieties should be used. Some powdery mildews develop races over time and it is important to check to which races the varieties are resistant. For example, Podosphaera xanthii has at least three different races (1, 2 and 3). Resistant varieties are available for races 1 and 2 but not for race 3.

Variety trials at the USU Extension Kaysville research farm indicate that we currently have race 3 in Utah because all varieties resistant to races 1 and 2 became infected with the mildew.

Increasing plant spacing between plants allows for better airflow. Better airflow leads to reduced humidity and faster drying of leaves and subsequent reduced infections. To prevent infections through spreading spores on clothes, work in healthy plants first before you go to infected sections, and wash clothes afterwards.

Chemical control

Wettable sulfur works very well and is accepted for organic production for powdery mildew of cucurbits and other vegetables. It can be used for ornamentals as well but should be tested on a couple of plants first to determine if there is any phytotoxicity. Some plants are sensitive to sulfur and it may cause burns on the leaves. Leaves will also get burned if sulfur is applied above 90°F. During the summertime, apply sulfur very early in the morning or late in the evening after it cools down. There should be at least 4 hours after an application before temperatures reach 90°F again. You should begin spraying as soon as the first small white spots are detected on plants. Scout fields to detect infections early. Once the first infections occur sulfur needs to be applied every 7 to 10 days throughout the growing season. Once a leaf is partially or fully covered in mildew, sprays will be ineffective. Kaligreen (Potassium bicarbonate) is another product that can be used but it is not always as effective as sulfur.

BACTERIAL SPECK OF TOMATO

Disease cycle

Bacterial speck of tomato is caused by Pseudomonas syringae pv tomato. The disease can be seed-borne and the bacteria can survive on debris from last year's tomatoes and on weeds. Splashing water from irrigation or rain can spread the bacteria from the inoculum source to neighboring plants. The disease only affects tomatoes. Bacterial speck is often said to prefer cool, moist conditions, but this does not apply in Utah where a lot of samples come to the Utah Plant Pest Diagnostic Laboratory during the hot summer months. The first symptoms are small brown spots on foliage (**Figure 140**) and green fruit. When fruit ripens the spots are surrounded by a yellow halo (**Figure 141**). Infection occurs when fruit is green, even if symptoms are not visible until fruit is ripe. The symptoms look very similar to another bacterial disease called bacterial spot of tomato. The two can be differentiated by growing out the bacteria on artificial medium. Bacterial spot has not been detected in Utah.

Figure 140: *Symptoms of bacterial speck on tomato leaves*

Figure 141: Symptoms of bacterial speck on tomato fruit

Management

Management for bacterial speck is protective. Once the plants are infected, there is nothing that can be done.

Cultural control

When transplants are grown from seed it is important to purchase certified disease-free seed to avoid introduction of bacteria to fields and yards. Transplants at nurseries should be carefully inspected for any brown spots on the foliage. Spots on leaves are often also surrounded by a yellow halo.

If the disease was present in tomatoes in the previous year, tomatoes should be planted in a different section of the yard the following year and all plant debris from the tomatoes should be destroyed to reduce the amount of inoculum present and minimize chances of infection from bacteria being splashed on the tomatoes from rain and irrigation. Good weed control near the tomatoes also reduces the chance of infection.

Chemical control

There are some copper based products (for example copper hydroxide) that can be used but they have to be applied as a preventative during the growing season following the manufacturer's label. For more information on bacterial speck of tomato, see the UC Davis IPM fact sheet **Tomato Bacterial Speck** and the University of Florida Extension fact sheet **Bacterial Speck of Tomato**.

CURLY TOP OF VEGETABLES

There are seven viruses in the Curtovirus group that cause diseases on vegetables. The viruses are spread by the beet leafhopper (Circulifer tenellus). In Utah, so far we have detected severe Beet curly top virus and pepper curly top virus. The most commonly affected plants are tomatoes and peppers. However, pumpkins, squash, spinach and common beets can be infected as well.

Figure 142: Tomato plant infected with a curly top virus. Notice the leaves curled upward

Figure 143: Purple veins on a tomato leaf infected with a curly top virus

Figure 144: *Pumpkin plant infected with a curly top virus*

Figure 145: *Spinach plant infected with a curly top virus*

Disease cycle

In late spring when weeds in the foothills dry up, leafhoppers start moving to fields to look for food. Often the first plants encountered are tomatoes. The leafhoppers feed on the plants, realize they do not like the taste and move on. That is why you often do not find any leafhoppers on tomato plants that show symptoms. On tomatoes, symptoms consist of yellowing leaves that are curled upward (Figure 142) and often, the veins on the underside of the leaves turn purple (Figure 143). Plants are permanently stunted. On peppers symptoms are stunting of the plants, and some plants turn yellow. Infected pumpkins are also stunted and leaves are yellow (Figure 144). The symptoms on pumpkins resemble nutrient deficiency. Leaves of infected spinach plants are yellow, plants are stunted and leaves are crinkled (Figure 145). On common beets, leaves turn yellow and can be distorted (Figure 146). In addition when beet tubers are cut, the vascular tissue is discolored (Figure 147).

Management

Management of curly top is difficult. There are no resistant tomato varieties.

Cultural control

Young plants are more susceptible than older plants. Covering tomato and pepper plants with a fine mesh netting for the first 6-8 weeks after

Figure 146: *Foliage of common beet plant infected with a curly top virus*

Figure 147: *Discoloration of vascular tissue in common beet (healthy beet, left and infected beet, right)*

transplanting to prevent leafhoppers from feeding can reduce disease incidence.

Figure 148: *Necrotic lesion on tomato leaf infected with tomato spotted wilt virus (TSWV)*

TOMATO SPOTTED WILT VIRUS OF PEPPER AND TOMATO

Tomato spotted wilt virus (TSWV) has more than 1,000 known hosts, many of them weeds that do not show symptoms.

Disease cycle

TSWV is transmitted by thrips including western flower thrips that are common in Utah. Thrips have to acquire the virus as larvae to be able to transmit it as adults. Therefore, adult thrips have to lay eggs on

Figure 149: *Ringspots on pepper leaf infected with TSWV*

Figure 150: *Brown concentric rings on green tomato fruit infected with TSWV*

infected plants because thrips larvae cannot fly. One possibility of infection is in the spring when adult thrips lay eggs on infected, non-symptomatic weeds and their offspring acquire the virus. Once they are adults they fly to pepper and tomato plants and transmit the virus. A second possibility of infection is purchasing infected transplants at a nursery. Early symptoms are necrotic spot on tomato leaves (**Figure 148**) and ringspots on peppers (**Figure 149**). On green tomato fruit, brown concentric rings can be observed (**Figure 150**). Ripe tomatoes often have blotchy colors ranging from yellow to red (**Figure 151**). Peppers will also show blotchy color patterns of green and red (**Figure 152**).

Management

Cultural control

Once a plant is infected there is no cure. Infected plants should be removed immediately and destroyed. They will not produce marketable fruit and just serve as a source of inoculum from which neighboring plants become infected. If problems with the disease occurred in the previous year, the use of resistant tomato and pepper varieties can be an option. Resistant varieties can be found

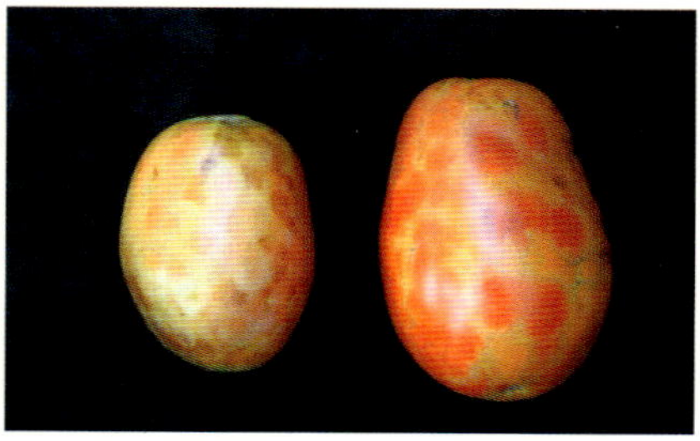

Figure 151: *Mature tomato fruit infected with TSWV*

Figure 152: *Mature jalapeno peppers infected with TSWV*

by an Internet search. Good weed control can reduce disease incidence, especially the removal of perennial weeds and volunteer tomatoes and peppers. The use of reflective mulch (silver colored) can reduce the number of thrips flying to the plants. Thrips control with insecticides is the most common way to prevent infection. For insecticide use in certified organic production, growers should check with their county Extension office or an entomologist to identify acceptable products.

TOBACCO MOSAIC VIRUS/ TOMATO MOSAIC VIRUS ON TOMATO AND PEPPER

Tobacco mosaic virus (TMV) and Tomato mosaic virus (ToMV) are closely related and the symptoms are the same. TMV was the first virus ever discovered and in contrast to many other plant viruses it can survive in plant debris for more than 50 years. This fact makes the virus very difficult to control.

Disease cycle

TMV/ToMV is seed borne and can be spread by handling infected plants or pruning plants with contaminated tools. Smokers can spread the virus on their hands after handling tobacco products that carry the virus. It is easy to spread the virus by hand. Just a tiny wound on the plant where the virus comes into contact with plant's sap is all that is needed. The virus does not have an insect vector which means there is no insects that can spread it. Most large-scale infections start out with a couple of plants infected through contaminated seed and then the virus is spread by hand or tools to other plants. Foliar symptoms can be very subtle and some tomato varieties may not show any foliar symptoms at all. Symptoms consist of a light and dark green mosaic pattern of the leaves (**Figure 153**). Fruit symptoms are more obvious. Brown spots and

Figure 153: *Mosaic pattern on tomato leaf caused by tobacco mosaic virus (TMV)*

Figure 154: *Brown spots on tomato fruit caused by TMV that extends into the flesh*

Figure 155: *Oak leaf pattern caused by TMV on pepper leaf*

circles appear on the skin of ripe fruit (**Figure 154**) that extend into the flesh under the skin. Leaf symptoms on pepper often show an oak-leaf pattern (**Figure 155**). Infected pepper fruit can show brown, necrotic spots and deformation.

Management

Cultural control

There is no cure for infected plants. Removal and destruction of infected plants is best. The plants should not be composted due to the longevity of the virus. There are TMV resistant hybrid tomatoes available but all heirlooms are susceptible. Cornell University posted a website with tomato varieties and their resistance level not only to TMV but other tomato diseases as well (**Vegetable MD Online**).

Pepper varieties listed as resistant include 'Jupiter', 'Bell Boy', 'Lady Bell' and 'North Star'. Other resistant varieties can be found online. For more information on TMV, see the Penn State University Extension fact sheet **Tobacco Mosaic Virus** and the University of Minnesota Extension fact sheet **Tomato-Tobacco Mosaic Virus Disease**.

POTYVIRUSES ON CUCURBITS

The group Potyviruses includes several viruses that infect cucurbits like zucchini, summer squash, winter squash and pumpkins. Among the Potyviruses are Papaya ring spot virus (PRSV) and Watermelon mosaic virus (WSV). In the last 2 years WSV caused significant yield losses to commercial growers.

Figure 156: *Mosaic symptoms caused by watermelon mosaic virus (WMV) on pumpkin*

Figure 157: Severe leaf deformation caused by WMV on pumpkin

Figure 158: Colorbreaking on "BabyBoo" pumpkin, part of the pumpkin stays green, caused by WMV

Disease cycle

Potyviruses are transmitted by aphids. Aphids feed on an infected plant and have virus particles stuck to their stylet. When they then feed on another plant, they deposit the virus particles in the plant during feeding and the plant becomes infected. Aphids do not carry Potyviruses in a persistent manner. They have to feed anew on an infected plant in order to acquire the virus again and transmit it.

Symptoms of Potyviruses are variable. Some viruses cause severe symptoms on leaves and fruit of susceptible varieties. Leaves can have subtle mosaic symptoms (**Figure 156**) or the symptoms can be severe, resembling herbicide (2,4-D) damage (**Figure 157**). Symptoms on fruit include color breaking (**Figures 158** and **159**), development of bumps (**Figure 160**) and smaller fruit and reduced yield.

Management

Cultural control

The use of resistant varieties is recommended when available. There are resistant zucchini, yellow squash and a few pumpkin varieties. There are no resistant winter squash varieties. Cornell University lists several resistant pumpkin varieties **Vegetable MD Online**, resistant zucchini varieties **Vegetable MD Online** and resistant summer squash varieties **Vegetable MD Online**. There are additional resistant varieties available.

Weeds and alfalfa can harbor Potyviruses. Good weed control especially of perennial weeds such as common mallow can reduce the

Figure 159: Colorbreaking on winter squash where - part of the squash stays green, caused by WMV

Figure 160: Deformation (warts) on young banana squash caused by WMV

amount of virus in the environment and reduce transmission. When alfalfa is grown nearby that has aphids, the application of an organically acceptable insecticide prior to cutting hay will reduce the amount of aphids moving to pumpkin and squash.

SEEDLING/TRANSPLANT DISEASES – DAMPING OFF

When growing plants from seed, there are a few things to consider that ensure high quality, healthy plants. There are several soil borne pathogens that can cause damping-off.

Disease cycle

Damping-off is caused by several different organisms that cause the disease including Pythium and Rhizoctonia. These fungi can survive in soil and on wooden benches. Once they come into contact with seedling roots, they colonize the roots and kill the plants. Plants turn brown to black and fall over (**Figure 161**).

Figure 161: *Damping off. The seedling in the middle is dying. Courtesy of Gerald Holmes, Valent USA Corporation*

Management

Cultural control

Preventing damping-off can be easily done with good sanitation. It is best to use new trays and pots to grow seedlings and transplants. If pots and trays are re-used from the previous year, make sure to clean them thoroughly and then put them in a 10% bleach solution for about 1 hour. After removing the pots and trays from the bleach, rinse them well with water so no chlorine residue is left. Tools used during sowing and benches should also be cleaned with a 10% bleach solution. Keep in mind that if you work in a certified organic system, bleach is not an option because it is not registered for organic production. When trays or pots are kept on wooden benches, put clean plastic tarp on the bench to prevent the plants from coming into contact with the pathogens. Placing pots and trays in individual saucers would isolate infections should one pot or tray show symptoms and prevent the spreading of the pathogens.

Seed should not be planted too deeply in the soil. Deep sowing puts additional stress on the seedling trying to come to the surface and exposes the plants longer to potential pathogens in the soil. Seedlings should be kept moist but never be excessively watered or left in water. Pythium especially likes it wet and its spores are motile and can swim in a film of water to roots and cause new infections.

Chemical control

There are no pesticides registered for damping-off in organic production.

Figure 162: *Dodder covering plants. The plant looks like tangled fishing line*

DODDER

Dodder (Cuscuta sp.) is a parasitic, seed-producing plant (Figure 162) that can colonize vegetables, ornamentals, alfalfa and potatoes. It can sometimes be seen on the side of the road looking like tangled fishing line.

Disease cycle

Seeds fall to the ground and germinate in the spring. The seedlings (Figure 163) locate a suitable host through the volatiles released by tomatoes and other plants. The chemicals are very distinct between plant species allowing dodder to find its preferred hosts. Once it comes in contact with a host it winds its vine around the host stem several times (Figure 164) and produces a root-like structure (haustorium) that penetrates the stem and establishes a feeding site. Nutrients and water from the host plant are now diverted to the dodder plant. When the contact between the dodder and host plant is established, the connection of the dodder to the ground will dry up. The plant continues to grow, attach itself to other parts of the plant and cover neighboring plants as well. Dodder flowers from late spring to fall and each plant can produce thousands of seed. Reports on seed longevity vary from 5 years to more than 20 years if no suitable host is present.

Management

Cultural control

Dodder is difficult to manage in an organic production situation. It is best to start out with seed that is free of dodder seed. If dodder was present in an area in the previous year, the amount of seedlings can be reduced by irrigating the area in the spring, waiting for the seedlings to germinate and die. Seedlings without a suitable host die within 5 to 10 days after germination. After the seedlings die, the area can be planted. This approach requires that

Figure 163: *Emerging seedlings. Courtesy of USDA APHIS PPQ Archive*

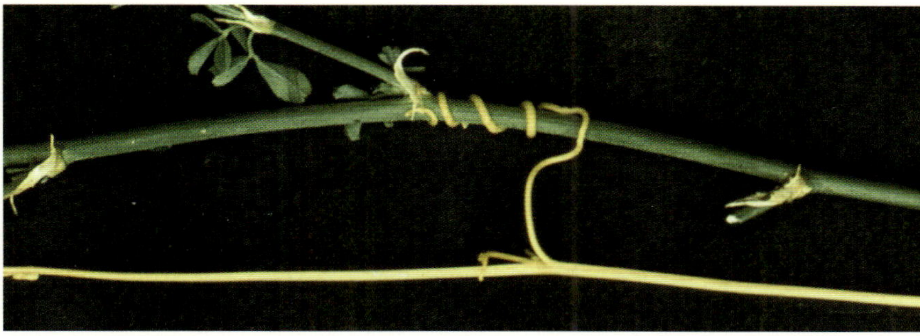

Figure 164: *Dodder plant attaches itself to a host. Courtesy of USDA APHIS PPQ Archive*

all weeds are removed as well since they can serve as a host, too. When dodder is encountered on perennial plants like alfalfa, cutting of dodder vines can reduce the amount of flowers produced and subsequent seed production. Vines that have been cut need to be removed from the field. Detached dodder vines can live and re-attach themselves to plants for several days before they die. For more information on dodder, see the Colorado State University Extension fact sheet **Dodder - A Plant Parasite**.

TABLE 29: IDENTIFICATION AND CONTROL OF COMMON DISEASES ON VEGETABLES

Plant Family	Disease or Disorder Name	Identification	Affected Plant Name(s)	Control
Composite (artichoke, chicory, lettuce, tarragon)	Fungal Root Rot	Wilting and reduced plant vigor, which occurs during forcing.	Chicory	Cultural practices that facilitate air movement will reduce disease severity.
	Leaf Blight	Reddish brown spots on leaf tips and margins; appear to be prematurely drying.	Lettuce	Hand remove blighted leaves.

Plant Family	Disease or Disorder Name	Identification	Affected Plant Name(s)	Control
Composite (artichoke, chicory, lettuce, tarragon)	Root Rot Disease	Fungal diseases reduce plant vigor and stands. Tips of leaves turn yellow, growing points die, whole stem and plant eventually dies. Buds are small and tough.	Artichokes, Tarragon	Reduce plant stress. Common stresses include insects, over watering, over cutting, drought and weed pressure.
	Viruses	Stunting of growth, interveinal yellowing and brittleness in older and lower leaves.	Artichokes, Chicory, Lettuce	Control aphids that transmit the disease.
	Tipburn (deficiency)	Nutrient deficiency which causes breakdown of the leaf tissue near the center of the head. Affected tissue becomes dry and brown or black.	Lettuce	Avoid excess fertilizer and water stress during head development. Keep plants evenly moist during growth.
Goosefoot (beet, spinach, swiss chard)	Leaf Spots	Fungal diseases that cause circular spotting on infected leaves.	Beet	Occurs when foliage remains wet for long periods. More common late in the year.
	Root Rots	Fungal diseases that cause decay and rotting of the root. May affect plant stands.	Beet	Crop rotation, improved soil drainage, and seed treatments are effective control options.
	Yellows	Yellow discoloration of plants.	Beet	Carried by leafhoppers. Cover plants with fabric mulch. No known control.

Plant Family	Disease or Disorder Name	Identification	Affected Plant Name(s)	Control
Gourd (cantaloupe, cucumber, pumpkin, summer and winter squash, watermelon)	Powdery Mildew	White fungal patches start on older leaves. The disease eventually spreads to all plant parts. The foliage dies, exposing fruits to the sun, which causes premature ripening.	Cantaloupe, Cucumber, Pumpkin, Summer and Winter Squash, Watermelon	Plant early-maturing or resistant varieties. Spring crops have less mildew problems than autumn plantings. Control weeds to eliminate hosts. Grow in full sun with good air circulation.
	Leaf Spot	Small transparent spots enlarge and darken, creating a target spot. Defoliation may cause fruit sun scald.	Cantaloupe, Watermelon	Practice crop rotation. Turn debris in as soon as possible after harvest and keep plants growing vigorously.
	Curly Top Virus	Young plants die without symptoms. Mature leaves yellow and die. New growth is dwarfed with shortened internodes and leaves are puckered and cupped out.	Cucumber	Transmitted by the beet leafhopper. Control insect. Remove affected plants. No other control.
	Virus	Leaves are light green, mottled, malformed, dwarfed and curled. Early infection affects fruit shape and flavor. Aphid transmitted disease.	Cantaloupe, Cucumber, Pumpkin, Summer and Winter Squash, Watermelon	Control aphids. Destroy severely infected plants.

Plant Family	Disease or Disorder Name	Identification	Affected Plant Name(s)	Control
Gourd (cantaloupe, cucumber, pumpkin, summer and winter squash, watermelon)	Wilt Disease	Leaves wilt on one or more vines. Plants often die. Streaking, slime formation or gummy exudates visible on stems. Diseases are caused by different pathogens.	Cantaloupe, Cucumber, Pumpkin, Summer and Winter Squash, Watermelon	Identify causal disease. Treat disease as recommended once identified.
Grass (popcorn, sweet corn)	Root Rots and Damping Off	Seedlings darken, wilt and die. Associated with cool, wet conditions in the spring.	Popcorn, Sweet Corn	Allow soils to dry before re-watering.
	Smut	White fungal galls that form on the tassel, stem or ear. Early plant infection will stunt growth and deform ears.	Popcorn, Sweet Corn	Remove and destroy galls and severely infected plants. Plant resistant varieties.
	Wilt Diseases	Wilting leaves, streaking and drying of leaves, stalk rotting, and plant lodging may occur. Plants often die.	Popcorn, Sweet Corn	Remove infected plants. Maintain clean garden practices.
Legume (beans, peas)	Curly Top Virus	Young plants die without symptoms. Mature leaves yellow and die. New growth is dwarfed with shortened internodes and leaves are puckered and cupped out.	Bean	Transmitted by the beet leafhopper. Control insect. Remove affected plants. No other control.

Plant Family	Disease or Disorder Name		Affected Plant Name(s)	Control
Legume (beans, peas)	Pod Rot	Irregular dark to gray brown spots that cover large contiguous areas. Infected leaves tear, making a ragged appearance.	Beans	Infections enter wounds under wet and damp conditions. Crop rotation and wide row spacing limit damage.
	Bean Blight	Small water soaked spots that enlarge and form large lesions on stems, leaves and pods.	Beans	Damp conditions favor this disease. Water carefully and allow soil to dry between irrigations.
	Fusarium Wilt	A downward curling of leaves and brittle stems. Stems and roots show yellow-orange discoloration within the vascular tissue. The disease occurs when soil temperatures exceed 70°F.	Peas	Plant resistant varieties. Plant early, so the crop develops before the soil reaches the optimum temperature for wilt development.
	Pea Enation Mosaic	Aphid transmitted virus disease. Leaves are mottled, crinkled and stunted and show white flecking on leaves and pods. Pods may be badly distorted.	Peas	Plant resistant varieties. Plant susceptible varieties early to avoid aphid infestation. Control aphids.

Plant Family	Disease or Disorder Name	Identification		Control
Legume (beans, peas)	Powdery Mildew	A powdery white fungus grows on the leaf and stem. Plants are dwarfed if infested early. Affected pods may develop small brown to black necrotic spots.	Peas	Plant early-maturing or resistant varieties. Spring seedings have less mildew problems than autumn plantings. Control weeds to eliminate hosts. Grow in full sun with good air circulation.
	Root Rot and Damping Off	Seedlings darken, wilt and die. Associated with cool, wet conditions in the spring.	Beans, Peas	Allow soils to dry before re-watering. Avoid compacted or wet soils. Seed in spring when soil is below 65°F. Avoid using too much nitrogen.
Lily (asparagus, chive, garlic, leek, onion)	Basal Rot	Fungal disease that attacks the area where roots and leaves join. The area rots and plant growth is slow and weak.	Leek, Onion	Use 5-year crop rotation. Solarize the soil where onions are to be planted. Avoid over-watering and improve soil drainage.

Plant Family	Disease or Disorder Name	Identification	Affected Plant Name(s)	Control
Lily (asparagus, chive, garlic, leek, onion)	Downey Mildew	Fungal disease that turns leaves a light tan to brown color. Furry growth, grayish violet in color, visible on the surface of infected leaves during moist periods.	Chives, Leek, Onion	Cultural practices that facilitate air movement and drying of leaves will reduce disease severity. Avoid overhead irrigation if regular problem.
	Neck Rot	Fungal disease that occurs during storage. Watery decay inside the bulb.	Onion, Garlic	Avoid excess moisture near harvest. Cure bulbs well before storing.
	Pink Root	Fungal disease that changes roots to a pink color. Roots eventually die and yields severely reduced.	Chives, Garlic, Onion	Use 5-year crop rotation. Solarize the soil where crops are to be planted.
	Root Rot	Tips of fern turn yellow, growing points die, whole stems and plants eventually die. Spears are small and skinny.	Asparagus	Reduce plant stress. Stresses include insects, over-watering, over cutting, drought and weed pressure.
	Iris Yellow Spot Virus	Dry, straw colored, diamond-shaped lesions on leaves. Leaves eventually die back.	Garlic, Leek, Onion	Control thrips which transmit the disease. Avoid drought stress. Do not over fertilize.
	Viruses	Viruses cause plants to decline and die. Yields decrease over several years.	Asparagus	Control aphids which transmit the disease.

Plant Family	Disease or Disorder Name	Identification	Affected Plant Name(s)	Control
Mint (basil, mint)	Anthracnose	Small water-soaked spots on leaves and stems.	Mint	Rotate planting areas, remove diseased plants and prune healthy plants to the ground in fall.
	Basil Shoot Blight	Fungal diseases that cause leaf spotting and premature loss of leaves. Dark streaks appear on the stems of older plants.	Basil	Keep the plants spaced far enough apart for adequate air circulation to keep plants dry.
	Mint Rust	Small whitish, slightly raised spots that turn reddish orange or brown on underside of leaves.	Mint	Avoid wet leaves overnight. Use drip irrigation or apply overhead water before mid-day.
	Root Rot Disease	Fungal diseases that cause decay and rotting of the roots and premature plant death.	Basil	Do not over water, practice crop rotations, and solarize the growing area.
	Verticillium Wilt	Leaf yellowing starting at the margin. Leaves eventually curl up and die.	Mint	Rotate planting areas, remove infected plants and do not over fertilize plants.
Mustard (broccoli, Brussels sprouts, cabbage, cauliflower, horseradish, kale, kohlrabi, mustard, radish, turnip)	Alternaria Leaf Spot	Damping off of seedlings. Leaf spots on leaves or heads are more common symptom. Spots form concentric circles and have a black sooty color.	Broccoli, Brussels Sprouts, Cabbage, Cauliflower	Avoid overhead irrigation. Practice good sanitation. Rotate crops.

Plant Family	Disease or Disorder Name	Identification	Affected Plant Name(s)	Control
Mustard (broccoli, Brussels sprouts, cabbage, cauliflower, horseradish, kale, kohlrabi, mustard, radish, turnip)	Powdery Mildew	A powdery white fungus grows on the leaf and stem. Plants are dwarfed if infested early. Affected pods may develop small brown to black necrotic spots.	Broccoli, Brussels Sprouts, Cabbage, Cauliflower	Plant early-maturing or resistant varieties. Spring crops have less mildew problems than autumn plantings. Control weeds to eliminate hosts. Grow in full sun with good air circulation.
	Root Rot	Fungal diseases that cause decay and rotting of the root. May affect plant stands.	Horseradish, Radish	Use crop rotation and improve soil drainage to improve control.
	Black Rot	Chlorosis of tissue beginning at leaf margins and spreading inward, creating v-shaped areas, veins within V blacken	Broccoli, Brussels Sprouts, Cabbage, Cauliflower	Use clean, disease-free seed or resistant cultivar. Rotate plantings and control weeds and insects.
	Boron (deficiency)	Nutrient deficiency which causes brown spotting on the head and hollow discolored stem below the head.	Broccoli, Cauliflower	Avoid excess fertilizer. May occur in high pH soils or where plants have been water stressed.
	Molybdenum (deficiency)	Nutrient deficiency which causes stunting of the plant and narrow, incompletely developed leaves to form.	Cauliflower	Use a complete fertilizer when growing transplants. Apply trace element mix to plants.

Plant Family	Disease or Disorder Name	Identification	Affected Plant Name(s)	Control
Mustard (broccoli, Brussels sprouts, cabbage, cauliflower, horseradish, kale, kohlrabi, mustard, radish, turnip)	Tipburn (deficiency)	Nutrient deficiency which causes breakdown of the leaf tissue near the center of the head. Affected tissue becomes dry and brown or black.	Brussels Sprouts, Cabbage	Avoid excess fertilizer and water stress during head development. Keep plants evenly moist during growth.
Nightshade (eggplant, pepper, potato, tomato)	Curly Top Virus	Young plants die without symptoms. Mature leaves yellow and die. New growth is dwarfed and leaves are puckered and cupped out. Fruit ripen prematurely and taste bitter.	Eggplant, Pepper, Potato, Tomato	Transmitted by the beet leafhopper. Control insect. Remove affected plants. No other control.
	Leaf Blights or Spots	Dark spots on stem, leaves or fruits. The diseases eventually spread to all plant parts. The foliage eventually dies, exposing fruits to the sun, which causes premature ripening.	Eggplant, Pepper, Potato, Tomato	Diseases promoted by cool, wet conditions. Do not overhead irrigate late in the day; let soil dry between waterings.
	Virus	Leaves are light green, mottled, malformed, dwarfed and curled. Early infection affects fruit shape and flavor. Viruses can be transmitted by aphids and leafhoppers, brushing against infected plants, or from tobacco products.	Pepper, Tomato	Control aphids. Destroy infected plants and weeds. Do not use tobacco products when handling plants.

Plant Family	Disease or Disorder Name	Identification	Affected Plant Name(s)	Control
Nightshade (eggplant, pepper, potato, tomato)	Various Wilt Diseases	Leaves wilt on one or more vines. Plants often die. Streaking, slime formation or gummy exudates visible on or in stems. Diseases are caused by different pathogens.	Pepper, Potato, Tomato	Identify causal disease. Plant resistant varieties that have V or F designated in their name. Crop rotation and soil solarization can help reduce wilt diseases.
	Blossom End Rot (BER disorder)	Blossom end rot is caused by a localized calcium deficiency brought on by poor water management, excessive nitrogen, root pruning and drought stress. Affected fruits become dry, brown or black on the flower end.	Pepper, Tomato	Better water and nutrient management can reduce BER.
	Cat-facing (disorder)	Catfacing is associated with cold weather during fruit set. Fruits are misshapen with unusual areas of growth.	Tomato	Early plantings often have cat-faced fruits on early trusses. Support structures, moist soils and warm weather help reduce these disorders.
	Sunscald (disorder)	During hot, dry weather fruits exposed to direct sunlight get sunburned. Exposed areas over-heat, dry out and do not color uniformly.	Eggplant, Pepper, Tomato	Maintain uniform soil moisture during hot weather. Big plants with good leaf cover have less sunscald problems.

Plant Family	Disease or Disorder Name	Identification	Affected Plant Name(s)	Control
Nightshade (eggplant, pepper, potato, tomato)	Tuber Greening (disorder)	Exposure of potato tubers to light in the garden or storage will form green pigments on the tuber surface. The chemicals produced (solanin) taste bitter after being cooked.	Potato	Keep tubers covered with soil in garden. Store in a dark, cool place. A small amount of green can be cut away but discard very green tubers.
	Tuber Greening (disorder)	Rough skins; cracking; small, irregular tuber shapes. Primarily caused by wet/dry soils or high soil temperatures.	Potato	Maintain uniform moisture conditions. Mulch heavily to regulate soil, water and temperature.
Parsley (carrot, celery, cilantro/ coriander, parsnip)	Damping Off or Seedling Rot	Death of new seedlings and yellowing of plants	Cilantro/ Coriander	Crop rotation. Use disease-free soil. Avoid crowding plants and discard affected plants.
	Leaf Blights	Fungal diseases that cause spotting on infected leaves.	Carrot, Parsnip	Occurs when foliage remains wet for long periods.
	Powdery Mildew	White fungal patches start on older leaves which will eventually die. The disease eventually spreads to all plant parts.	Celery	Plant resistant varieties. Use appropriate fungicides for control and water so the leaves have time to dry during the day.

Plant Family	Disease or Disorder Name	Identification	Affected Plant Name(s)	Control
Parsley (carrot, celery, cilantro/ coriander, parsnip)	Root Rots and Spots	Fungal diseases that cause decay and rotting of the root. Leads to forking and off-shaped roots.	Carrot, Parsnip	Crop rotation. Soil solarization
	Yellows	Yellow discoloration of plants.	Carrot, Parsnip, Cilantro/ Coriander	Carried by leafhoppers. Cover plants with fabric mulch. No known control.
	Black Heart (disorder)	Brown or black discoloration of the young leaves in the center of the plant. Affected tissue dies. Injury is not visible until later in the season. This disorder is a localize deficiency of calcium which is essential for cell development. Similar to BER or tipburn.	Celery	Control black heart applying calcium-rich fertilizers to the soil. Use bone meal, blood meal or calcium sprays. Avoiding water stress is a good way to minimize this problem.

INDEX

INTRODUCTION

Amendment (4, 5)
Certified Organic (4, 11-13)
Certified Organic Agriculture/ Farming (13)
Chemical (4, 11-12)
Clay (2, 3)
Climacteric fruits (15, 16)
Climate (1)
Community gardening or gardens (1, 20)
Community supported agriculture (CSA) (20)
Compaction (2)
Companion planting (4)
Compost (3, 15)
Container gardening (4)
Containers (20)
Cover crops (15)
Crop rotation (15)
Disease(s) (9)
Farmers market (15, 20)
Fertilize (4, 5, 11-13)
Flavor (15, 16)
Garden myth (4, 5, 11)
Genetically Modified Organisms (GMO) (GE) (12)
Insect (4, 9)
Insecticide (4)
Integrated Pest Management (15)
Irrigate (irrigation) (3, 9)
Manure (3, 4, 12, 15)
Mulch (4)
National Organic Program (NOP) (12, 13)
Natural enemies (4, 12)
Nitrogen (5)
Nutrient(s) (2, 3, 4, 12, 15-17)
Nutrient deficiencies (9)
OMRI website or Organic Materials review (4, 11, 13)
Organic farming (12)
Organic matter (2-5)
Pest (4, 9, 11-12, 15)
Pesticides (4, 11, 13)
pH (5, 16)
Phosphorus (5)
Potassium (5)
Potting mix (3)
Raised bed & raised bed gardening (3, 4)
Salt (5)
Sand (2, 3)
Soil test (4, 5)
Topsoil (3)
U.S. Department of Agriculture (USDA) (4, 11-13, 18)
Varieties/variety (15)
Weed(s) (9, 20)

GARDEN PREPARATION

American Disabilities Act (ADA) limited mobility (25, 57, 58)
Certified arborist (26)
Certified Organic (label) (27, 31)
Certified organic agriculture (32)
Chemical(s) (26, 33)
Clay (24)
Climate (28, 29, 50, 53)
Close-row (45)
Cold frame (30)
Cold hardiness/tolerance (27, 48)
Community gardening or gardens (24, 26)
Compaction (soil) (57, 58)
Compost (24, 25, 58-60)
Container gardening (57, 58)
Containers (42, 44, 53, 57, 58)

Cool season (41, 45, 47, 50, 51)
Crop rotation (41, 46)
Days to harvest (28, 31)
Days to maturity (27)
Disease(s) (26, 28-33, 42, 46, 61)
Drip irrigation (60, 61)
Fertilizer (55, 56, 58, 60, 61)
Flavor (29)
Frost (25, 26, 28, 47-50, 53)
Garden layout (23, 41)
Genetically Modified Organisms (GMO) (GE) (27, 28, 32, 33)
Greenhouse (30)
Hardening (55, 56)
Heirloom (27-31, 34-39)
High tunnel (30)
Hybrid (27-32, 34-39)
Insect (28, 30, 32, 33, 46)
Irrigate (irrigation) (25, 26, 30, 60, 61)
Mulch (30, 51, 60)
Nitrogen (24, 55, 59)
Nutrient(s) (24, 25, 32, 56, 60, 61)
Nutrient deficiencies (60)
Open pollinated (27-31)
Organic matter (24, 59, 60)
Pest (26-30, 32, 46)
Pesticides (26, 33)
Phosphorus (24, 55)
Pollination (chart) (30)
Pollution (59)
Potassium (24, 55)
Potting mix (53, 55, 57, 58, 60)
Raised bed & raised bed gardening (44, 46, 57-60)
Rootstock (30)
Salt (24, 59, 60)
Sand (24)
Season extension (58)
Site selection (23, 26)
Soil test (24, 60, 61)
Topsoil (24, 60)
U.S. Department of Agriculture (USDA) (27, 31, 33)
Varieties/variety (27-31, 34-38, 50, 53)
VFN (32)
Warm season (41, 45, 47, 51)
Weed(s) (23, 25, 26, 57, 58, 60, 61)

ORGANIC GARDENING TECHNIQUES

Bee(s) (84)
Beneficial insects (70, 73)
Biological (70, 71, 77, 79)
Certified arborist (100-102)
Certified Organic (65, 66)
Chemical(s) (69-73, 75, 107)
Chilling requirements (81, 85)
Climate (79, 85, 88, 90, 92, 97, 107)
Cold frame (108, 110)
Cold hardiness/tolerance (82, 83, 86, 97, 107)
Companion planting (70, 71)
Compost (65-70, 75, 77)
Containers (97)
Cool season (67, 107)
Cover crops (65, 68, 76, 79)
Cultural control (71)
Crop rotation (74, 76, 79)
Disease(s) (65, 66, 69, 70, 75, 77, 79, 82, 86, 94, 97, 100, 102, 105, 108)
Drip irrigation (108)
Fertilize (65-67, 69, 72, 77, 78, 94, 97, 98)
Flame weeding (77)
Flavor (87-97)
Floating row cover (74, 107, 109)
Freeze-free period (107)
Frost (82, 83, 85, 96, 109, 110)
Garden myth (82, 94)
Greenhouse (67, 107, 108, 110, 111)
Heirloom (83)
High tunnel (108, 110, 111)
Hybrid (83)
Insect (65, 69-75, 77, 82, 84)
Insecticide (66)
Iron chlorosis (98)
Irrigate (irrigation) (69, 76, 82, 98, 108)
Legumes (72)
Loam (96, 97)
Low tunnel (109, 111)
Locate (97)
Manure (68, 69, 110)
Mechanical (control) (75-77)
Mulch (72, 74-77, 98, 105, 107, 108)
Nitrogen (67, 72)

Nurse cropping (72)
Nutrient(s) (66-69, 78, 79, 98)
Nutrient deficiencies (69, 98)
Organic farming (78)
Organic matter (68, 87, 97, 98)
Pest (65, 66, 69-72, 74, 75, 77-82, 86, 96, 98, 109)
Pesticides (65, 71, 72, 75, 78)
pH (66, 68, 69)
Physical control (71, 74)
Planting (86, 87, 98)
Pollination (chart) (81, 84, 85, 90-94)
Pollution (69)
Potting mix (66, 67)
Pruning (81, 82, 85, 96, 98-105)
Raised bed & raised bed gardening (108, 109)
Root flare (87)
Rootstock (85, 86)
Row cover (108)
Salt (66)
Sand (96, 97)
Season extension (79, 107, 108, 111)
Site selection (83)
Soil test (68, 69, 98)
Solarization (77, 108)
Stale seedbeds (76, 77)
Thin (94, 95, 101, 102, 104)
Training (102)
Trap crop (71-73)
USU Botanical Center (Kaysville) (83, 87)
USU Research Farm (Kaysville) (103)
U.S. Department of Agriculture (USDA) (65, 82, 83)
Varieties/variety (69, 77, 81-98)
Warm season (67, 107, 108, 110)
Weed(s) (65, 66, 68, 69, 72, 75-79, 96, 107, 108)

GARDEN SOIL

Amendment (117, 118, 123-129)
Chemical(s) (123)
Clay (115-119, 124, 127, 131)
Compaction (121, 124, 128)
Compost (123, 125-128, 131-135)
Disease(s) (121, 132)
Fertilize (116, 118, 129, 133, 134)
Garden myth (115, 118, 121, 127, 129)
Irrigate (irrigation) (116, 121-123)
Loam (117-119, 127)
Manure (123, 126, 129)
Mulch (125, 128)
Nitrogen (119, 128, 129, 131-134)
Nutrient(s) (115-119, 121, 124, 125, 127, 129, 131)
Nutrient Deficiencies (122)
Organic Matter (115-119, 122, 124-134)
Pest (121)
pH (119, 121-123, 131)
Phosphorus (119, 122)
Potassium (119, 123)
Raised bed & raised bed gardening (117, 122, 124)
Salt (118, 119, 121, 123, 124, 127, 129)
Sand (115, 116, 118, 119, 126, 127, 131)
Silt (115-117, 119)
Sodic (122, 123)
Soil test (115, 118, 119, 123, 124, 127)
Topsoil (116-118, 127)
Weed(s) (128, 132, 135)

ORGANIC GARDEN CARE

Abiotic disorder (160-162)
Amendment (143, 144, 162, 181)
Bee(s) (173-177, 180)
Beneficial insects (179, 180, 182)
Biological (179, 180)
Botanical (179)
Certified arborist (182)
Certified Organic (label) (142, 144, 179, 180)
Certified organic agriculture (146)
Chemical (140, 180, 184, 185)
Chicken (162-165, 185)
Clay (140, 181)
Climate (167, 173)
Compaction (160, 184, 185)

Compost (141, 145, 146, 156, 158, 181, 183-185)
Cover crops (158-160, 181, 183-186)
Cultural control (179, 180)
Disease(s) (163, 181)
Drip irrigation (167, 169, 170, 172)
Fertilize (139-158, 162, 183)
Frost (161, 162, 183)
Garden myth (142, 144, 147, 168, 180)
Genetically Modified Organisms (GMO) (GE) (148)
Insect (142, 176, 179)
Insecticide (179, 180)
Integrated Pest Management (IPM) (180)
Iron chlorosis (142, 143, 161)
Irrigate (irrigation) (143, 160-162, 167-172, 181, 182)
Legumes (146, 158-160, 183-185)
Manure (141, 144-146, 158, 183)
Mechanical (control) (179, 180)
Mulch (182, 184, 185)
Natural enemies (158, 179)
Nitrogen (139-141, 143, 145-160, 162, 181, 183-186)
Nutrient(s) (139-149, 163, 185, 186)
Nutrient deficiencies (143, 145)
OMRI website or Organic Materials review (142, 144, 146, 179, 180)
Organic matter (140-147, 156, 158, 160, 161, 168, 181, 184-186)
Personal protective equipment (180)
Pest (139, 142, 165, 171, 175, 179, 180, 185, 186)
Pesticide (148, 161, 179, 180)
Phosphorus (139-141, 143, 145, 146, 148-150, 156)
Planting (182)
Pollination (162, 173, 182)
Pollution (140, 141, 144)
Potassium (139, 140, 142, 145)
Potash (140, 142, 143, 146)
Prune (162, 182)
Raised bed & raised bed gardening (183)
Salt (142, 146, 161)
Sand (140, 168, 169)
Season extension (161, 181)
Silt (140)
Soil test (140-142, 144-146, 149, 156, 161)
Sunscald (161, 182)
U.S. Department of Agriculture (USDA) (144, 146, 179, 180)
Varieties/variety (150)
Warm season (161, 183)
Weed(s) (146, 158, 160, 179, 181, 184, 186)
Winter injury (southwest) (161, 182)

GARDEN PEST CONTROL

Abiotic disorder (191)
Bee(s) (190, 195, 200, 202, 213, 215, 218, 239, 240, 245-247, 257)
Beneficial insects/organisms (189, 190, 197, 198, 200, 212, 213, 215, 224-226, 233, 246, 252)
Biological (190, 193, 200, 202, 213, 215, 219, 223, 226)
Botanical (201)
Certified Organic (label) (189, 201, 207, 209, 210)
Certified organic agriculture (231, 232, 264, 267)
Chemical(s) (189, 190, 193, 221, 235, 252, 258, 260, 261, 267, 268)
Chicken(s) (199, 230, 235, 241)
Climate (197)
Compost (198, 252, 265)
Cover crops (251, 252)
Cultural control (190, 193, 197, 200, 202, 213, 251, 253, 258, 259, 261-263, 265-269 274)
Crop rotation (208, 252, 270, 271, 274-277, 279-281)
Days to harvest (275)
Degree-days (DD) (196, 197)
Disease(s) (189, 191, 199, 204, 211, 220, 230, 249, 257-267, 269-281)
Drip irrigation (253, 275)
Fertilizer (226, 230, 243, 252, 253, 270, 274-278, 281)
Flame weeding (255)
Flavor (271)

Floating row cover (199, 212)
Frost (247, 258)
Greenhouse (191, 217-219, 222, 223, 225)
Heirloom (265)
High tunnel (217)
Insect (189, 191, 194-199, 203-213, 215, 217-223, 226, 227, 229-231, 233-240, 242, 245-247, 249, 257, 264, 270, 274, 277, 278)
Insecticide (192, 207-213, 220, 224, 226, 237, 340-247, 264, 267)
Integrated Pest Management (IPM) (189, 191, 193, 195, 197, 200, 202, 213, 226, 227, 230, 235)
Iron chlorosis (199)
Irrigate (irrigation) (199, 225, 228, 243, 252, 258, 260, 261, 268, 264, 275, 278)
Legumes (241, 252, 254, 272)
Manure (198, 226, 251)
Mechanical (control) (190, 192, 193, 199, 202, 213, 251, 253)
Mulch (192, 198, 203-206, 208, 209, 211, 213, 238, 245, 252, 253, 264, 270, 280, 281)
Natural enemies (189, 193, 196, 200, 202, 212, 213, 215, 217, 219, 223-227, 234, 236, 239, 241, 244, 246, 247)
Nitrogen (250, 252, 273, 279)
Nutrient(s) (191, 198, 249, 250, 268)
Nutrient deficiencies (262, 270, 277, 278)
Organic farming (208)
Organic matter (198, 200, 243, 249, 251, 252, 262, 270, 277, 278)
Personal protective equipment (247)
Pest (189-205, 209, 210, 213, 215-218, 220-227, 231, 233, 235, 238-242, 244-247, 249, 250, 257)
Pesticides (189, 190, 193, 197, 200-202.213, 220,221, 223-226, 231, 247, 267)
pH (27.7)
Pollination (202, 257)
Pollinators (190, 193, 196, 197, 212, 213, 218, 252)
Prune (199, 236, 241, 258, 259, 276, 279)
Site selection (243)
Soil test (250)
Solarization (273-276, 279, 281)
Stale seedbeds (253)
Sunscald (238, 271)
Trap crop (198)
USU Botanical Center (Kaysville) (250)
USU Research Farm (Kaysville) (260)
Varieties/variety (212, 213, 258-260, 263-266, 272, 273, 276, 277, 279, 280)
Weed(s) (189, 191, 199, 200, 206, 230, 238, 245, 249-255 260-264, 266, 268, 270 273, 274, 277, 278)

TABLES

1. Listing of Climacteric and non-climacteric fruits and vegetables.
2. Suggested Vegetable Varieties for Utah.
3. Traditional Row Spacing.
4. Close-row Planting.
5. Vegetable Planting Groups and Suggested Vegetable Planting Dates for the Wasatch Front (Outdoors).
6. Average Last Spring Frost and Suggested Vegetable Planting Dates for Various Locations in Utah.
7. Optimal Soil Temperature Ranges for Seed Germination and Days to Germination of Garden Plants.
8. Suggested Schedule for Starting Transplants Indoors.

9. Suggested Schedule for Starting Transplants Indoors in Washington County Area.
10 Online Retailers that Sell USDA Certified Organic Seed.
11. Soilless Potting Mix Recipe.
12. Traditional Recommendations of Compatible Plant Associations.
13. Tree Fruit Pollination Guide.
14. Common Soil Amendment Characteristics.
15. Common Composting Problems and Solutions.
16. Average Nutrient Concentrations and Rates of Availability for Various Organic Materials.
17. Commonly Available Organic Fertilizers.
18. Fertilization Recommendations for Various Fruit and Vegetable Garden Plants.
19. Commonly Used Cover Crops, Their Growth Characteristics, and Seeding Rate Recommendations.
20. 10 Common Abiotic Fruit and Vegetable Plant Disorders for Utah Gardens.
21. Irrigation Set Time Recommendations for Common Drip Irrigation.
22. Irrigation Guidelines for Various Garden Plants and Growth Stages.
23. Identification and Control of Common Insect Pests on Vegetables.
24. Quick Guide to Naturally Occurring Beneficial Predators.
25. Quick Guide to Commercially Available Parasitoids.
26. Quick Guide to Entomopathogens.
27. Quick Guide to Entomopathogens.
28. Insecticides for Organic Fruit Production.
29. Identification and Control of Common Diseases on Vegetables.

FIGURES

1. USDA certified organic label. Available at www.ams.usda.gov.
2. Most garden plants require six to eight hours of direct sun daily. iStock Photo #15597591.
3. If positioned poorly, tall garden plants may shade lower growing plants. iStock Photo #7571098.
4. Consider placement of garden pathways before planting garden beds. Photo courtesy of Shawn Olsen.
5. Using good sanitation practices, like picking-up and discarding fruit at the end of the growing season, is one technique to reduce the likelihood of pests popping up in your garden. Photo by Katie Wagner.
6. Male and female flower parts on corn plants. iStock Photo #12021993.
7. Example Garden Plan. Illustration by Olivia Yeip.
8. Gardener planting onion sets. iStock Photo #19462054.
9. Tomato plants trained-up a vertical structure with their lower branches pruned to provide ideal growing conditions for herbs planted underneath
10 Soil Thermometer. iStock Photo #12552284.
11. Red spinach seedlings growing under florescent lights. Photo by Travis Snyder.

12. A container garden. Photo courtesy of Shawn Olsen.
13. Unframed raised bed. iStock Photo #20400823.
14. Raised bed made of lumber. iStock Photo #3131210.
15. Raised bed planted in block pattern. iStock Photo #19215584.
16. Soaker hose placed around tomato plant. Photo by Ron Nichols, USDA Natural Resources Conservation Service.
17. Seedling emerging from potting mix. iStock Photo #590441.
18. Earthworms are an indication of soils with adequate organic matter content. iStock Photo #12472009.
19. Lady bird beetle adult gorging on aphids. iStock Photo #12578718.
20. Floating row cover. iStock Photo #11828062.
21. Straw mulch. iStock Photo # 20683904.
22. Asparagus, a long-lived garden perennial. Photo by Katie Wagner.
23. USU Student Organic Farm. Photo by Amanda Hawks.
24. Demonstration orchard at the USU Botanical Center. Photo by Shawn Olsen.
25. Pollination chart of apple varieties. Illustration by Olivia Yeip.
26. Effect of different dwarfing rootstock on the same apple variety. Illustration from Virginia Cooperative Extension fact sheet, Tree Fruit in the Home Garden. Illustration altered by Olivia Yeip.
27. Illustration of tree planting. Illustration from USU Extension fact sheet, Planting Landscape Trees. Illustration altered by Olivia Yeip.
28. Apple cluster that should have been thinned to one fruit earlier in the season. iStock Photo #14366053.
29. Basic pruning tools. Illustration by Olivia Yeip.
30. Basic plant framework. Illustration from USU Extension fact sheet, Pruning the Orchard. Illustration altered by Olivia Yeip.
31. Basic pruning cut - Left: Thinning, Right: Heading. Illustration by Olivia Yeip.
32. Prune fruit trees when buds are dormant. iStock Photo #9036171.
33. Central Leader. Illustration by Olivia Yeip.
34. Modified Leader. Illustration from Virginia Cooperative Extension fact sheet, Growing Pears in Virginia. Illustration altered by Olivia Yeip.
35. Open Center. Illustration by Olivia Yeip.
36. Quad V. Illustration by Olivia Yeip.
37. Four-cane Kniffin system for grapes. Illustration from University of Minnesota Extension fact sheet, Growing Grapes for Home Use. Illustration altered by Olivia Yeip.
38. Pruning raspberries. Illustration from University of Missouri Extension fact sheet, Pruning Raspberries, Blackberries and Gooseberries. Illustration altered by Olivia Yeip.
39. Pruning black and purple raspberries. Illustration from University of Missouri Extension fact sheet, Pruning Raspberries, Blackberries and Gooseberries. Illustration altered by Olivia Yeip.
40. Pruning trailing blackberries. Illustration from University of Missouri Extension fact sheet, Pruning Raspberries, Blackberries and Gooseberries. Illustration altered by Olivia Yeip.

41. Blackberries growing on a trellis. Photo by Katie Wagner.
42. Lettuce planted in black plastic mulch. iStock Photo #21833999.
43. Looking inside a plastic low tunnel. Photo by Travis Snyder.
44. Plastic low tunnel over raised bed. Photo by Travis Snyder.
45. Cold frames in front with greenhouse in back. iStock Photo #14420335.
46. Looking inside a plastic high tunnel. Photo by Dennis Hinkamp.
47. High tunnel made of PVC pipe hoops and covered with plastic. Photo by Dennis Hinkamp.
48. Soil texture triangle. Courtesy of: soils.usda.gov.
49. Loam textured garden soil. iStock Photo #3327143.
50. Till or mix amendments into existing soil. Drawing by Barbara Gustaveson.
51. Soil test in progress. Photo courtesy of Grant Cardon.
52. Plant wilting can be a symptom of multiple garden stresses. Photo by Katie Wagner.
53. Garden furrows can serve as walkways. Photo by Katie Wagner.
54. Organic mulch ready to spread in the garden. iStock Photo #14570773.
55. Simple compost pile. iStock Photo #12146723.
56. Compost bins constructed from pallets. Photo by Katie Wagner.
57. Grapes may not require additional fertilizer. Photo by Travis Snyder.
58. Bountiful harvests grow from properly nourished plants. Photo by Travis Snyder.
59. Lake water polluted by fertilizer run-off. iStock Photo #10618937.
60. Iron chlorosis on strawberry leaves. iStock Photo #26013032.
61. Label on bag of organic fertilizer. Photo by Travis Snyder.
62. Perennial garden plants, like strawberries, benefit from a slow and steady release of nutrients. Photo by Katie Wagner.
63. Composted animal manures provide a good source of plant nutrients. iStock Photo #7184696.
64. Buckwheat cover crop in bloom; seeds will form soon. Photo by Katie Wagner.
65. Rhode Island Red laying hen. Photo by Travis Snyder.
66. Slugs and snails are considered a delicacy to hungry backyard hens. iStock Photo #4658141.
67. Chard growing in the garden. Photo by Katie Wagner.
68. Drip irrigation system tested and garden row ready to plant. Photo by Katie Wagner.
69. Drip irrigation layout. iStock Photo #7505075.
70. Irrigating the orchard. iStock Photo #9215546.
71. Dripline of tree. Courtesy of International Society of Arboriculture.
72. Queen surrounded by workers. Photo by James Barnhill.
73. Langstroth hive. Photo by James Barnhill.
74. Package of honey bees. Photo by James Barnhill.
75. Beekeeper tending hive. iStock Photo #7522093.
76. Honey-filled comb ready for harvest. Photo by James Barnhill.
77. Extracted and filtered honey. Photo by James Barnhill.
78. Illustration of 'Pesticide' umbrella concept. Illustration by Olivia Yeip.

79. Take precautions to protect bees and other beneficial insects. Photo by Travis Snyder.
80. Plan on taking a much deserved break – after completing fall garden chores! iStock Photo #20434906.
81. Some garden vegetables, like carrots, can be mulched-over with leaves or straw and harvested late into the fall. iStock Photo #20434906.
82. Plan to prune fruit trees early spring before bud break. iStock Photo #11774923.
83. Fall pumpkin field. iStock Photo #4519162.
84. Winter cover crop planted in raised bed. Photo by Katie Wagner.
85. Bumblebee visiting sunflower. Photo by Travis Snyder.
86. Earwig trap. Photo by Diane Alston.
87. Diagram of IPM building blocks. Illustration from USU Extension fact sheet, The Integrated Pest Management Concept. Illustration altered by Olivia Yeip.
88. Squash bugs on pumpkin. iStock Photo #4092480.
89. Demonstrating use of a hand lens. Photos by Diane Alston.
90. Pherocon AM yellow sticky trap for monitoring cherry fruit fly. Photo by Diane Alston.
91. May 10, 2013, pest advisory of spray application timing for codling moth control. Available at utahpests.usu.edu.
92. Table of short- and long-term pest management tactics. Illustration from USU Extension fact sheet, Important Components of a Successful Pest Management Program. Illustration altered by Olivia Yeip.
93. Alyssum used as a ground cover. iStock Photo #9562434.
94. Corrugated cardboard strip with codling moth cocoon and pupa. Photo by Diane Alston.
95. Syrphid fly adult feeding at a flower. iStock Photo #29463716.
96. Bacillus thuringiensis (Bt) is an organically certified chemical control option for tomato hornworm. iStock Photo #26508495.
97. Home gardener applying an organic pesticide with a hand-pump sprayer wearing personal protective equipment. iStock Photo #19965418.
98. Praying mantis. Photo by Travis Snyder.
99. Lady beetle larva, pupa, and adult. Photo 1: Photo by Travis Snyder, Photo 2: iStock Photo #25480531, Photo 3: iStock Photo #14485738.
100. Green lacewing adult. iStock Photo #29352540.
101. White cocoons attached to a host caterpillar. iStock Photo #9362781.
102. Larvae infected with nematodes. Photo by Ricardo Ramirez.
103. Diverse garden planting. Photo by Katie Wagner.
104. Cilantro flowers are attractive to many natural enemies. iStock Photo #33472428.
105. Asian lady beetle. iStock Photo #1166430.
106. Ant protecting aphids. iStock Photo #8758604.
107. Kestrel feeding on prey. iStock Photo #22658664.
108. Barn owl nesting in tree cavity. iStock Photo #1804467.
109. Robin perched on handle. iStock Photo #19756148.

110. Bat hanging on tree bark. iStock Photo #5790828.
111. Aphids on cabbage plant. Photo by Marion Murray.
112. Spider mite damage. Photo by Marion Murray.
113. Codling moth damage to apple. Photo by Marion Murray.
114. Woolly apple aphid. Photo by Marion Murray.
115. San Jose scale. Photo by Marion Murray.
116. Blister mites. Photo by Marion Murray.
117. Pear psylla damage. Photo by Marion Murray.
118. Greater peachtree borer. Photo by Marion Murray.
119. Peach twig borer. Photo by Marion Murray.
120. Thrips damage. Photo by Marion Murray.
121. European paper wasp. Photo by Marion Murray.
122. Adult Western cherry fruit fly on coloring fruit. Photo by Marion Murray.
123. Western cherry fruit fly larve in cherry. Photo by Marion Murray.
124. Raspberry horntail. Photo by Marion Murray.
125. Raspberry crown borer. Photo by Marion Murray.
126. Rose stem girdler. Photo by Marion Murray.
127. Root weevil damage. Photo by Marion Murray.
128. Clover growing next to a vegetable garden at the USU Botanical Center. Photo courtesy of Shawn Olsen.
129. Field bindweed is a common and troublesome perennial weed in Utah. iStock Photo #3377320.
130. Buckwheat cover crop at Salt Lake County Jail garden. Photo by Katie Wagner.
131. Black plastic mulch. iStock Photo #21833999.
132. Shallow cultivation of garden weeds. iStock Photo #12126190.
133. Stirrup hoe. Photo by Mark Williams.
134. Wheel hoe. Photo by Mark Williams.
135. Grubbing hoe. Photo by Mark Williams.
136. Shepard's Crook – Characteristic symptom of fire blight. Photo by Claudia Nischwitz.
137. Apple branch with fire blight canker. Photo by Claudia Nischwitz.
138. Bacteria oozing from infected apple. Photo by Claudia Nischwitz.
139. Black fruiting structures, chasmothecia, on powdery mildew on maple leaf. Photo by Claudia Nischwitz.
140. Symptoms of bacterial speck on tomato leaves. Photo by Claudia Nischwitz.
141. Symptoms of bacterial speck on tomato fruit. Photo by Claudia Nischwitz.
142. Tomato plant infected with a curly top virus. Notice the leaves curled upwards. Photo by Claudia Nischwitz.
143. Purple veins on a tomato leaf infected with a curly top virus. Photo by Claudia Nischwitz.
144. Pumpkin plant infected with a curly top virus. Photo by Claudia Nischwitz.
145. Spinach plant infected with a curly top virus. Photo by Claudia Nischwitz.
146. Foliage of common beet plant infected with a curly top virus. Photo by Claudia Nischwitz.

147. Discoloration of vascular tissue in common beet (healthy beet, left and infected beet, right). Photo by Claudia Nischwitz.
148. Necrotic lesion on tomato leaf infected with tomato spotted wilt virus (TSWV). Photo by Claudia Nischwitz.
149. Ringspots on pepper leaf infected with TSWV. Photo by Claudia Nischwitz.
150. Brown concentric rings on green tomato fruit infected with TSWV. Photo by Claudia Nischwitz.
151. Mature tomato fruit infected with TSWV. Photo by Claudia Nischwitz.
152. Mature jalapeno peppers infected with TSWV. Photo by Claudia Nischwitz.
153. Mosaic pattern on tomato leaf caused by tobacco mosaic virus (TMV). Photo by Claudia Nischwitz.
154. Brown spots on tomato fruit caused by TMV that extends into the flesh. Photo by Claudia Nischwitz.
155. 'Oak leaf' pattern caused by TMV on pepper leaf. Photo by Claudia Nischwitz.
156. Mosaic symptoms caused by watermelon mosaic virus (WMV) on pumpkin. Photo by Claudia Nischwitz.
157. Severe leaf deformation caused by WMV on pumpkin. Photo by Claudia Nischwitz.
158. Colorbreaking on "BabyBoo" pumpkin, part of the pumpkin stays green, caused by WMV. Photo by Claudia Nischwitz.
159. Colorbreaking on winter squash - part of the squash stays green, caused by WMV. Photo by Claudia Nischwitz.
160. Deformation (warts) on young banana squash caused by WMV. Photo by Claudia Nischwitz.
161. Damping off. The seedling in the middle is dying. Photo courtesy of Gerald Holmes, Valent USA Corporation.
162. Dodder covering plants. The plant looks like tangled fishing line. Photo by Claudia Nischwitz.
163. Emerging seedlings. Photo courtesy of USDA APHIS PPQ Archive.
164. Dodder plant attaches itself to a host. Photo courtesy of USDA APHIS PPQ Archive.

PICTURES

Front Cover

- Vegetables in basket. iStock Photo #14393094.
- Grape vines. iStock Photo #21865524.
- Carrots. iStock Photo #5420085.
- Bee. iStock Photo #17042287.

Inside

- Inside Cover: Vegetables in basket. iStock Photo #31854578.
- Pg #1 Community garden. iStock Photo #19990898.

- Pg #2 Watering. iStock Photo #17009985
- Pg #3 Hands in soil. iStock Photo #17836521.
- Pg #7 Introduction cover: Farmers market. iStock Photo # 4691841.
- Pg #9 Old Main at Utah State University. Photo by Donna Barry.
- Pg #13 Vegetables for sale. Clipart Photo #63299403.
- Pg #15 Apricot. iStock Photo #13470751.
- Pg #17 Grouped vegetables. Depositphotos #1480737.
- Pg #18 Food storage. iStock Photo #16706453.
- Pg #19 Little girl with tomatoes. iStock Photo #7145510.
- Pg #20 Pushing a wheelbarrow. iStock Photo #19969520.
- Pg #21 Garden preparation cover: Worm. iStock Photo #8280446.
- Pg #27 Radishes. iStock Photo #8793275.
- Pg #47 Okra plant. Photo by Katie Wagner.
- Pg #53 Plants growing. iStock Photo #3417480.
- Pg #63 Organic gardening techniques cover: Compost. iStock Photo #8691221.
- Pg #81 Raspberries. iStock Photo #16567877.
- Pg #113 Garden soil cover: Asparagus. iStock Photo #22632079.
- Pg #125 Hands planting. iStock Photo #15832262.
- Pg #135 Rain boots shoveling. iStock Photo #20560375.
- Pg #137 Organic garden care cover: Girl gardening. iStock Photo #13943406.
- Pg #160 Growing tomatoes. iStock Photo #18712044.
- Pg #160 Cracked soil. iStock Photo #3131895.
- Pg #161 Frost damage on plant. Photo by Marion Murray.
- Pg #161 Salt damage on plant. Photo by Marion Murray.
- Pg #161 Pesticide damage on plant. Photo by Marion Murray.
- Pg #161 Sunscald injury on plant. Photo by Katie Wagner.
- Pg #161 Iron chlorosis on plant. Photo by Marion Murray.
- Pg #161 Blossom end rot on tomato. Photo courtesy of Utah Pests.
- Pg #162 Damaged corn. Photo by Marion Murray.
- Pg #185 Garden furrows. Photo by Katie Wagner.
- Pg #187 Garden pest control cover: Caterpillar. iStock Photo #16233125.

Back Cover

- Plants growing. iStock Photo #19099030.
- Gardening tools in soil. iStock Photo #10922562.
- Hummingbird. iStock Photo #26681279.
- Hand pruning a tree. iStock Photo #9036171.

USU EXTENSION COUNTY OFFICE LISTING

Beaver County
Courthouse
105 E. Center Street, P.O. Box 466
Beaver, UT 84713
(435) 438-6450
extension.usu.edu/beaver
Hours: Monday-Friday 8a.m. - 5p.m.

Box Elder County
01 South Main
Brigham City, UT 84302
(435) 695-2542
extension.usu.edu/boxelder
Hours: Monday-Friday 8a.m. - 5p.m.

Cache County
179 N. Main Street, Suite 111
Logan, UT 84321
(435) 752-6263
extension.usu.edu/cache
Hours: Monday-Friday 8a.m. - 5p.m.

Carbon County
120 E. Main Street Courthouse
Price, UT 84501
(435) 636-3233
extension.usu.edu/carbon
Hours: Monday-Friday 9a.m. - noon, 1p.m. - 5p.m.

Davis County
28 E. State Street, P.O. Box 618
Farmington, UT 84025
(801) 451-3412
extension.usu.edu/davis
Hours: Monday-Friday 8a.m. - 5p.m.

Duchesne County
50 E. 100 S., P.O. Box 978
Duchesne, UT 84021
(435) 738-1140
extension.usu.edu/duchesne
Hours: Monday-Friday 8:30a.m. - 5p.m.

Emery County
75 E. Main Street, P.O. Box 847
Courthouse, Room 113
Castle Dale, UT 84513
(435) 381-2381
extension.usu.edu/emery
Hours: Monday-Friday 8:30a.m. - 5p.m.

Garfield County
Courthouse
55 S. Main Street, P.O. Box 77
Panguitch, UT 84759
(435) 676-1113
extension.usu.edu/garfield
Hours: Monday-Thursday 8a.m. - 5p.m. (Closed Fridays)

Grand County
125 W. 200 S.
Moab, UT 84532
(435) 259-7558
extension.usu.edu/grand
Hours: Monday-Friday 9a.m. - 5p.m.

Iron County
585 N. Main St. #5, P.O. Box 69
Cedar City, UT 84721
(435) 586-8132
extension.usu.edu/iron
Hours: Monday-Friday 8:30a.m. - noon, 1 - 5p.m.

Juab County
Juab County Center
160 N. Main St. Nephi, UT 84648
(435) 623-3450
extension.usu.edu/juab
Hours: Monday-Thursday 7a.m. - noon, 1 - 6p.m. (Closed Fridays)

Kane County
180 W. 300 N.
Kanab, UT 84741
(435) 644-4901
extension.usu.edu/kane
Hours: Monday-Thursday 9a.m. - 5p.m. (Closed Fridays)

Millard County (Delta)
83 S. Manzanita Ave.
Delta, UT 84624
(435) 864-1480
extension.usu.edu/millard
Hours: Monday, Wednesday & Friday 8a.m. - 4:30p.m.

Millard County (Fillmore)
50 S. Main Street
Fillmore, UT 84631-0568
(435) 743-5412
extension.usu.edu/millard
Hours: Tuesday & Thursday 8:30a.m. - 4:30p.m.

Morgan County
48 W. Young Street, P.O. Box 720
Morgan, UT 84050-0720
(801) 829-3472
extension.usu.edu/morgan
Hours: Monday-Thursday 7a.m. - 6p.m. (Closed Fridays)

Ogden Botanical Garden
1750 Monroe Blvd.
Ogden, UT 84401
(801) 399-8080
extension.usu.edu/weber/htm/horticulture/
Hours: Monday-Friday 1 - 5p.m.
Saturday 10a.m. - 2p.m.

Piute County
Courthouse
550 N. Main Street, P.O. Box 39
Junction, UT 84740
(435) 577-2901
extension.usu.edu/piute
Hours: Monday-Friday 9a.m. - 5p.m.

Rich County
20 S. Main, P.O. Box 8
Randolph, UT 84064
(435) 793-2435
extension.usu.edu/rich
Hours: Monday-Friday 9a.m. - 5p.m.

Salt Lake County
2001 S. State Street S-1200
Salt Lake City, UT 84190-2350
(801) 468-3170
extension.usu.edu/saltlake
Hours: Monday-Friday 8a.m. - 5p.m.

San Juan County
Courthouse
117 S. Main St., P.O. Box 549
Monticello, UT 84535
(435) 587-3239 ext. 9
extension.usu.edu/sanjuan
Hours: Monday-Friday 9a.m. - 5p.m.

Sanpete County
325 W. 100 N. Street
Ephraim, UT 84627
(435) 283-7597
extension.usu.edu/sanpete
Hours: Monday-Friday 8a.m. - noon, 1 - 5p.m.

Sevier County
250 N. Main
Richfield, UT 84701
(435) 893-0470
http://extension.usu.edu/sevier
Hours: Monday-Friday 8a.m. - noon, 1 - 5p.m.

Summit County
45 E. 100 N., P.O. Box 127
Coalville, UT 84017-0127
(435) 336-3217
extension.usu.edu/summit
Hours: Monday-Friday 8a.m. - 5p.m.

Swaner Preserve & EcoCenter
1258 Center Drive
Park City, UT 84098
(435) 649-1767
swanerecocenter.org
Hours: Thurs & Fri 11a.m. - 4p.m.
Sat 10a.m. - 4p.m. (Sun-Wed Closed)

Thanksgiving Point
3003 N. Thanksgiving Way
Lehi, UT 84043
(801) 768-7443
thanksgivingpoint.com/
Hours: Monday-Friday 10a.m. - 8p.m.

Tooele County
151 N. Main Street
Tooele, UT 84074-2141
(435) 277-2400
extension.usu.edu/tooele
Hours: Monday-Thursday 7a.m. - 6p.m. (Closed Fridays)

Uintah County
152 E. 100 N.
Vernal, UT 84078
(435) 781-5452
extension.usu.edu/uintah
Hours: Monday-Friday 8a.m. - 5p.m.

USU Botanical Center
700 S. 150 E.
Kaysville, UT 84037
(801) 593-8969
utahbotanicalcenter.org/
Hours: Monday-Friday 1 - 5p.m.
Saturday 10a.m. - 2p.m.

USU RESOURCES AND CITED FACT SHEETS

TOP 10 QUESTIONS AND ANSWERS FOR ORGANIC FRUIT AND VEGETABLE GARDENING IN UTAH

- **Wasatch Community Gardens**
  http://wasatchgardens.org

- **Salt Lake County Urban Farming**
  www.slco.org/urbanfarming

- **American Community Garden Association (ACGA)**
  www.communitygardens.org

- **Slow the Flow**
  www.slowtheflow.org

- **Organic Materials Review Institute**
  www.omri.org

INTRODUCTION

- **Organic Materials Review Institute**
  www.omri.org

- **National Sustainable Agriculture Service**
  https://attra.ncat.org/organic.html

- **USDA Food Safety and Inspection Service**
  http://www.fsis.usda.gov/wps/portal/fsis/home

- **USDA National Organic Program**
  http://www.ams.usda.gov/AMSv1.0/nop

- **Organic Gardening Fundamentals (Fact sheet)**
  http://extension.oregonstate.edu/mg/metro/sites/default/files/Organic_gardening.pdf

- **2012 Production Guide for Storage of Organic Fruits and Vegetables**
  http://nysipm.cornell.edu/organic_guide/stored_fruit_veg.pdf

- **USU Extension Canning**
  http://extension.usu.edu/canning/

- **USDA Complete Guide to Home Canning**
  http://nchfp.uga.edu/publications/publications_usda.html

- **The Ball Canning Company: Blue Book of Preserving**
  http://www.freshpreserving.com/home.aspx

- **Community Supported Agriculture**
  www.csautah.org

GETTING STARTED AND SITE SELECTION

- **Soil Test Website**
  www.usual.udu.edu

- **Topsoil Quality Guidelines for Landscaping (fact sheet)**
  http://extension.usu.edu/files/publications/publication/AG-SO-02.pdf

- **Urban Gardens and Soil Contaminants**
  http://www.misa.umn.edu/prod/groups/cfans/@pub/@cfans/@misa/documents/asset/cfans_asset_287228.pdf

- **Critical Temperatures for Frost Damage on Fruit Trees (fact sheet)**
  http://extension.usu.edu/files/publications/factsheet/pub__5191779.pdf

- **From Neglected Parcels to Community Gardens**
  http://wasatchgardens.org/files/images/FromNeglectedParcelsToCommunityGardens.PDF

VARIETY SELECTION

- **Electronic Code of Federal Regulations**
  http://www.ecfr.gov/cgi-bin/text-idx?c=ecfr&sid=9186ff5094dac441c85451ade630c3c4&rgn=div8&view=text&node=7:3.1.1.9.32.3.354.5&idno=7

- **Utah Freeze Dates**
  http://climate.usurf.usu.edu/reports/freezeDates.php

- **Creating an Heirloom Vegetable Garden (fact sheet)**
  http://www.coopext.colostate.edu/adams/sa/pdf/June2009-Heirloom.pdf

- **Hybrid Varieties and Saving Seed (fact sheet)**
  http://aggie-horticulture.tamu.edu/archives/parsons/vegetables/seed.html

- **Hybrid and Heirlooms (fact sheet)**
  http://urbanext.illinois.edu/hortihints/0102a.html

- **Tomato, Part 1 (fact sheet)**
  http://aggie-horticulture.tamu.edu/archives/parsons/vegetables/tomato.html

- **Tomato, Part 2 (fact sheet)**
  http://aggie-horticulture.tamu.edu/archives/parsons/vegetables/tomat2.html

- **Safety of Genetically Engineered Food**
  http://anrcatalog.ucdavis.edu/pdf/8180.pdf

- **Genetically Engineered Foods: Food Safety of Genetically Engineered Crops**
  http://biomedsci.cornell.edu/graduate_school/shared/gradschool/Outreach/Genetically_Modified_Organisms/fs10_foodsafety.pdf

- **Genetically Engineered Foods: In the Marketplace**
  https://scholarworks.iupui.edu/bitstream/handle/1805/812/GE%20foods%20in%20the%20marketplace.pdf?sequence=1

- **What are GMO's?**
  http://www.ars.usda.gov/Research/docs.htm?docid=7205

- **Genetically Modified Foods**
  http://edis.ifas.ufl.edu/fs084

GARDEN LAYOUT AND PLANTING

- **Territorial Seed Company**
  http://gardenplanner.territorialseed.com/

• **Intensive Gardening Methods (fact sheet)**
http://pubs.ext.vt.edu/426/426-335/426-335.html

• **Fruit and Vegetable Production Fact Sheets (fact sheet)**
https://extension.usu.edu/htm/publications/by=category/category=696

• **Utah Climate Center**
http://climate.usurf.usu.edu/

• **Dixie Gardener**
http://www.dixiegardener.org/

• **Soil Temperature Conditions for Vegetable Seed Germination**
http://www.aces.edu/pubs/docs/A/ANR-1061/ANR-1061.pdf

• **Vegetable Planting Guide**
http://www.ext.colostate.edu/mg/gardennotes/720.pdf

STARTED PLANTS FROM SEED

• **Utah Climate Center**
http://climate.usurf.usu.edu/

• **Dixie Gardener**
http://www.dixiegardener.org/

• **Growing Your Own Transplants at Home (fact sheet)**
http://extension.usu.edu/files/publications/publication/Horticulture_Home Horticulture_2011-01pr.pdf

CONTAINER AND RAISED BED GARDENING

• **Selecting and Using Organic Fertilizers (fact sheet)**
http://extension.usu.edu/files/publications/factsheet/hg-510.pdf

• **Herb Container Gardens (fact sheet)**
http://extension.usu.edu/boxelder/files/uploads/hg524.pdf

• **USU Analytical Laboratory**
http://www.usual.usu.edu/

• **Raised Bed Gardening (fact sheet)**
http://extension.usu.edu/files/publications/publication/Horticulture_Garden_2012-01pr.pdf

• **Designing a Basic PVC Home Garden Drip Irrigation System**
http://extension.usu.edu/files/publications/publication/Horticulture_Home_2008-02pr.pdf

ORGANIC VEGETABLE GARDENING: AN OVERVIEW

• **Table 10: Online retailers that sell USDA Certified Seed**
www.Jonnyseeds.com
www.teritorialseed.com
www.burpee.com
www.parkseed.com
www.sustainableseedco.com
www.seedsofchange.com
www.highmowingseeds.com
www.groworganic.com
www.snowseed.com
www.seedsavers.org
www.rareseeds.com
www.mvseeds.com

- USU Analytical Laboratory
http://www.usual.usu.edu/

- Potting Mixes for Certified Organic Production
https://attra.ncat.org/attra-pub/summaries/summary.php?pub=47

- National Sustainable Agriculture Information Service (ATTRA)
https://attra.ncat.org/organic.html

TREE FRUIT AND SMALL FRUIT: AN OVERVIEW

- Utah Home Orchard Pest Management Guide (USU publication)
http://extension.usu.edu/files/publications/factsheet/home-orchard-pest-mgmt-guide.pdf

- Pruning the Orchard (fact sheet)
http://extension.usu.edu/files/publications/publication/HG_363.pdf

- Tree Fruit Recommendations (fact sheet)
http://extension.usu.edu/boxelder/htm/fruit/variety

- Apple Production and Variety Recommendations for the Utah Home Garden (fact sheet)
http://extension.usu.edu/files/publications/publication/Horticulture_Fruit_2012_02pr.pdf

- USU Botanical Center
http://usubotanicalcenter.org/

- Strawberries in the Garden (fact sheet)
http://extension.usu.edu/files/publications/publication/Horticulture_Fruit_2008-06pr.pdf

- Red Raspberry Production in Utah (fact sheet)
http://extension.usu.edu/files/publications/factsheet/raspberry-production04.pdf

- USDA Plant Hardiness Zones
http://planthardiness.ars.usda.gov/PHZMWeb/

- Pollination of Fruit Trees (fact sheet-Colorado)
http://www.ext.colostate.edu/pubs/garden/07002.html

- Pollination of Fruit Trees (fact sheet-Washington State)
http://www.spokane-county.wsu.edu/spokane/eastside/Fact%20Sheets/C105%20Pollination%20of%20Fruit%20Trees%2005.pdf

- General Chilling Requirements of Various Fruits and Nuts
http://www.ag.arizona.edu/pubs/garden/mg/fruit/foundation.html

- Rootstocks and Dwarf Fruit Trees (fact sheet)
http://umaine.edu/fruit/growing-fruit-trees-in-maine/rootstocks-and-dwarf-fruit-trees/

- Planting Landscape Trees (fact sheet)
http://extension.usu.edu/files/publications/publication/NR_FF_017pr.pdf

- Apple Varieties for Cooking, Baking, and Cider (fact sheet)
http://extension.wsu.edu/maritime-fruit/pages/appleusechart.aspx

• A Comparison of 10 Fall Bearing Raspberry Cultivars for Northern Utah (fact sheet)
http://extension.usu.edu/files/publications/publication/Horticulture_Fruit_2013n-01pr.pdf

• Dixie Gardener Fruits
http://dixiegardener.org/htm/fruits

• Colorado Grape Grower's Guide
http://www.ext.colostate.edu/pubs/garden/550a.pdf

PRUNING FRUIT TREES AND SMALL FRUIT

• International Society of Arboriculture (ISA)
www.isa-arbor.com

• Pruning the Orchard (fact sheet)
http://extension.usu.edu/files/publications/publication/hg_363.pdf

EXTENDING THE GROWING SEASON

• USU Utah Climate Center
http://climate.usurf.usu.edu/

• USU Production Horticulture Publications
*http://extension.usu.edu/production-hort/ **this was listed as tunnel.usu.edu in the book on pg. 111*

• Greenhouses for Homeowners and Gardeners
http://palspublishing.cals.cornell.edu/nra_order.taf?_function=detail&pr_booknum=nraes-137

• Mississippi University Extension Greenhouse Design Publications
http://msucares.com/pubs/plans/books/greenhouses.html

GARDEN SOIL AND SOIL TESTING

• Topsoil Quality Guidelines for Landscaping (fact sheet)
http://extension.usu.edu/files/publications/publication/AG-SO-02.pdf

• USDA-NRCS Web Soil Survey
http://websoilsurvey.nrcs.usda.gov/app/HomePage.htm

• Understanding Your Soil Test Results
http://extension.usu.edu/files/publications/publication/AG_Soils_2008-01pr.pdf

• Understanding Your Soil Test Report
http://www.mtregional.org/Docs/Resources/Understanding_Soil_Tests_hg512.pdf

• USUAL Soil Testing Laboratory
http://www.usual.usu.edu/

THREE COMMON SOIL PROBLEMS

• Blueberries in Utah? Difficult, but Maybe Not Impossible (fact sheet)
http://extension.usu.edu/files/publications/publication/Horticulture_Furit_2009-01pr.pdf

• Solutions to Soil Problems II. High pH (Alkaline Soil)
http://extension.usu.edu/files/publications/publication/AG_Soils_2003-02.pdf

• Understanding your Watershed: pH (fact sheet)
http://extension.usu.edu/files/publications/publication/NR_WQ_2005-19.pdf

• USUAL Soil Testing Laboratory
http://www.usual.usu.edu/

• Soil, Water, and Plant Tissue Testing in Utah Orchards (fact sheet)
http://extension.usu.edu/files/publications/publication/AG-FG-02.pdf

• Water Salinity and Crop Yield (fact sheet)
http://extension.usu.edu/files/publications/publication/AG-425_3.pdf

• Salinity and Plant Tolerance (fact sheet)
http://forestry.usu.edu/files/uploads/AGSO03.pdf

• Soil Salinity and Ornamental Plant Selection (fact sheet)
http://extension.usu.edu/files/publications/publication/HG_Landscaping_2008-02pr.pdf

• Understanding your Soil Report (fact sheet)
http://www.mtregional.org/Docs/Resources/Understanding_Soil_Tests_hg512.pdf

• Solutions to Soil Problems I. High Salinity (Soluble Salts)
http://extension.usu.edu/files/publications/publication/AG_Soils_2003-01.pdf

• Solutions to Soil Problems IV. Soil Structure (Compaction)
http://extension.usu.edu/files/publications/publication/AG_Soils_2003-04.pdf

ORGANIC MATTER AND SOIL AMENDMENT

• Solutions to Soil Problems V. Low Organic Matter
http://extension.usu.edu/files/publications/publication/AG_Soils_2003-05.pdf

• Using Compost in Utah Gardens (fact sheet)
http://extension.usu.edu/files/publications/factsheet/HG_Compost_02.pdf

• Using Mulches in Utah Landscapes and Gardens (fact sheet)
http://extension.usu.edu/files/publications/factsheet/HG_Compost_04.pdf

• Preparing and Improving Garden Soil (fact sheet)
http://extension.usu.edu/files/publications/factsheet/pub__8066784.pdf

BACKYARD COMPOSTING

• The Composting Process (fact sheet)
http://extension.usu.edu/files/publications/publication/AG-WM_01.pdf

• Backyard Composting in Utah (fact sheet)
http://extension.usu.edu/files/publications/factsheet/HG-Compost-01.pdf

• Composting References
http://extension.usu.edu/smac/htm/composting

GARDEN SOIL FERTILITY

• Diagnostic Testing for Nitrogen Soil Fertility (fact sheet)
http://extension.usu.edu/files/publications/publication/AG_282.pdf

• Understanding Your Watershed: Nitrogen
https://extension.usu.edu/files/publications/publication/NR_WQ_2005-15.pdf

• Understanding Your Watershed: Phosphorus
https://extension.usu.edu/files/publications/publication/NR_WQ_2005-18.pdf

• Understanding Your Watershed: Dissolved Oxygen
https://extension.usu.edu/files/publications/publication/NR_WQ_2005-16.pdf

• OMRI Website
www.omri.org

• Selecting and Using Organic Fertilizers (fact sheet)
http://extension.usu.edu/files/publications/factsheet/HG-510.pdf

• Organic Fertilizers (fact sheet)
http://www.ext.colostate.edu/mg/gardennotes/234.html

• Cover Crops for Utah Gardens (fact sheet)
http://extension.usu.edu/files/publications/publication/HG-521.pdf

• Cover Crop in Organic Systems Western Implementation Guide
http://tilth.org/files/r-e/ocp/cover-crop-in-organic-systems

• Considerations for Raising Small Populations of Backyard Poultry in Population-dense Communities
http://extension.usu.edu/files/publications/publication/AG_Poultry_2009-02pr.pdf

• Housing Backyard Chickens
http://extension.usu.edu/files/publications/publication/AG_Poultry_2008-01pr.pdf

• Principles of Feeding Small Flocks of Chickens at Home
http://extension.usu.edu/files/publications/publication/AG_Poultry_2008-02pr.pdf

• Biosecurity Principles: Protecting Your investment
http://extension.usu.edu/files/publications/publication/AG_Poultry_Health_Biosecurity_01pr.pdf

• Handling Baby Poultry
http://extension.usu.edu/files/publications/publication/AG_Poultry_2010-01pr.pdf

GARDEN IRRIGATION

• Garden Water Use in Utah (fact sheet)
http://digitalcommons.usu.edu/cgi/viewcontent.cgi?article=1181&context=extension_histall

• Strawberry Irrigation (fact sheet)
http://extension.usu.edu/files/publications/publication/Horticulture_Fruit_2008_05pr.pdf

- **Irrigation Basics of Eastern Washington Vineyards**
http://cru.cahe.wsu.edu/CE Publications/EM061E/EM061E.pdf

- **USU Extension Fruit Fact Sheet**
https://extension.usu.edu/htm/publications/by=category/category=186

- **USU Extension Vegetable Fact Sheets**
https://extension.usu.edu/htm/publications/by=category/category=194

- **USU Extension Turf Fact Sheets**
https://extension.usu.edu/htm/publications/by=category/category=858

- **Western Regional Climate Center**
http://www.wrcc.dri.edu/climatedata/comparative/

PESTICIDE APPLICATION

- **OMRI website**
www.omri.org

- **Reducing Pesticide Poisoning of Bees (fact sheet)**
http://extension.usu.edu/files/publications/factsheet/Pesticides_No__19.pdf

FALL GARDEN CARE

- **Irrigation System Maintenance (fact sheet)**
https://extension.usu.edu/files/publications/factsheet/HG_Irrigation_2004-01.pdf

- **Sunscald Injury or South West Winter Injury on Deciduous Trees (fact sheet)**
http://extension.usu.edu/files/publications/factsheet/nr_ff_021pr.pdf

INTEGRATED PEST MANAGEMENT

- **Utah Pest Website**
http://utahpests.usu.edu/

- **Local Extension County Offices**
*http://extension.usu.edu/htm/counties **listed simply as extension.usu.edu in book***

- **Utah IPM Pest Advisories**
*http://utahpests.usu.edu/ipm/ **listed as ipm.usu.edu in text of book, which does not hyperlink correctly*

- **Utah Plant Pest Diagnostic Lab**
http://utahpests.usu.edu/uppdl/

- **Utah Pests video fact sheets**
http://utahpests.usu.edu/htm/video-fact-sheets

- **Utah Tree Fruit IPM Advisories**
http://utahpests.usu.edu/ipm/htm/fruits

- **Alpha Scents**
www.alphascents.com

- **Great Lakes IPM**
http://www.greatlakesipm.com/

- **Gardens Alive**
http://www.gardensalive.com/

- **Peaceful Valley**
https://www.groworganic.com/

- **Gempler's**
http://www.gemplers.com/